The Canadian
Mutual Fund Bible

The Canadian
MUTUAL FUND BIBLE
A Complete Guide

MARK NEWSOME
Director, Wood Gundy Private Client Investments Inc.
THOMAS HOLYOAKE BOX
BA, LLB

MACMILLAN CANADA
TORONTO

Canadian Cataloguing in Publication Data

Newsome, Mark

The Canadian mutual fund bible

Includes index

ISBN 0-7715-7566-1 (bound) ISBN 0-7715-7550-5 (pbk.)

1. Mutual funds. I. Box, Thomas Holyoake. II. Title.

HG5154.5.N49 1998 332.63′27 C97-932061-5

1 2 3 4 5 TG 01 00 99 98 97

Macmillan Canada

A Division of Canada Publishing Corporation

Toronto, Ontario, Canada

Printed in Canada

CONTENTS

Important Notice

This book is intended to be a general guide to assist the reader in understanding Canadian mutual funds, but it does not purport to treat each topic exhaustively. The book is not intended to and cannot take the place of the professional advice all investors should seek and consider in light of their own particular circumstances before they make any investment decision. While the information presented has bee obtained from sources the authors believe to be reliable and every effort has been made to ensure accuracy, it cannot be guaranteed. Individual mutual funds and groups of funds are mentioned in this text for purposes of example and discussion only; references to them are not to be construed as recommendations for purchases or sales, nor are they to be taken as definitive comments on the quality of the funds or the funds' management.

Wherever possible, the data has been reported as of December 31, 1996 since annual data is most readily available on a calendar year basis, and presenting all data on the same basis facilitates comparisons and analysis. Moreover, it is the authors' view that, for the most part, short-term developments are insignificant. Current quotations may be obtained from the financial press or one's financial consultant.

The comments and opinions expresses in this book are those of the authors alone, and are not to be attributed to any corporation or other entity with which they may be associated.

ACKNOWLEDGEMENTS

We are indebted to many people for their assistance in producing this book. Andrew Cook and Darlene Reid provided invaluable research assistance. Rob Bell and the staff at BellCharts provided us with additional data and attempted to answer our many technical questions. Bill Bamber, John Carswell, Guenther Kleberg, George Hood, Frank Dickson, Bret Mecredy-Williams, Stephen Smith, and Jeffery Zahn all reviewed the manuscript and made numerous constructive suggestions. John Carswell, President of Canso Fund Management Ltd., also provided us with insights into the intricacies of bond fund management. Brian Murphy graciously supplied advice on tax issues, and the advice of Dan Richards regarding the organization of the book was most useful. We are also grateful for the support and encouragement of Gerry McCaughey and the contributions of Sonia Baxendale and Meri Rawlings-Taylor. When administrative efficiency was essential, Nathalie Hetu provided it. The staff at Macmillan Canada, and Alison Maclean and Shannon Potts in particular, made the process of publication as painless as possible. Although it does not need repeating, responsibility for any errors or omissions is solely ours.

We owe a special thanks to Alix Box and Heather Newsome for enduring endless discussions about the book, and for supporting the project throughout its protracted genesis, in the steadfast belief that it would be finished.

PREFACE

The Myths of Mutual Funds

Although a great deal is written about mutual funds, there is an enormous amount of misinformation about them, as well as an alarming lack of basic understanding about what is important.

MYTH: SHORT-TERM PERFORMANCE IS IMPORTANT

It is an indisputable fact that investor interest is greatest for funds with the highest short-term records. Funds that top the performance charts over one month or one year inevitably experience a subsequent surge in sales. The remarkable thing, though, is that these funds are virtually never at the top of the charts over five years or ten years. The reality is that stellar short-term performance is typically the product of an unusually audacious investment approach. Over the long term, this approach is as likely to produce disproportionately poor results. Consistency is the most reliable guide to future performance, and only truly long-term records provide insight into a fund's consistency.

MYTH: SMALL FUNDS OUTPERFORM BIG FUNDS

If this were true, we should expect to see small funds dominating the performance lists. In fact, they don't. Although there are far more small funds than "giant" funds (those with more than $1 billion in assets), three of the nine Canadian stock funds with the highest ten-year records are giant funds. The *Templeton Growth Fund* has continued to outperform with assets of more than $6 billion, and the superior long-term performance of the U.S.-based *Fidelity Magellan Fund* has been sustained even with assets of more than $20 billion.

MYTH: MARKET TIMING INCREASES RETURNS

The myth of market timing is appealing because the benefit of hindsight seduces investors into believing that it is possible to anticipate the movements of the market. The fact is that the effect of timing investments is relatively minor. An investor who "bought low" by contributing $5,000 to the *Templeton Growth Fund* each year on the market's lowest day between 1969 and 1991 would have amassed $1.29 million and realized an average annual return of 18.4 percent. An investor who "bought high" by contributing $5,000 to the same fund each year on the market's highest day would have amassed $1.12 million and realized an average annual return of 17.4 percent. It is far more important to invest than to worry about when to invest.

MYTH: THE MORE FUNDS, THE BETTER

The importance of diversification cannot be ignored, but diversification does not mean that if some is good, more must be better. The obsession with having more funds is motivated primarily not by investment considerations but by the marketing campaigns of fund companies. Asset allocation is the current mantra of the fund industry, and there has been a massive proliferation of both new categories of funds and "systems" to aid investors in spreading their investments among the different types of funds. It is no coincidence that these asset allocation systems charge investors additional fees. The reality is that truly superior funds already provide investors with adequate diversification.

MYTH: THE PROSPECTUS IS A GOOD SOURCE OF INFORMATION

Securities laws require mutual fund managers to tell investors that there is important information contained in the prospectus. What they don't have to tell you is that the prospectus is generally written by lawyers, and is best understood by other lawyers. Precision is (apparently) much more important than clarity, and the result is that most prospectuses are completely unintelligible to the average investor.

Even more frustrating is the fact that a great deal of the information in the prospectus does not address the real concerns of investors. For example, there is a mandatory description of "risk factors" in every prospectus, but it is usually far too vague to be useful. You will search in vain for a straightforward answer to the question: "Can I lose money?"

MYTH: YOU CANNOT LOSE MONEY IN A BOND FUND

There are really two myths here. The first myth is that you can't lose money in bonds. Too many investors confuse fixed returns and certainty of repayment with a lack of financial risk. Inflation is the scourge of interest-bearing investments, and the fact that a bond investor can expect to be repaid does not mean that the money repaid will have the same purchasing power as the money that was originally invested.

The second myth is that bond funds are as safe as bonds. Nothing could be further from the truth. While a bond investor is eventually repaid when the bond matures, bond funds have no maturity date—there is no point at which the investor is repaid. The investor can sell the bond fund, but there is absolutely no guarantee that the amount invested can be recovered.

MYTH: COSTS ARE AN IMPORTANT FACTOR IN CHOOSING FUNDS

This myth is pernicious because it focuses attention on unimportant issues at the expense of important issues. The fund manager's ability is the primary factor affecting a fund's future performance. Over the long term, costs have a minimal impact on overall return, and in any event, the value added by good management will more than compensate for costs of the fund investment. The difficulty is that comparing costs is undemanding, while evaluating good management requires commitment and effort, and the financial press are too often fascinated by superficial information.

MYTH: YOU SHOULD NEVER BUY A LOAD FUND

The myth about loads is based on two misconceptions. The first misconception is that no-load funds charge no fees. Not so. All funds involve costs, and the costs of some no-load funds are higher than the comparable costs of some load funds. The second misconception is that paying a load lowers investment returns. The reality is different. While there is no appreciable difference in the performance of load and no-load funds, there is a difference in the success of their investors. On average, investors who buy load funds do *better* than no-load investors—because load investors are more likely to adopt a more successful long-term "buy-and-hold" investment approach.

MYTH: THE MORE VOLATILE THE FUND, THE GREATER ITS RISK

While most people understand that financial risk is the potential for losing money, analysts, academics, and journalists think that financial risk is volatility. Volatility can be an important indicator of the anxiety an investment may cause an investor, but it has very little to do with the investment's potential for loss. A decline in the price of an investment is a "risk" only if the investor panics and sells the investment. It took the U.S. market only about a year to recover entirely from the decline and "crash" of 1987, and the Canadian market only slightly longer.

MYTH: INDEX FUNDS ARE BEST

The culprit in this myth is a misguided belief that since it is impossible to identify managers who can outperform the market over the long term, it is irrational to incur the higher costs of active management. Wrong on two counts. First, choosing a fund that outperforms the market isn't impossible. The key is to identify the right indicators. Second, index funds aren't a panacea. They may not underperform by much, but they will never outperform.

MYTH: DOLLAR COST AVERAGING MAXIMIZES RETURNS

The conventional wisdom is that dollar cost averaging is a strategy for maximizing investment returns in mutual funds. Virtually every mass-market book on investing offers an explanation of how dollar cost averaging works, yet none compares the relative real-life performance of dollar cost averaging and lump-sum investing.

The reality is that dollar cost averaging almost never maximizes investment returns. Lump-sum investing is nearly always a more profitable way to invest. The reason is, simply, that the benefits of compounding are maximized in a lump-sum investment. In dollar cost averaging, the earliest contributions get the full benefits of compounding. The later contributions derive virtually no benefits from compounding. As Sir John Templeton so wisely observes, "the best time to invest is when you have money."

Dispelling the Myths

This book does not offer a list of recommended funds. In our view, the whole notion of identifying the current high fliers is flawed, since this year's stars are as likely as not to be next year's dogs. Instead, our focus is on providing investors with the tools to make informed judgements about the funds which are most likely to meet their expectations. In an environment of conflicting marketing campaigns, accurate information is essential and our objective is to dispell the many myths of mutual fund investing.

We do not provide voluminous data about funds. We don't tell you how big a fund is, or what its portfolio mix was on June 30, 1995. A lot of that information is irrelevant, and the remainder is available from other sources that will be more current than any book could possibly be. All in all, listing the "stats" for a group of funds seems to us a better way to fill up the space between the covers than to truly inform investors. Neither do we offer "profiles" of star managers. We think the phenomenon of the star manager is misguided, and in any event, we don't think investors need, or care, to know what the manager's hobbies are, or what the manager's parents hoped for their progeny. Instead, our approach emphasizes the application of research, logic and discipline to the process of evaluating funds. We try to identify what is important in evaluating and choosing a mutual fund, and explain why it is important to the reader.

The approach will not assist investors in picking the fund with the highest return next year, but it will protect them from choosing inappropriate funds. While the process is rigorous, it isn't rigid. Although we have been careful to ensure that the standards we use to evaluate funds are logical and demanding, we also recognize that other standards may be appropriate. However, by choosing funds without logically derived and clearly defined standards, investors lose many of the benefits of mutual fund investing, leaving themselves vulnerable to much of the risk identified with picking individual stocks.

We have divided the book into several parts. Part 1 puts mutual funds in context. Mutual funds are simply a means of investing. Understanding the basics of investing helps enormously in appreciating how mutual funds work and what makes a fund good or bad. Part 2 examines the characteristics of different kinds of mutual funds, highlighting the factors that contribute to superior performance. An income fund can mirror the bond market; a growth fund will often reflect a stock market. Part 3 discusses the issues of management, taxes, and costs in substantial detail, explaining what factors are truly important. Part 4 draws together the various elements developed in the preceding parts to develop a process for evaluating mutual funds, and illustrates how to choose the mutual fund that is most suitable for your specific objectives. Each part builds on the preceding parts. Readers who are familiar with other investments may find the material in Part 4 sufficient, while those with less experience will find that the information in earlier parts provides a basis for the later sections on evaluating funds.

For those who want to use the book as a reference, Part 5 includes a number of appendices that provide technical information about various secondary issues, and a series of lists identifying funds with a track record of at least five years.

In addition, we have incorporated a number of research "tools" in the text. There is an Executive Summary at the beginning of each chapter, and Chapter 20, which summarizes the important issues in evaluating a fund, includes numerous cross-references to various chapters throughout the text. Unfamiliar words and phrases are highlighted in the text, and defined and explained in a comprehensive glossary. We hope that these features make the book more convenient to use.

PART ONE
INVESTMENT BASICS

There is nothing exotic or exceptional about mutual funds. They are merely a way of investing. They have some unique characteristics, but they work fundamentally in the same way that other kinds of investments work. A stock fund will often mirror the stock market, and an income fund will often reflect the bond markets. Many of the same considerations that are important in choosing good stocks and bonds are also important in mutual fund investing.

Our view is that understanding how mutual funds work is essential to making informed and intelligent choices about the most suitable funds. In turn, a basic grasp of the fundamentals of investing is necessary to appreciate how mutual funds work.

Unfortunately, the fundamentals of good investing are too frequently ignored. For example, while most commentary about mutual funds pays lip service to the idea that mutual funds are long-term investments, many sources continue to pump out reams of data about short-term developments and performance. The *Globe and Mail*, for example, publishes "Daily Fund Action," which tracks daily price changes in various funds categories. Although this "data" is useless in assisting investors to evaluate and choose suitable funds, its publication could create the erroneous impression that short-term market movements are significant.

Part 1 is devoted to outlining the important investment principles of mutual funds. Chapter 1 provides an overview of their rationale and a brief analysis of their advantages and limitations. Chapter 2 describes the mechanics of mutual fund operation. Chapters 3 to 5 explain the details of asset classes, investment returns, and risk. Finally, Chapter 6 examines the process of managing risk.

CHAPTER ONE

RATIONALE

EXECUTIVE SUMMARY

This chapter describes the general characteristics of mutual funds, and explains their basic advantages and limitations.

1. A mutual fund is a way of investing that pools the resources of many individual investors to achieve common objectives.

2. Mutual funds offer several advantages:
   - By pooling resources, individual investors are able to purchase a broader range of investments, and may thereby significantly reduce the risk of loss.
   - By pooling resources, investors are able to afford the services of professional investment managers, who have specialized expertise in choosing investments.
   - They are a convenient and easy way to invest.

3. Although they offer considerable benefits, mutual funds also have some limitations:
   - Individuals must surrender some control over their financial affairs.
   - With the exception of money market funds, mutual funds generally work best for investors who intend to make long-term investments.

INTRODUCTION

What are mutual funds, and why are they so popular?

A ***mutual fund*** is simply a pooling of individual investments into a fund administered by people who have special expertise in managing large amounts of money. This ***manager***, on behalf of the investors, invests the combined resources to achieve the particular objectives of the fund.

One of the major reasons for the enormous growth in the mutual funds industry in recent years is mutual funds' versatility. There are mutual funds designed to meet a wide range of investment objectives, and the features offered by most funds make them ideal for investors with limited resources. Low minimum purchases and monthly purchase plans make them even more accessible.

But the appeal of mutual funds is certainly not limited to "small" investors. The cost and convenience of mutual funds compare very favourably with the expense of hiring a professional to manage a personal account. In addition, the past performance of mutual fund managers can be easily ascertained, while the historical record of those who manage individual accounts is much harder to evaluate. Often the reported performance of such a private money manager really reflects the combined results of a variety of individual accounts (which may be quite different from the specific account of an individual investor).

Characteristics of Mutual Funds

There are a number of basic differences between mutual funds and other types of investments. Let's consider a few of the more important differences.

- A mutual fund is based on the idea of an investment ***portfolio***. A portfolio is merely a selection or "basket" of investments owned by an investor. Mutual fund investors are the indirect owners of the portfolio held by the fund.

- Although the fund makes investments on behalf of the investors, it is the portfolio manager, rather than the individual investors, who makes the investment decisions. Investors are entitled to a proportionate "slice" of the profit (or loss) from a fund's ownership of various investments.

- Unlike investments such as ***term deposits*** or ***guaranteed investment certificates (GICs)***, mutual fund investments are not guaranteed by the Canada Deposit Insurance Corporation.

- The system of regulation for mutual funds includes rigorous disclosure and audit requirements and ensures that investors are protected from any improper dealings by the manager. We'll discuss this in greater detail in Chapter 2.

- A mutual fund's rate of return is not predetermined. While term deposits, GICs, and bonds all offer a "set" rate of return, the return on a mutual fund is variable and depends on both market conditions and the kinds of investments made by the fund's manager. The return from a mutual fund can in fact be negative—the value of the fund can drop. The returns that are advertised by funds are *past* returns and do not necessarily indicate what the future holds. Much of this book is devoted to providing the information you'll need to identify those funds that are most likely to sustain historically superior performance.

- Unlike stocks and bonds, most mutual fund units are purchased directly from and sold to (or ***redeemed*** by) the fund itself rather than other investors.

- The price of most mutual fund units is not affected by the buying and selling of the mutual fund units themselves, as is the case for stocks and bonds, but is determined solely by the value of the investments that the fund holds.

- Unlike GICs and other fixed-term investments, mutual funds have no predetermined ***maturity***, or due date, when the investment ends. They are "perpetual" investments.

Advantages of Mutual Funds

Mutual funds offer the investor four major advantages: diversification, professional management, convenience, and liquidity.

Diversification

Diversification means *not* putting "all your eggs in one basket." Owning a variety of investments may greatly reduce the danger that a single poor choice will prove disastrous.

The difficulty for many smaller investors is that they lack the resources to develop a diversified portfolio. Just to duplicate the ***Dow Jones Industrial Average*** would require investments in 30 different stocks. The problem is compounded by the fact that minimum purchase commissions on such individual stock transactions can severely impair returns. Since an investment of about $5,000 is needed to avoid the consequences of minimum purchase costs, even partial diversification can be an expensive proposition for the average individual. In addition, the amount of time required to do the research necessary to establish a properly diversified portfolio is prohibitive for most investors.

In contrast, a mutual fund investment permits individual investors to participate in a much wider range of securities than is usually feasible on an individual basis yet avoid the transaction costs associated with small individual positions. For many funds, the minimum investment is $500, which is a fraction of the amount necessary to develop a properly diversified individual portfolio.

Professional Management

Professional money managers are likely to do a better job of investing than the average individual could ever hope to do. There are a number of pitfalls in "going it alone."

- Many investors underestimate the emotional requirements for profitable investing. Successful investors evaluate opportunities dispassionately. Too many investors get emotionally involved in the choices they make. They refuse to acknowledge the bad choices they make, and fail to adapt to changing situations.

- Many investors rely on the mass media as their primary source of financial information. The problem is that commentary from these sources often comes from journalists rather than investment professionals, and is intended ultimately to sell newspapers rather than educate the consumer. Information from these sources can be incomplete, can often be out of date, and can be unbalanced. A little knowledge can be a very dangerous thing.

- Many investors lack the training or experience to make informed judgements about the merits of an investment, even when accurate information is available.

- The financial markets are constantly changing, and even competent investors often simply do not have the time to review adequately the vast array of investment alternatives, or to monitor and evaluate selections on a regular basis.

- Many investors just aren't that interested in actively managing their investments. Even those who are keenly aware of their financial needs may find financial information either boring or intimidating, and many would prefer to leave the work to others.

For all of these reasons, the professional acumen of mutual fund managers is invaluable. And the great thing about mutual funds is that the cost of these essential skills is usually reasonable.

Convenience

"Knowledge is power," and information about mutual funds is readily available. The performance of mutual funds is widely reported in the financial press, making it easy to obtain information about current prices and developments.

Every fund is required to inform investors about the nature and status of their investment both at the outset and on a continuing basis. All funds are required to report semi-annually to unitholders, and many provide quarterly reports as well. These reports set out in general terms the performance of the fund since the last report, the fund manager's outlook for the future, and at least a partial breakdown of the fund's portfolio. While there will always be those who feel that the information provided is incomplete, receiving a single report from a mutual fund that summarizes the performance of a diversified portfolio of investments is far more convenient than wading through the documents for each security. This benefit is enormously magnified for foreign investments, since timely information about such investments is often much more difficult to obtain.

It's also very easy to invest in a mutual fund. Funds are sold by a broad array of outlets, including brokerage houses, banks and trust companies, insurance companies, and dedicated sales forces, in addition to the sales divisions of the funds themselves. Most funds (and certainly all the major ones) have efficient client service departments, and transactions are processed the day the order is received by the fund.

There is a wide selection of fund types, targeted at most investment preferences. There are funds that emphasize capital appreciation, funds that offer steady income, funds that "balance" investment objectives, and an increasing number of funds that specialize in investments ranging from real estate to precious metals to financial derivatives. Many fund sponsors offer "families" or groups of funds, with individual funds in a number of categories, providing investors the opportunity to develop a comprehensive portfolio. We'll discuss the characteristics of these types of funds in later chapters.

There is also a broad range of payment options. Sales charges can be levied when the investment is purchased or redeemed, and many fund sponsors offer ***no-load funds***, which impose no sales charge. It is important to recognize that "no-load" does not mean "no cost": all mutual fund investments—without exception—entail costs of various kinds.

Finally, there is an array of features that extend the convenience of mutual funds. Among the most common are–

- **monthly purchase plans**
  Money can be automatically drawn from an account to purchase fund units.
- **automatic reinvestment**
  The monthly (or quarterly or annual) ***distributions*** can be invested in more units without charge rather than being paid out to the investor.
- **systematic withdrawals**
  The investment can be drawn on at regular intervals to provide current income.

- **allocation services**
  Many funds now offer "services" to apportion an investor's assets between a number of funds within a fund family.

Liquidity

Liquidity is the ease with which an investment can be bought and sold. A liquid investment can be sold without its price being noticeably affected, while an illiquid investment can only be sold with some difficulty, and often only at a discounted price.

Most mutual funds are quite liquid. In the first place, mutual funds are permitted to invest only a small proportion of the portfolio in illiquid investments. Secondly, units or shares in a mutual fund are bought and sold directly from the fund company. The price of the unit is determined solely by the value of the portfolio's investments in the markets–there is no discounting.

Limitations of Mutual Funds

Although the advantages of mutual funds are considerable, there can also be disadvantages. First, while the cost of mutual fund management is reasonable, it is somewhat inflexible. Investors who want to tailor an investment portfolio to their circumstances must often incur additional fees to coordinate investments among a variety of mutual funds. In some cases, the fees charged by the management of the mutual funds could well exceed those levied by a private money manager. Whether or not the benefits of the mutual fund format outweigh these fee considerations is a very personal decision.

Second, most mutual funds are by their nature long-term investments. They are generally ill-suited to situations in which the invested capital will be required in less than three to five years. Investors who buy a bond or even a GIC have the assurance that the amount available to them at maturity is known with reasonable certainty, but mutual fund investors do not have that assurance.

Third, the fact that actual investment decisions regarding the fund's portfolio are beyond the control of the individual investor can sometimes be a problem. For example, the taxation of mutual funds is rather inflexible.

The finances of a mutual fund are usually arranged so that the fund itself pays no tax on the profits from its investing. Instead, any taxable income is passed on to the fund's unitholders, and may create unanticipated tax liabilities. In addition, the lack of specific maturity dates can complicate an investor's financial planning.

A Note on Real Estate Investment Trusts and Royalty Trusts

Real estate investment trusts (***REITs***) are superficially similar to mutual funds. Like mutual funds, they purchase and hold a portfolio on behalf of the investors in the trust, and distribute the income from the investments to the investors pro rata. In a REIT, the portfolio consists of real estate rather than company shares or government bonds. Real estate is accorded special tax consideration, and REITs also provide a mechanism for passing the tax advantages of a real estate investment on to the investors in the trust.

In a number of important respects, however, REITs are quite different from conventional mutual funds. The most important difference is that there are a fixed number of investors in a REIT. The units of the trust trade on stock ***exchanges***, and investors who wish to buy or sell units do so through the exchange rather than from the trust itself.

The advantage of exchange trading is that it increases the liquidity of the trust units. For the trust to sell and redeem the units of investors, trust managers would have to reassess the value of the portfolio fairly frequently. Since real estate can sometimes be difficult to value, this reassessment would constitute a significant financial burden. Since the units trade on an exchange, the obligation on the trust to assess the value of the portfolio is reduced, and buyers and sellers are free to negotiate the best possible price. Many mutual funds that specialized in real estate were converted to REITs precisely to take advantage of the increased liquidity offered by exchange trading.

Royalty trusts are similar to REITs in some ways. In a royalty trust, the "portfolio" consists of income-producing resource properties like mines and oil or gas wells. Investors in a royalty trust share the income from the resource property. In addition, royalty trusts are set up to enable the individual investors to take advantage of the various tax concessions for which resource properties are eligible.

The appeal of royalty trusts is that they pay a high dividend, much of which is tax-free for the investor. What is often not understood about the royalty trust is that much of the pay-out to the investor constitutes a return of the capital rather than true "profit." This is important because the return of capital increases the tax liability an investor faces on the sale of the investment. We'll take a closer look at this issue in Chapter 16.

It is also important to recognize that the assets in the portfolio of a royalty trust are ***wasting assets***. Unlike a real estate investment, the value of a resources-producing asset gradually declines as the resources are extracted. If the trust is unable to replace the properties in its portfolio, the value of the trust units will eventually decline to zero. Notably, the cost of acquiring additional properties will reduce the pay-outs to investors. Furthermore, unless investors set aside (or reinvest) a portion of the return from the royalty trust, they could eventually be left with nothing.

CHAPTER TWO

ORGANIZATION AND OPERATION: AN OVERVIEW

EXECUTIVE SUMMARY

This chapter provides an overview of the basic structural and organizational features of mutual funds.

1. There are two basic types of funds:
   - closed-end funds
   - open-end funds

Most investors are concerned with open-end funds.

2. There are several different categories of funds:
   - money market funds
   - equity or growth funds
   - income funds
   - balanced funds

The categories have different objectives and characteristics.

3. Mutual funds are established by sponsors, which take responsibility for ensuring that the new fund satisfies various regulatory requirements, including the preparation of a prospectus and the assignment of administrative functions.

4. The prospectus is a mutual fund's most important disclosure document. It contains a wealth of information, but it can often be difficult to read. The various financial statements of a fund are more useful tools in many ways.

5. The actual operation of a mutual fund is simple. The money invested by unitholders is used by the fund's investment adviser and portfolio manager to purchase a variety of investments. The choice of investments depends both on the objectives of the fund and on the manager's evaluation of specific investment opportunities.

6. The process of purchasing a mutual fund investment is simple and generally straightforward. Purchases and sales take place at the fund's net asset value, which is calculated daily for most funds. Most funds offer a broad variety of options and features to improve their convenience to investors.

7. Although mutual funds are not insured by the Canada Deposit Insurance Corporation, mutual fund investors are protected in a variety of ways.

8. In addition to regular mutual funds there are two specialized types of investments that have a number of similarities to them:
   - segregated funds
   - labour-sponsored venture capital funds

These types of funds are subject to somewhat different regulation than conventional open-end funds.

INTRODUCTION

In Chapter 1 we looked at the basic advantages and disadvantages of mutual funds. In this chapter, we'll take a closer look at how funds are organized.

Types of Funds

There are two basic types of funds.

Closed-End Funds

There are currently about 20 ***closed-end funds*** in Canada. There are many, many more available in the United States. Investing in closed-end funds is very similar to investing in public companies. Investors purchase shares in the fund, and the fund purchases a portfolio of investments. Closed-end funds are offered for sale by the sponsor for a limited time, and the total amount of money that may be invested, or the number of ***shares*** that may be issued, is limited. When the fund has reached the limits set out in the prospectus, no further purchases are possible, and the fund is "closed." Thereafter, shares in a closed-end fund are bought and sold from other investors in the stock market, rather than directly from the fund. Shares in closed-end funds frequently trade at a discount from, or more rarely, a premium to the value of the fund's portfolio. Closed-end funds are discussed in greater detail in Appendix A.

Occasionally, a closed-end fund will be converted to an open-end fund. The usual reason for this "***mutualization***" of a closed-end investment fund is that the shares or units of the closed-end fund have been trading at a discount and that opening the fund will allow the unit price to rise.

Open-End Funds

The ***open-end fund*** is by far the more common form of fund, and is the primary focus of this book. Open-end funds differ from closed-end funds in a number of ways. Units in an open-end fund are bought and sold directly from the fund rather than being traded on stock exchanges. Units of the fund are continuously offered for sale by the fund and the price of the units is determined solely by the value of the investments in the fund portfolio:

the price of shares in an open-end fund are never sold at either a premium or a discount. There is no limit on the number of units or the size of an open-end fund.

Most open-end mutual funds are structured as ***unit trusts***, but some are established as ***investment companies***. An investment company is a corporation with share capital. Investors purchase shares in the company, and the company in turn purchases a portfolio of ***securities*** (***stocks***, ***bonds***, etc.), which constitutes the assets of the corporation. The income from the securities, together with any profit from the buying and selling of the securities, results in a profit (or loss), which is passed on to investors as ***dividends*** of the fund.

A unit trust does not have a share structure. In these funds, the fund is a ***trustee*** for the unitholders, holding the portfolio of investments on behalf of the investors. The income from the investments (***interests***, dividends or ***capital gains***) is passed to the unitholders in the form in which it is received by the trust.

This difference in the way income is reported by the fund can have tax implications, which we'll return to in Chapter 16.

Categories of Funds

All funds, whether open-end or closed-end, fall into one of four basic categories:

- money market
- equity or growth
- income
- balanced

These categories are distinguished from each other by a number of factors, including–

- the fund's objectives
- the kinds of investments the fund makes
- the degree to which prices and returns fluctuate
- the anticipated rate of return

Figure 2-1. The Relationship between Return and Variability of Return for Fund Categories

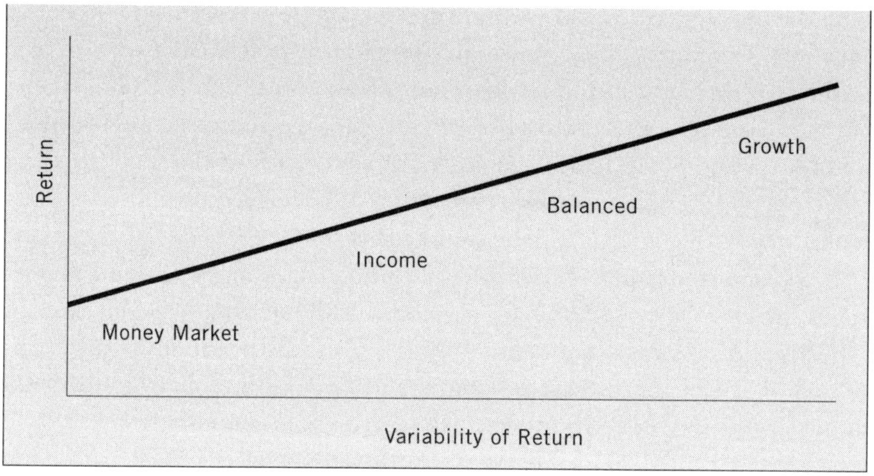

Figure 2-1 shows the basic relationship between return and variability of return for different fund categories. Generally speaking, ***money market funds*** invest in cash and cash-equivalent securities and are characterized by low but stable return. ***Equity*** or ***growth funds*** invest in stocks or equities. Although the returns of these funds are generally higher, these returns also tend to vary more widely from year to year. ***Income*** and ***balanced funds*** occupy intermediate positions. In Chapter 3, we'll look in greater detail at the different kinds of investments available to mutual funds. In Part 2, we'll examine some of the other differences between types of funds in greater detail.

Mechanics

How a Fund is Established

A mutual fund is very similar to an investment club, in which the members pool their resources to purchase investments, and share in any profits of the club. However, since mutual funds are offered to the general public, they are more closely regulated than informal investment clubs.

Mutual funds are established by ***sponsors***. Very often, the sponsor is the first investor in a fund, putting up "seed capital" to ensure that the fund has sufficient resources to purchase an initial portfolio of investments. The sponsor is responsible for the preparation of the various documents that describe the organization of the fund and explain to investors how it will be operated. In addition, the sponsor arranges for the provision of services that a fund requires. For instance, the sponsor will arrange for a bank or trust company to serve as ***custodian*** of the investments purchased by the fund, and for an auditor to review the financial statements of the fund. In some cases, the sponsor also secures a ***distributor***, which is responsible for advertising, marketing, and selling the fund to investors.

The sponsor is also responsible for choosing a manager, and (sometimes) an ***investment adviser*** for the fund. Although the basic investment objectives of the fund are defined by the prospectus, the investment approach and specific investment choices are determined by the portfolio manager and investment adviser. These professionals' characteristics are therefore critically important to the performance of the fund, and we'll examine them in some detail in Chapter 14.

The sponsor often benefits from the establishment of the fund in one or more of the following ways:

- It may act as the manager of the fund and is paid a management fee to do so.

- It may act as the portfolio manager or distributor for the fund and receives part of the management fee.

- It may offer other financial services to the public and attracts customers for its other services through the mutual funds it sponsors. This is particularly true when the sponsor is a bank or trust company.

Most mutual funds, and certainly all the major ones, are part of one fund group or another. The funds in each group are typically administered by a common sponsor, but each fund in the group has distinct investment objectives and policies, and may use the services of a specific investment adviser or portfolio manager. Mackenzie Financial Corporation, for example, is the sponsor for 30 separate funds organized into three fund groups.

Important Documents

There are a number of documents governing the structure of operation of a mutual fund. The most important ones include–

- the Declaration of Trust
- the custodian agreement
- management agreements

In addition, there are a number of documents that explain a fund's operation to investors. These documents are called ***disclosure documents*** and include–

- the prospectus
- financial statements
- the annual information form

We'll look briefly at each of these disclosure documents to highlight the most important features.

The Prospectus

The ***prospectus*** is the basic disclosure document required to be issued in connection with sales of securities. According to securities legislation, its purpose is to provide the prospective investor with "full, true and plain disclosure" of all material facts relating to the securities. Securities laws in Canada provide certain rights to purchasers of securities issued pursuant to a prospectus if it contains a misrepresentation or fails to disclose a material fact. There are detailed requirements governing the contents of a prospectus.

Most Canadian mutual funds are now issued pursuant to a ***simplified prospectus***. The simplified prospectus system for mutual funds in intended to provide investors the legal protection provided by a prospectus, combined with all up-to-date additional information afforded by the ***continuous disclosure*** requirements. The simplified prospectus itself is intended to be a concise presentation in plain language of relevant information about the fund an investor should know before making a decision to buy its securities. It incorporates by reference and is accompanied by the fund's annual information form and its audited financial statements, which include a balance sheet, a statement of income, a statement of investment portfolio, a statement of transactions and a statement of changes in net assets. All these documents together form the fund's permanent information record.

Funds that are available only to ***sophisticated investors*** require a substantial minimum investment and are subject to less rigorous disclosure requirements. In such cases, the funds may be offered to the public by way of an ***offering memorandum***. (In Ontario, the minimum investment is $150,000; in British Columbia, it is $97,000.)

Securities law requires that prospective investors be provided with a copy of the prospectus at the time of purchase. Although the prospectus contains a wealth of information concerning issues such as investment objectives, practices and restrictions; management; the valuation of fund units; and sales charges, it is fundamentally a legal document and it is often rather dry and dull. In addition, the information it contains is necessarily somewhat general. Considerable progress has been made by a number of fund companies towards making the prospectus more accessible and relevant to the average investor, but there is still room for improvement.

The Purchase and Sale of the Fund

Mutual funds are purchased and sold at their ***net asset value***, the total value of the investments in the fund portfolio (less any liabilities) divided by the number of units in the fund. For example, a fund with 20 million units or shares and an investment portfolio worth $100 million will have a net asset value of $5. Investors purchasing the fund will pay $5 *per unit* or *share*. Since the purchase takes place at net asset value, the transaction does not affect the price.

Net asset value depends on the value of the investments in the portfolio. If the value of the investments in the portfolio rises, the net asset value of the fund will also rise; if the value of the portfolio holdings declines, the fund's net asset value will also drop. In many cases, the value of the fund's investments is determined daily, based on their market price at the close of business. However, for investments that do not trade frequently, the process of establishing value is more involved and far less reliable.

The Management of the Fund

The prospectus is required to identify the manager of the fund. As we'll discuss in Chapter 14, the manager is responsible for the operation of the fund and in particular for decisions about portfolio investments on behalf of the unitholders. Often, the prospectus authorizes the manager to delegate various functions and responsibilities to "subadvisers." And, although securities legislation requires that unitholders approve any change in the manager of the fund, there is generally no obligation on the part of the manager to seek the approval of unitholders when reassigning these responsibilities. As a result, it is often difficult to determine precisely who is responsible for the fund's portfolio.

The Investment Objectives and Policies of the Fund

Although investors are constantly advised to read the prospectus, it is generally unhelpful in identifying the fund's investment objectives. There are several reasons for this.

- The descriptions of the fund's investment objectives are typically too general to be useful guides to the way in which the fund will be managed.

- Depending on how the management of the fund is structured, the portfolio manager may have great discretion in choosing the fund's investment portfolio within the specified objectives of the fund. The choice of portfolio manager accordingly has enormous implications for the investment approach that the fund adopts, and a change in the portfolio manager can precipitate an abrupt change in the investment approach.

- Securities regulations require unitholder approval for any change in the ***fundamental investment objectives*** of the fund, but exactly what constitutes a "fundamental investment objective" is rarely specified. As a result, the manager may change many of the fund's characteristics, including the risk profile. The fundamental investment objective of the *AIC Advantage Fund*, for example, is to "maximize return in a manner which is consistent with the preservation of capital by investing primarily in Canadian equity securities." Over the past few years, this fund has achieved impressive returns by investing in companies with a focus on the wealth management industry, but this focus is clearly not a fundamental investment objective and is therefore open to change without notice.

- While various investment practices (such as buying on margin, or short-selling) are prohibited by present legislation, some funds authorize the manager to use these practices in the event the prohibitions are lifted.

The Risks of the Fund

Although the prospectus devotes a great deal of attention to disclosing the "risk factors" of the investment, for the most part this disclosure is inadequate. In part, this is because the concept of ***risk*** has a variety of meanings, as you'll see in Chapter 5. In part as well, it is because the language of investment analysis is often quite technical. In particular, reviews of the risks of ***derivatives*** are typically complicated, as the following excerpt illustrates:

> The Fund may invest in, and use derivative instruments for hedging and non-hedging purposes... There can be no assurance that a Fund's hedging strategies will be effective. There may be an imperfect historical correlation between changes in the market value of the investment, or attribute of the investment (including currency exposure) being hedged, and the instrument with which the investment or attribute is hedged, and any historical correlation may not continue for the period during which the hedge is in place...
>
> In addition, there is the risk of loss by a Fund of margin deposits in the event of bankruptcy of a dealer with whom the Fund has an open position in an option or forward contract...

For the average investor, this description of potential risks is incomprehensible.

Fees and Expenses

One issue that the prospectus does a very good job of explaining is the matter of fees and expenses. However, while most investors perceive this issue to be important, in fact fees and expenses are usually the least important factors in choosing a mutual fund investment. In Chapter 18, we discuss fees in detail.

For those who want to wrestle with the minutiae of the prospectus, we've provided a fuller outline in Appendix B.

Financial Statements

Financial statements for the preceding five years must accompany, or be incorporated in, the simplified prospectus. While many investors ignore these statements, they contain information that is useful in evaluating a mutual fund. They disclose, for example, the fund's ***management expense ratios*** for the preceding five years. The management expense ratio indicates what portion of a fund's profit goes to paying expenses, and can therefore be helpful in evaluating the efficiency of management.

In addition to the financial statements required of any business, such as the ***balance sheet*** and ***statement of earnings***, two financial statements are unique to mutual funds.

- The ***statement of investment portfolio*** describes the investments of the fund on a specific date. Funds are required to report this information twice a year, but many funds put out quarterly reports.
- The ***statement of portfolio transactions*** itemizes the investments that the fund has bought and sold since the last report.

Taken together, these statements are useful in assessing ***portfolio turnover***, which indicates the frequency with which the fund's investments are traded. As we'll see in Chapter 15, portfolio turnover is an important indicator of the fund manager's investment approach. In addition, we'll see in Chapter 16 that portfolio turnover has a significant effect on the potential tax liability of a mutual fund investment.

Annual Information Form

The ***annual information form*** essentially fills in the gaps between the information that securities regulators require in full prospectuses, and the data that is included in the simplified prospectus permitted for most mutual funds. This form is available to investors upon request, and discloses–

- names of officers and directors of the fund
- remuneration and financial circumstances of officers and directors
- major share- or unitholders of the fund and the manager
- names of those who perform the principal functions of the fund
- interests of management in transactions that may materially affect the fund
- a five-year history of management fees
- greater detail with respect to investment objectives and practices
- significant holdings of other investments

Operations

The basic operation of a mutual fund is deceptively simple. Investors' funds are used by the manager as they are received to purchase a variety of investments which are combined in a portfolio. The choice of investments is dictated first by the fundamental investment objectives and ***investment policies*** specified in the prospectus, and second by the manager's investment approach. The portfolio of a growth fund will emphasize equities, while that of an income fund will emphasize debt securities.

The value of a mutual fund increases in two ways. First, the various investments that the mutual fund manager makes may generate income. Second, the value of the investments may rise. Since the net asset value of a fund reflects the value of the investments in the portfolio, an increase in the value of those investments will result in an increase in net asset value.

Features

Despite the variety of features offered by mutual funds, the process of investing in mutual funds is quite simple.

- The purchase and redemption (or sale) of a fund is effected after the close of the financial markets on any day when the fund's net asset value is calculated. The ***settlement date*** for the transaction (when payment must be made) is three business days following the transaction date.

- Most funds calculate net asset value daily and permit purchases and redemptions daily. The net asset value of some funds (notably those investing in ***illiquid*** investments such as real estate) is set only weekly, monthly, or even quarterly. These funds thus offer fewer opportunities for redemption than other funds.

- The dollar amount of the investment is divided by the current net asset value to establish the number of units that will be purchased. Fractions of units are possible. For example, an investment of $6,000 in a mutual fund with a current net asset value of $14.58 will purchase 411 units plus 523/1000 of a unit. While this is an awkward way of expressing fractions, it is currently the industry standard.

There is almost always a minimum amount required for an initial purchase, and a lower minimum for additional purchases. The minimums vary widely. Many funds have minimums as low as $1,000, while several have minimums of $150,000. Most funds impose lower minimums on investments for tax-advantaged plans such as ***registered retirement savings plans (RRSPs)***.

- Many, but not all, funds impose sales charges on the purchase of units. Sales charges imposed when the units are purchased are called ***front-end loads***, while sales charges levied when the investment is sold are called ***deferred sales charges***. Front-end loads are often negotiable, while deferred sales charges typically decline with the length of the investment. We'll return to fees in greater detail in Chapter 18.

- Most funds offer the convenience of periodic purchase plans. In these plans, a fixed amount is withdrawn from the investor's bank account at regular intervals for the purchase of fund units. The frequency of the withdrawals varies from monthly to quarterly. Purchases are made at the prevailing net asset value.

The idea underlying these plans is called ***dollar cost averaging***. By investing a set amount at regular intervals, the investor buys more shares or units when the price is low, and fewer units when the price is high. As a result, the average price of the investment is reduced. While dollar cost averaging is frequently advertised as a way to maximize investment returns, the returns from lump-sum investing are almost always greater. Such programs are useful only as a method of forced saving. For those who are interested, a more detailed explanation of dollar cost averaging can be found in Appendix C.

- Fund groups generally permit ***switches*** from one fund to another within the same family of funds at a reduced cost. Groups that are sold by dealers may impose a modest additional sales charge (which is often negotiable and is typically limited to a maximum of 2 percent of assets). Other groups impose only fixed administrative "fees." Almost all groups restrict the number of low-cost transfers. As we'll see in Chapter 16, however, switches can entail tax liability.

- From time to time, the fund will make a ***distribution*** of the profits from the fund. Since the net asset value of a fund reflects the value of all its assets, including cash in the bank, unit values decline when distributions are paid.

For tax reasons, distributions must be made at least once per year, but many funds make distributions more frequently. The distributions of money market funds are most frequent, with some funds making distributions weekly. The frequency of distributions of income funds depends on the fund portfolio. While most make distributions monthly or quarterly, a few make distributions only semi-annually or annually. Growth funds typically make only annual distributions.

The amount of the distributions also varies. Some funds—notably income funds—attempt to make the amount of their distributions consistent. The amount of the distribution of other funds—particularly growth funds—will vary considerably from year to year.

The amount of the distribution can be spent, or it can be reinvested in the fund at the current net asset value. Most funds have automatic reinvestment plans. It is important to remember that a fund's reported performance is based on the assumption that distributions are reinvested. Investors who choose to spend the distributions often forget to consider this in comparing the performance of their investment to the fund's reported performance.

- To address the problem of irregular distributions for investors who require a regular income from the investment, most funds offer systematic withdrawal plans, which permit investors to automatically redeem sufficient units to provide predetermined cash payments.

Using systematic withdrawals can have three important consequences. In cases where the fund was purchased on a deferred sales charge basis, the withdrawals may be subject to the deduction of sales charges. In addition, the systematic withdrawal of amounts that exceed distributions and appreciation will ultimately result in encroachment on (and possible exhaustion of) the original investment. Finally, any systematic withdrawals will have tax implications.

- Many funds, and certainly all the major fund groups, provide their unitholders with a virtual avalanche of reports and newsletters. Securities law requires funds to provide financial reports at least twice a year, but many funds issue quarterly reports, and several publish monthly bulletins. Many fund companies provide regular reports on the fund manager's outlook and periodic commentary on the financial markets. Some funds make their commentaries available by telephone as well. A number of funds offer financial planning software of various kinds. Finally, the Internet provides yet another avenue for communication between fund managers and investors. Unfortunately, the volume of this information is no assurance of its quality.

- At the end of each year, the fund provides a tax receipt that distinguishes the income from the fund as interest, dividends, or capital gains. For funds held in tax-advantaged plans, like RRSPs and registered retirement income funds (RRIFs), the income is not subject to tax. For investments that are not tax sheltered, the income must be reported.

- Several fund groups have devoted considerable effort to making statements more useful, by identifying the individual investor's ***adjusted cost base*** and rate of return.

Investor Protections

There are a number of investor safeguards built into the way in which mutual funds are organized and regulated.

- The securities and other assets of a fund are held for safekeeping by a ***custodian***, separate and apart from the assets of the fund manager. Chartered banks and trust companies may act as custodians.

This prevents improper dealings with the investments of the fund. While this may seem an unlikely event, such a separation offers real protection. For example, in the collapse of the Alberta-based Principal Group, only the mutual fund investors were protected from loss because the fund's investments were segregated from the company's other assets.

- Funds are required to appoint ***auditors*** to review the way in which the financial statements of the fund are prepared.

The general role of the auditor is to ensure that the accounting procedures of the fund conform to "generally accepted accounting principles." In particular, the auditors have a role in ensuring that the stated value of the investments in the fund matches the net asset value.

- Certain significant changes in the affairs of a mutual fund, such as changes in the fundamental investment objectives, the manager, the auditor, or any decrease in the frequency of calculating not asset value, can only be made with the approval of the unitholders, which must be obtained at a meeting convened for that purpose. The purpose of this requirement is to ensure investors have some control over the way in which their money is managed.

- There is a general portfolio content rule, called the market exposure rule which restricts a mutual fund from buying securities of any issuer if, after the purchase is made, more than 10 percent of the fund's net assets would be invested in that issuer's securities. In addition, the fund may not hold more than 10 percent of any class or series of a class of securities of such issuer. This restriction does not apply to certain government securities.

This market exposure rule is designed to ensure that there is a minimum level of diversification in the fund portfolio, and to prevent the portfolio manager from taking inordinate risks with investors' resources. There are also specific rules governing investments in real estate, and other illiquid assets.

- There are extensive rules governing investments in derivatives

These rules are intended to prevent the use of riskier types of derivatives, and thereby limit the potential for uncontrolled loss. Mutual funds may only use ***permitted derivatives***, which may be broadly characterized as derivatives for which a reasonably clearly identifiable market exists.

A mutual fund is not restricted in its use of permitted derivatives if they are used only for hedging. A ***hedge*** is a technique for reducing risk by pairing investments so that price changes in one investment are offset by opposing price changes in the other. The use of permitted derivatives includes hedging all or a portion of the currency exposure of an investment.

A mutual fund may not use permitted derivatives to do indirectly what it is restricted from doing directly when investing in securities. In addition, it may not use permitted derivatives to obtain any ***leverage*** in addition to what is already permitted. Leverage is the synthetic enlargement of an investment, magnifying the opportunity for profits or losses. Because options can provide leverage, a mutual fund may not invest more than 10 percent of its assets in options. Finally, a mutual find may not be exposed to unlimited liabilities through the use of derivatives: it is required to hold sufficient assets in connection with its derivatives liabilities to ensure that they can be discharged. We'll return to the use of derivatives in our discussion of financial assets in Chapter 3. Additional information is contained in Appendix F.

- The fund must report regularly to unitholders. Provincial securities regulators impose minimum standards on the information that must be reported to unitholders. In Ontario, this information includes financial statements, such as the balance sheet, statement of investment portfolio, statement of portfolio transactions, and statement of changes in financial position. In addition, trade confirmations must be delivered to an investor promptly and disclose the price per unit or share at which the transaction was effected and the amount deducted for sales, service, and other charges. Finally, account statements must be delivered at least annually and disclose:

> the number and market value at the date of purchase or redemption of securities purchased or redeemed during the period since the date of the last statement...and showing the total market value of all securities of the mutual fund held by the client.
>
> [RRO, 1990, Reg.1015, sec.123(5)]

- The basis on which fund performance is calculated and advertised is controlled. For example, money market funds must calculate ***indicated yield*** according to a specified formula and disclose the indicated yield whether or not any other measure of performance is employed. ***Standard performance data*** must be at least as prominent as other performance data in any advertising or promotional material. For all funds except money market funds, standard performance data is the fund's compound annual return over one, three, five, and ten years, together with disclosure of the assumptions on which the calculations are based. In addition, the advertisement of performance data for multiple funds must be uniform.

These requirements are intended to prevent fund sponsors from emphasizing the performance of their "best" funds in such a way that confusion about performance of other funds might result.

A Note on Hybrid Funds

Segregated Funds

Segregated funds are a special type of open-end investment fund particular to the life insurance industry. They are essentially variable life insurance policies in which the value of the benefit is determined by the market price of a portfolio of investments. While they superficially resemble conventional mutual funds in some ways, they differ in important respects.

Proponents of segregated funds usually highlight their advantages:

- The most widely advertised advantage of segregated funds over conventional mutual funds is that a minimum of 75 percent of the principal amount invested in a segregated fund is guaranteed by the sponsoring insurance company. Although this guarantee sounds wonderful, the reality is less impressive. To qualify for the guarantee, investors must retain the investment for a minimum of ten years (fifteen years in some cases) or until death. As we'll see in future chapters, the likelihood of actual loss over ten years in a properly managed fund is almost nil. In addition, there is no guarantee of any return beyond the return of the amount invested. In other words, the funds make no promises about potential profits. Nevertheless, the comfort of a guarantee is extremely attractive to some investors.

- Another advantage is that segregated funds may be rendered creditor-proof in certain circumstances because they are a form of life insurance. Unlike conventional mutual funds—even those held in a tax-sheltered plan—these investments are generally protected from creditors if a preferred beneficiary (a spouse or dependent child) is designated.

- In addition, the entire value of the investment passes to designated beneficiaries, while the estate remains responsible for any tax liability.

But segregated funds also have some drawbacks:

- Since segregated funds are regarded as an insurance product rather than as "securities," they are governed by the various insurance acts, rather than by securities acts, and are largely exempt from the close scrutiny to which conventional mutual funds are subject. For those who are interested, we've provided a comprehensive list of the differences in regulation in Appendix D.

  The differences in the regulation of segregated funds and conventional funds have been the source of considerable debate within the industry. In July 1997, in response to criticisms about the limitations in the regulation of segregated funds, the Canadian Life and Health Insurance Association (CLHIA) released new guidelines regarding their operation. While addressing some of the critics' concerns, these new guidelines still differ from the rules under which conventional funds operate. Most importantly, the guidelines apply to less than 30 percent of the industry: more than 70 percent of these funds are sold under group plans, to which the guidelines do not apply. In addition, the CLHIA guidelines are purely voluntary: there is no requirement that the manager of a segregated fund adhere to these guidelines, and more significantly, there is no sanction for noncompliance. Finally, the guidelines require the disclosure of payments to salespeople only when these payments may be charged against the assets of the fund. Unlike the voluntary code governing conventional funds, there is no requirement that payments to salespeople by the insurer be disclosed.

- Although the assets of a segregated fund are separate from the general assets of the sponsoring insurance company, the assets which determine the fund's obligation to an investor are not necessarily the assets which comprise the fund's portfolio.

- The commissions on segregated funds are generally less negotiable.

Perhaps the most interesting fact about these funds is that very often the management of their investment portfolios is handled by the managers of conventional mutual funds. The *Manulife Vistafunds,* for example, are managed by Altamira, and the *Transamerica Growsafe Funds* are managed by Guardian Capital.

Labour-Sponsored Investment Funds

Labour-sponsored venture capital corporations are a type of fund authorized by the federal government in 1991 to stimulate investment in small businesses and thereby encourage employment. Various provincial governments have subsequently joined the federal initiative. Although these funds are subject to provincial securities legislation and are regulated in some respects like mutual funds, some of the rules designed to protect mutual fund investors do not apply to these funds.

The mandate of these funds is to invest in small- to medium-sized companies for which there is often not a public or published market. This focus has three major consequences:

- Given the nature of the investments these funds are intended to make, they are more speculative. There are fewer limits on the amount that can be invested in individual securities or illiquid investments.

- These funds are more difficult to value accurately. Small- to medium-sized businesses are typically private, or closely-held corporations for which there may be little or no market in which their shares can be sold. Thus, the mechanisms by which prices and values are established operate less efficiently. The prospectus of the *Integrated Growth Fund* (now *Canadian Venture Opportunity Fund*) describes this difficulty as follows:

> Most [conventional] mutual funds value their investments at the closing market price at which they can be bought and sold... The valuations [of investments in labour-sponsored funds] may not reflect the prices at which investments can actually be sold, partic-

ularly after taking into account associated selling costs such as sales commissions and legal fees.

- These funds are often less liquid. The illiquidity of their portfolios and the difficulties of accurately establishing net asset values may require these funds to control and sometimes limit the right of investors to redeem units. Heavy redemptions in circumstances where net asset values can only be estimated might unduly depress net asset values for remaining investors. As a result, aggregate annual redemptions are limited to 20 percent of the asset value of the fund.

The other feature that sets labour-sponsored funds apart from conventional mutual funds is the unique tax treatment they are accorded. Both the federal and provincial governments offer tax credits on purchases of these funds. The purpose of the tax incentives was to encourage investment in these funds by providing a "cushion" against the risks of investing in small and fledgling businesses. The reality is that tax incentives, rather than investment merits, have become the focus of the marketing campaigns for these funds. With the combination of the tax credits and the maximum tax deductions available for RRSPs, the total tax relief appears to approach 80 percent. Although widely quoted in comparing these funds to conventional mutual funds, this calculation is grossly misleading because conventional mutual funds do not include the RRSP-based tax relief in promoting their value.

For those who are interested, we've included a more detailed discussion of the investment restrictions, risk factors, and tax considerations of labour-sponsored funds in Appendix E.

CHAPTER THREE

FINANCIAL ASSETS

EXECUTIVE SUMMARY

This chapter provides an introduction to the basic types of investments.

1. Investments can be divided into types or asset classes on the basis of their characteristics. The most basic asset classes include–
   - equities (stocks)
   - fixed-income investments
   - cash and cash equivalents
   - real estate
   - commodities and financial futures

2. The most typical equity is the common stock of a company. Equities constitute ownership in a business. They provide an opportunity for profit to the investor in two ways. As the company grows, the value of a share in the business also grows and becomes more valuable, so that the share can be sold for more than its purchase price. In addition, the company can pay a portion of its profit to the owners of the company as dividends.

3. There are an enormous number of factors that can affect the profitability of equities, and investors (including fund managers) use various approaches to identify the most promising investments.

4. Fixed-income assets are loans. The simplest example is a bond. Like other loans, the profit of these investments comes from the interest that borrowers pay. As a result, the price of bonds and other fixed-income investments is tied very closely to changes in interest rates. As interest rates rise, the value of a bond declines; as interest rates drop, the value of a bond rises.

5. Cash refers to both money in the bank and debt investments that mature within one year. Short-term debt investments are included with cash because they are highly liquid and because their price does not vary substantially as a result of changes in interest rates.

6. An investment in real estate can be either an equity or a debt. Equity investments in real estate are determined by appraisal rather than by auction on an exchange. This situation creates special difficulties for investors.

7. Debt investments in real estate are called mortgages. They can be purchased directly or by way of mortgage-backed securities. Mortgages and some mortgage-backed securities are different from bonds and other fixed-income investments because the income for investors is complicated by the repayment of the principal of the debt.

8. Commodities include tangible things such as oil, gold, coffee, and grain, and some intangible things like contracts for financial instruments. They are purchased or sold in anticipation of changes in their prices. Since the price of commodities can fluctuate unpredictably, they can be risky.

9. Derivatives are investments that are based on, or derived from, another investment. A commodity future is a derivative because the investment is not in the commodity itself, but is a contract based on the commodity. Although there are a variety of uses for derivatives, they can also easily be misused. In addition, there can be significant difficulties in establishing the value of some derivatives. Taken together, the difficulties of valuation and the potential for misuse can result in significant investment losses.

10. Foreign assets are really no different from domestic assets. However, they are dealt with separately because foreign investments present additional risks. The most obvious concern is the fluctuation in exchange rates between foreign markets and the domestic market. A devaluation of the foreign currency can severely reduce (or eliminate) profits. In addition, administrative procedures differ markedly from domestic practice even in developed markets, and can make foreign investments cumbersome. In developing markets, there is often far less regulatory supervision; thus, the valuation of investments in these "emerging" markets can be particularly uncertain.

INTRODUCTION

Investments can be divided into types or asset classes on the basis of their differing characteristics. The basic asset classes are–

- equities (stocks)
- fixed-income investments
- cash and cash equivalents
- real estate
- commodities and financial futures

Investors, including the portfolio managers of mutual funds, combine these asset classes in various ways, depending on their specific objectives. In this chapter, we'll look at the general characteristics of these asset classes and the way in which investors profit from them.

In addition, we'll examine two special types of assets:

- foreign assets
- derivatives

Foreign assets are merely investments beyond our borders. Derivatives are investments that are based on, or derived from, an underlying asset. Both these sorts of investments are becoming increasingly important, and it is therefore important to understand their characteristics.

Equities

Equities such as ***common stocks*** represent ownership of an interest in a business. Like the owners of any business, an equity investor has two expectations: first, that the business will make a profit and distribute at least some of the profit to the shareholders as dividends; second, that some of the profit will be used to expand the business, increasing the value of the business.

Analysts use a number of criteria to categorize and compare equities. Some of these criteria are described on the following page.

- **market capitalization**

  Market capitalization is a measure of the size of a corporation, determined by multiplying the number of shares by the price per share.

  "Blue chip" stocks are shares of large, well-established companies and generally have market capitalizations over $500 million. They often pay regular dividends, and the returns are consequently reasonably stable.

  "Small-cap" stocks are the opposite of blue chip stocks: they have smaller market capitalizations (under $300 million). They are far less likely to pay dividends, and their returns are typically less secure, but they often have the potential for greater growth than the blue chips.

- **earnings pattern**

  Investments may also be distinguished on the basis of their earnings. ***Value stocks*** often have strong earnings relative to their price. The earnings of ***growth stocks*** are typically quite modest in relation to their price, but they have greater potential for growth. ***Cyclical stocks***, as their name suggests, have earnings that fluctuate in relation to the business cycle for their industry

- **economic sector**

  The alternating periods of strength and weakness in the economy are called the ***business cycle***. At different stages in the business cycle, different kinds of businesses will do best. Industrial products, for example, do well when the economy is growing. Resources stocks typically do best in the latter stages of an economic expansion.

- **geographical location**

  Different countries have different business cycles. As a result, the stocks of foreign companies, domestic companies, and domestic companies doing business in foreign countries will do well at different times.

Valuing Equities

There are two basic methods of evaluating equity investments:

- fundamental analysis
- technical analysis

Fundamental analysis is based on the view that the future value of an investment can be anticipated from characteristics of the business itself, including the current soundness of the company and expectations about profitability of the business.

The most widely used measure of stock values is the relationship between the price of a stock and the per-share profit of the company. This is called the ***price/earnings ratio***, or ***p/e ratio***. The historical average p/e ratio for the Canadian market (represented by the ***Toronto Stock Exchange Composite Index 300*** (***TSE 300***) is approximately 16 times earnings. This means that if a company earns $1 per year per share, the price of the stock has historically been around $16. It is important to understand, though, that this is a long-term average that varies over time and from industry to industry and country to country. The average p/e ratio in Canada tends to fluctuate widely because the Canadian market is concentrated in resources sectors. Since the U.S. market is more diversified, its average p/e ratio is often regarded as a more reliable ***benchmark***. The long-term historical average p/e ratio of the ***Standard & Poor's 500 Index*** (***S&P 500***) is 14 times earnings.

Within fundamental analysis, there are two basic "schools." ***Value investing*** focuses on the current soundness of the company, examining for example its ***liquidation value***. Liquidation value is the price that would be realized if the company were dissolved and the assets sold off. If the company's share price is less than its liquidation value, the stock is undervalued: for whatever reason, investors are unwilling to pay the true value of the company. In the absence of any sound explanation for the depressed price, it is presumed that the market will ultimately recognize the true value of the company and bid up the price of the stock. Value stocks usually have substantial liquidation values relative to price and often have low p/e ratios.

Disney is a good example of a value company. Prior to the appointment of Michael Eisner as chief executive, the value of the stock had languished despite the fact that the company owned an extensive library of classic animated films. By restoring and re-releasing the animated classics and distributing them on video, Eisner successfully realized a new source of income from the previously unrecognized value of the film library, and the price of the stock soared.

Growth investing emphasizes the prospects of a business. Growth investors weigh the current price of the investment against the expected income from the business. The focus of growth investing is therefore the identification of factors that will affect the anticipated profit of the company. The p/e ratios of growth stocks are often quite high because investors are willing to pay higher prices in anticipation of high future profits, and the liquidation values of these stocks are typically quite low relative to price.

Wal-Mart is an excellent example of a growth stock. Sam Walton started his business in 1952 as a single five-and-dime store in Fayetteville, Arkansas. By offering a distinct mix of products and employing innovative techniques to lower costs, he created a novel approach to merchandising that has been enormously successful. The company first sold its shares to the public in 1970 at $16.50 per share; since then, the stock has "split" two-for-one on ten separate occasions. An investor who purchased one share in 1970 would currently have 1,024 shares with a total value of over $27,600. The ***compound annual return*** (which we'll discuss in Chapter 4) has been approximately 50 percent.

Technical analysis is based on the view that historical trends in the fluctuation of prices, and the volume of shares traded, can be used to predict future price movements. Instead of examining the financial circumstances of a company, technical analysis focuses on the market behaviour of the stock, and attempts to anticipate changes in the demand for particular stocks, since this variation is expected to result in price changes. In the words of economist John Maynard Keynes, these analysts try to determine "what average opinion expects average opinion to be."

The chief analytical tool of technical analysts is ***charting***, in which the prices and volumes of stock transactions are plotted on graphs. By presenting market information in graphical form, analysts attempt to identify trends and, more particularly, changes in trends that serve as signals to buy or sell securities. Most technical analysts also rely on other indicators of market behaviour such as the "confidence index" and the "market breadth indicator" to confirm the emergence and development of trends.

In short, technical analysis attempts to figure out ahead of time what other investors are going to do. In situations of near "hysteria," this approach can sometimes forecast very short-term tendencies in the overall market, but its use in identifying longer-term trends or specific investment opportunities is extremely limited.

A Note on Preferred Shares

Preferred shares also represent an ownership interest in a business. They are distinguished from common shares because the right to dividends or the claim on corporate assets in the event of dissolution is *in preference to* that of common shares. Moreover, unlike common stock, the dividend on preferred shares is usually "fixed" at a particular rate (although the possibility of changes in the rate or amount of preferred dividends may be features of a particular share issue). However, unlike bonds and debentures (which we address below), the right to dividends on preferred shares is not absolute: the payment of dividends may be suspended if earnings decline sharply.

Stocks and Mutual Funds

The manager of a mutual fund uses the same methods as individual investors to choose stocks for a fund's portfolio. In fact, an equity or stock fund is really nothing more than a portfolio of stocks that comes complete with professional investment advice and management. The success of the fund will depend in large measure on the skill of the manager, and we'll look at the approaches used to select stocks in Chapter 13.

Fixed-Income Investments

Fixed-income securities include debt investments that last longer than one year, such as bonds, ***debentures***, and ***mortgages***. We'll deal with bonds and debentures in this section and address mortgages in the section on real estate.

The basic difference between bonds and equities is that, while equities represent ownership in a business, bonds and debentures are essentially loans. Bond investors are entitled to receive interest payments. Generally speaking, bonds have specific collateral, while debentures do not. (However, government bonds are still called bonds, even though they have no specific collateral.)

The fact that a bond is a loan has three significant consequences:

- The price of bonds is closely related to interest rates.
- The length of a bond investment is limited. While most equity investments are perpetual, bonds have a maturity date when the loan is to be repaid.
- The ability of the borrower to repay the debt is important.

Setting Interest Rates for Bonds

The interest rate on a bond is called the ***coupon***. It is almost always "fixed." (It is for this reason that bonds are referred to as "fixed-income" investments.) The coupon is determined by the issuer of the bond. Three important factors affect the coupon:

- **the prevailing interest rates**
  The coupon will reflect the interest rates prevailing in the economy. When interest rates are high, issuers will offer high coupons. When interest rates are low, issuers can offer low coupons.

- **the term of the bond**
  The relationship between interest rates and the term of the bond is called the ***yield curve***. Normally, the yield curve is "positive," meaning that bonds issued for longer terms have higher coupons than shorter bonds. The reason is that investors expect additional compensation for assuming the "risk" of relatively greater uncertainty about interest rates further in the future. Occasionally, this usual pattern is disrupted, and an ***inverted yield curve*** develops, usually as a result of moves by the U.S. Federal Reserve Bank to limit the supply of money in the economy. (The Bank of Canada can also tighten the supply of money in the Canadian economy, but the impact of "the Fed" is vastly greater.)

- **the quality of the bond**
  The quality of a bond reflects the ability of the issuer to make the promised interest payments, and is based on its ***credit rating***. Bonds issued by the government of Canada and by provincial governments have the highest ratings because there is virtually no chance that these issuers will default on the obligation to make interest payments. Bonds issued by large companies with a solid history of earnings are rated lower than government bonds and must offer a higher coupon to compensate, but are still ***investment grade***. Bonds issued by borrowers with little or no history of earnings must offer even higher coupons. These bonds are often called ***high-yield*** or ***"junk" bonds***.

The Relationship between Interest Rates and Bond Prices

Since the coupon of a bond issue almost never varies, while interest rates are constantly changing, the value of a bond will reflect the relationship between its coupon rate and the prevailing interest rates. As interest rates rise, the value of a bond falls, since the fixed coupon rate of the bond becomes less attractive than prevailing rates. As interest rates decline, the value of a bond rises, since the fixed coupon of the bond becomes more attractive than prevailing rates.

As Figure 3-1 shows, the relationship between interest rates and bond prices can be compared to the movement of a teeter-totter, with bond prices at one end and interest rates at the other.

Figure 3-1. Interest Rates versus Bond Prices

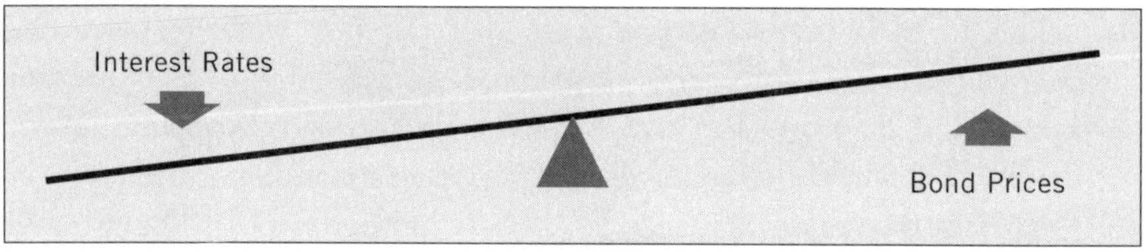

A simplified example will illustrate the relationship. Although bonds are both issued and redeemed at ***face***, or ***par value***, in the intervening period they can be bought and sold in the bond market. A $1,000 bond with a coupon rate of 10 percent will produce an income of $100 per year. If the prevailing interest rate is 10 percent, a purchaser will pay $1,000 to receive the income of $100. If, however, the prevailing interest rate increases to 11 percent, new bonds will be issued with coupons that reflect this higher interest rate, and an investor paying $1,000 will receive an income of $110. These new bonds will therefore be more attractive than the old bonds.

The old bond can, however, be made more attractive with a ***discounted*** price. This has two effects. The first is that the income of $100 will now be more than 10 percent of the purchase price. The second is that the investor can now realize a profit from the difference between the price paid for the bond and the $1,000 payable when the bond matures.

On the other hand, the old bond will become more valuable if the prevailing interest rate drops to 9 percent, and the price of the bond will attract a ***premium*** because its interest rate is higher than that available on new bonds.

There are at least two factors that will affect the degree to which changes in interest rates precipitate changes in the price of a bond:

• term to maturity

The longer the term to maturity, the greater the effect a change in prevailing interest rates will have on the price of the bond. In our example above, the longer the 1 percent increase in income is available—that is, the longer the time before the bond is redeemed at par—the greater the value of the incremental income. This means that the value of bonds with longer maturities fluctuates much more than the value of bonds with shorter maturities. Figure 3-2 illustrates this relationship between maturity and price.

Figure 3-2. The Effect of Maturity on Changes in Bond Prices

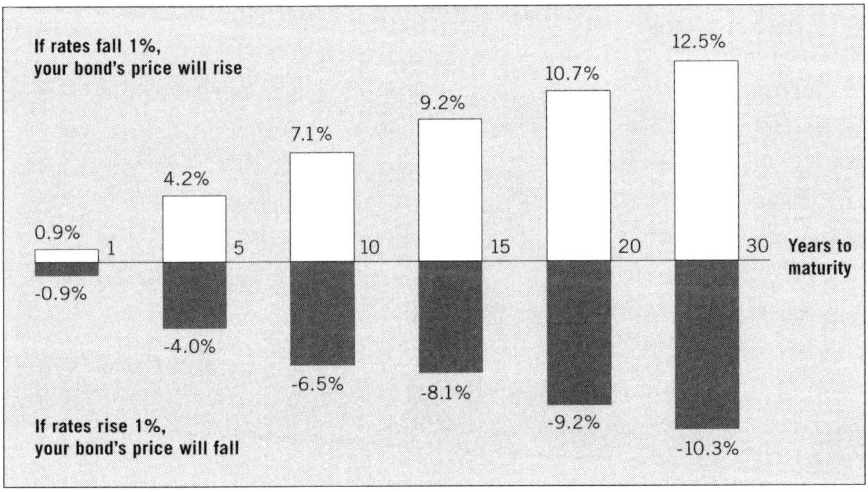

• coupon

For a given term to maturity, the price of bonds with a lower coupon will typically change more in response to changes in interest rates than will the price of bonds with a higher coupon. For example, the value of a bond with a coupon rate of 6 percent will drop more than the value of bond with a coupon rate of 12 percent if interest rates increase. ***Zero coupon bonds***, or ***strip bonds***, on which the value of the interest payments has been built into the discounted price of the bond, display the greatest fluctuations in price.

A Note on Duration

While it is reasonably convenient to compare stocks on the basis of p/e ratios, comparing bonds with different maturities, coupons, and credit qualities is more problematic. Bond managers therefore use the concept of duration to compare bonds. Duration combines coupon and maturity and is essentially a measure of how quickly the bond pays for itself by taking into account the number of payments (maturity) and the size and timing of those payments (coupon). Duration is also indirectly a measure of risk. For every 1 percent change in interest rates, a bond (or other fixed income security) will change in value by a percentage equal to its duration. The shorter the duration, the faster the cost of the bond investment is recouped and the lower the reinvestment or default risk.

Bonds and Mutual Funds

Mutual funds invest in bonds in exactly the same way that individuals do, and investing in a bond fund or income fund is very similar to investing in a number of different bonds. In choosing bonds for a fund portfolio, the manager will weigh the relative advantages of the higher interest rates usually offered by bonds with longer maturities against the smaller price fluctuations, or ***volatility***, of bonds with shorter maturities.

The difference between individual bonds and bond funds—and it is a major difference—is that bond funds do not have a maturity date. Because bond funds hold bonds with a variety of maturities, there is no specific point at which an investment in a bond fund is repaid. You'll see how this can be important later on.

Cash and Cash Equivalents

Cash and cash equivalents are short-term debt instruments. As such, they are loans producing a fixed income. They are distinguished from longer-term assets by two factors. First, cash and cash-equivalent assets are very liquid. This means that the value of such investments can be realized immediately. Cash, of course, is already realized; cash equivalents include investments with a very short term to maturity such as bonds with a term of less than one year, ***treasury bills***, ***commercial paper*** and ***banker's acceptances***.

The other feature that distinguishes these short-term investments from other fixed-income assets is that the value of these assets changes very little—they always trade close to their par or stated value. Because the time frame of these investments is short, the total incremental value of any discrepancy between the coupon rate and the prevailing rates will be small, and changes in prevailing interest rates will consequently have little effect on the price. As a result, it is most unlikely that investors will be hurt, even if interest rates change dramatically.

Cash Equivalents and Mutual Funds

All mutual funds hold some cash-equivalent investments, and some funds specialize in them. As with funds specializing in bonds, funds that specialize in cash-equivalent investments have no maturity date and thus differ from individual cash-equivalent investments.

Real Estate

An investment in real estate can take two forms: direct investment, or ownership, which is a type of equity; and mortgages, which are a kind of debt investment.

Direct Investment (Ownership)

For many individuals, ownership of real estate has far more to do with lifestyle choices than with investing: economic benefits are very often secondary considerations in the decision to buy a house. Some of the most important factors in choosing real estate as an investment include the following:

- **location**
  It is often said that the three most important factors in choosing real estate investments are "location, location, and location." Property that has a desirable location or that is close to services such as transportation systems or social amenities is generally more valuable than more isolated parcels of real estate.

- **potential for income**
  In essence, this factor reflects the current value of a future flow of

income. A property that commands high rents is—all other things being equal—worth more than one that commands low rent. In addition, the term, or length, of the lease and the certainty of the rent are important.

- **carrying costs**

  In many cases, an equity interest in real estate is purchased using borrowed money. (Most people do this when they buy a house. They borrow from the bank and use the borrowed money to pay the vendor.) As a result, interest rates can have an important effect on the value of real estate. When interest rates are high, and it costs a lot to borrow, the price investors are willing to pay for real estate often declines. Conversely, when interest rates are low, and money can be borrowed inexpensively, investors are typically willing to pay higher prices.

- **liquidity**

  Unlike shares in a company, no two parcels of real estate are the same: each parcel has a unique combination of characteristics. As a result, real estate can often be somewhat illiquid. Liquidity reflects the ease with which an investment can be sold. Investments that are highly liquid usually have a readily established price and can generally be sold at that price. The price of somewhat less liquid investments may have to be discounted to conclude a sale. Illiquid investments have a limited market and may be difficult to sell.

A Note on Appraised Values

Since each parcel of real estate is unique, the value of one parcel can be only a rough guide to the value of other properties. The value of real estate is therefore determined by appraisal rather than by auction, as is the case with shares of companies traded on public exchanges. An appraisal is really nothing more than an educated guess about value, based on an evaluation of the income, replacement costs, sale prices of similar properties, and other factors.

This fact creates special difficulties for investing in real estate. If the appraised value of a parcel is artificially high, an investor will overpay for the asset. Conversely, there is no assurance that a parcel can be sold at its appraised value. In either case, an investor's potential profit may be diminished.

Mortgages

A mortgage is a loan secured by real estate. It differs from other debt investments because the amount borrowed is typically ***amortized***, or repaid gradually over the term of the debt in blended payments of principal and interest.

Individuals can invest in mortgages in two different ways. The investor can hold a mortgage directly from the borrower. The lender is responsible for collecting the payments and assumes the full risk that the borrower may not be able to pay.

Alternatively, the investor can purchase a ***mortgage-backed security (MBS)***. These securities are simply "pools" or "bundles" of mortgages with a total value of $10 million to $30 million; they are packaged by financial institutions like banks and reissued or resold to investors in units of $5,000. The financial institution collects the monthly payments on behalf of the investors, and distributes the payments to them in proportion to their share in the "pool." Some MBSs are closed or ***non-prepayable***, which means that the mortgages in the pool do not permit the borrowers the privilege of early repayment of the debt. As a result, the payments to investors are regular. Other MBSs are ***prepayable***, which means that the mortgages in the pool allow borrowers the option of early repayment. The effect of this feature is that the income from prepayable MBSs is typically irregular, since it is impossible to know beforehand what proportion of the borrowers in the pool will take advantage of the prepayment privilege.

MBSs have been offered in Canada since 1987. In the United States, the MBS market is massive. Approximately 75 percent of all mortgages are converted into MBSs. In Canada, the market is much smaller, representing only about 2.5 percent of residential mortgages, but it is growing rapidly.

Real Estate and Mutual Funds

Mutual funds invest in real estate directly or through mortgages and MBSs. Funds that invest in real estate must file a full prospectus rather than the simplified version permitted for most other funds. As we'll see in Chapters 7 and 8, the peculiar difficulties of investing in these assets also present problems for the funds that invest in them. Indeed, the conversion of a number of real estate mutual funds to REITs over the past few years has been fuelled largely by the desire to circumvent the problem of illiquidity. Since mutual funds can be redeemed only when net asset values are calculated, funds that invest in real estate can typically be redeemed much less frequently than funds in which net asset values are established daily. Because REITs are traded on exchanges, investors are able to sell their investments when they choose.

Commodities

Commodities include tangible things such as oil, gold, coffee, and grain, and some intangible things such as contracts for financial instruments. Investors buy and sell commodities in anticipation of changes in their prices.

However, predicting commodity prices can be tricky because, in addition to the usual difficulties of predicting demand and supply, ***speculation*** has an important effect on commodities markets. Speculation is high-risk investing, and speculators are investors who make large "bets" on the future price of an asset. Because these bets are not based entirely on random outcomes, speculators differ from gamblers. Speculation in commodities is characterized by the use of leverage, which magnifies the potential returns (or losses). As a result, the activities of speculators can cause dramatic swings in the price of an asset.

The most sensational example of the effect of speculation on the price of commodities is the attempt by the Hunt brothers to capture the world silver market. The Hunts and their associates began purchasing silver in July 1979, using borrowed funds to make down payments on silver to be delivered in the future. In August and September, the increased demand created by this activity pushed the price from $8.00 to $16.00 per ounce. This demand dramatically increased the value of the silver that the Hunts had already agreed to purchase, and this increased value was used by the Hunts as collateral for further loans, which were used to make down payments on even more silver. By the end of 1979, the price had reached $34.50, and by the middle of January 1980, the price had hit $50.00. Securities regulators, concerned about the potential effects of the Hunts activities, imposed a variety of trading restrictions that effectively prevented further purchases. In the absence of speculative pressures, the price dropped precipitously, reaching $21.00 by the beginning of March 1980. As the price declined, the value of the Hunts' collateral also declined. The Hunts were obliged to sell the silver they had acquired to cover their loans, and the resulting flood of silver into the market severely depressed the price. By the end of March, the price had dropped to $10.80.

As this example illustrates, the activities of speculators can dramatically affect the demand for a commodity, causing its price to fluctuate enormously. In conjunction with more ordinary changes in market conditions, it is very easy for both speculators and ordinary investors to be caught on the wrong side of these price shifts.

This example also illustrates the mechanism by which commodities are traded. Few speculators buy actual commodities: instead they purchase ***commodity futures***. A commodity future is a contract to buy the commodity at some point in the future. It is a type of derivative, which we discuss in further detail below.

Commodities and Mutual Funds

While there are a number of funds that buy commodities or commodity futures in the United States, only two of these funds are available in Canada.

Derivatives

As the name implies, derivatives are investments that are derived from an underlying asset. Instead of investing directly in stocks, bonds, real estate, or commodities, an investor can purchase an investment that offers the opportunity to trade in that asset in some fashion. A ***future***, for example, enables investors to establish the price they will pay in the future to acquire a particular asset. An ***option*** permits investors to deal in the underlying security at a pre-determined price for a fixed period of time.

Derivatives can be used a number of ways in managing investment portfolios. Some of these uses are quite conservative. Derivatives are, for example, often used to hedge investments. A hedge is a technique for reducing loss by pairing investments so that price changes in one investment are offset by opposing price changes in the other. By pairing a derivative with an asset, a fund manager can limit the investment risks of that asset. For example, a stock put (which is a type of option) gives the holder the right (but not the obligation) to sell the underlying stock at a specified price. By investing in both the stock and the put, it is possible to fix a minimum price at which the stock can be sold. Derivatives such as futures also enable funds to maintain necessary cash while allowing exposure to more potentially profitable asset classes.

More recently, a number of mutual funds have used derivatives for more aggressive purposes. Derivatives are increasingly used to manage the ***currency risk*** associated with foreign investments. They can also be employed to simulate exposure to foreign markets while preserving the fund's eligibility for tax-advantaged plans such as RRSPs. Finally, derivatives permit a fund manager to leverage an investment, synthetically enlarging the investment to magnify profits (or losses).

Problems with Derivatives

Despite the opportunities they offer, derivatives present a number of limitations. Many of the more complex derivatives are difficult to value. This difficulty has major implications for the net asset values of funds that employ them. In addition, some derivatives are illiquid. This too will affect net asset values since illiquid investments can frequently be sold only at significantly discounted prices.

While problems of valuation alone are significant, they are usually manageable. A more serious drawback is that many derivatives are inherently leveraged. An option, for example, typically entitles an investor to deal in 100 shares of the underlying stock. This characteristic, combined with difficulties in valuation, can make derivatives very unstable and creates the potential for unlimited loss. To some degree, losses from the use of derivatives are due to the failure of management in the companies and institutional investors that employ them to understand them and adequately limit and monitor their use. A number of articles written following the derivative "crisis" in early 1994 focused on lapses in supervision and risk management procedures. Unfortunately, though, a considerable part of the problem is far more intractable. Although rules and policies exist in most jurisdictions to regulate the use of derivatives, adherence to these rules is largely a matter of self-regulation, and is difficult to monitor. These difficulties of enforcement become more pronounced as the derivatives become more complex, and can be difficult to manage in periods of turmoil, when "normal" financial relationships are disrupted.

Derivatives and Mutual Funds

The use of derivatives in mutual funds has increased dramatically in the past six years. In addition to such conservative uses as cash flow management and hedging, several funds now use derivatives more aggressively to circumvent foreign content restrictions on tax-advantaged plans such as RRSPs. In addition, a small number of funds actively employ derivatives to boost returns.

For those who are interested, a fuller discussion of derivatives can be found in Appendix F. In our view, while "conservative" uses of derivatives are unobjectionable, more aggressive uses are misguided because derivatives involve a great deal more potential for loss than conventional investments. The widely publicized losses suffered by such sophisticated investors as Metallgeselschaft, Barings Bank, Proctor & Gamble, the municipality of Orange County, California, and mutual fund manager Paine Webber are strong indications that where derivatives are involved, mistakes can have extreme consequences out of proportion to the benefits they offer.

Foreign Assets

Investing in foreign assets presents a unique set of circumstances. The potential for growth is much greater in many foreign markets than in Canadian markets, but foreign markets also present a number of difficulties.

- Many foreign markets are more volatile than the domestic Canadian market. Volatility signifies the degree to which prices fluctuate: higher volatility indicates more extreme fluctuations. As we'll see in Chapter 5, volatility, although often misunderstood, is frequently used as a measure of the riskiness of an investment.

- Many foreign economies have fixed ***exchange rates***, which tend to create rigidities in financial markets and distort the valuation of assets in foreign currencies. Typically, fixed exchange rates peg the foreign currency too high, with the result that the values of the foreign assets are inflated. Often, fixed exchange rates are coupled with foreign exchange controls.

- Potential currency devaluation represents a real threat to investments in some foreign markets. The devaluation of the Mexican peso in January 1995 is a classic example. While growth in the earnings of equities may adjust to changes in relative currency values, debt investments offer no such prospect: devaluations result in a permanent reduction in return.

- The accounting principles on which asset valuations are based vary from market to market and may distort the "real" value of the asset relative to domestic assets. The extent of this problem varies. In Japan, for example, the capital cost of fixed assets in a business is typically depreciated much more rapidly than is the case in North America. The effect of this convention is to depress current earnings but increase the earnings outlook for future years. Here's another example: in markets characterized by very high ***inflation***, the use of exchange rates prevailing at the end of the fiscal year to establish financial statement values can create a misleading impression of the company's performance.

As a result of these features, concentration of investments in individual emerging markets can be dangerous. In early 1994, the Hong Kong market lost nearly 30 percent of its value in the first quarter of the year, and in 1995, the devaluation of the Mexican peso triggered a decline of about 20 percent in the value of the Mexican market.

Mutual funds are a very convenient way to invest in foreign markets, but they are also susceptible to these pitfalls. The value of some Latin American mutual funds, for example, declined by nearly 30 percent over 1994 and 1995 as a result of the Mexican peso débâcle.

CHAPTER FOUR

INVESTMENT RETURNS

EXECUTIVE SUMMARY

This chapter provides an introduction to the calculation and evaluation of investment returns.

1. The return of an investment is its profitability. Return has two components:
   - the current income of the investment
   - the capital appreciation, or increase in value, of the investment

The combination of income and capital appreciation represents the total return of the investment.

2. The return of a portfolio depends on–
   - the mix of asset classes
   - the choice of specific investments within each of those classes

3. While GICs, term deposits, and Canada Savings Bonds report future returns, the returns reported for mutual funds are past returns. There are three principal ways in which mutual fund returns are reported:

   - Simple returns are returns over one year or less. They reflect the change in the value of an investment over the period, including any dividends or distributions that have been paid.

- Compound annual returns show the return of the investment in terms of annual performance, and are more convenient in comparing investments. Because they take into account the effect of compounding, they can exactly reflect an investor's investment experience. The major drawback of compound returns is that they obscure the fact that returns are not constant.

- Year-over-year returns show the annual return for each year. They are cumbersome to use in comparing investments, but do illustrate the fact that returns vary from year to year.

4. Inflation, taxes, and sales charges or commissions all reduce an investor's actual profit, and the calculation of investment returns must be adjusted for their effects.

5. There are a number of ways to compare returns:
   - with the average return of a group of investments or mutual funds
   - with a benchmark or independent standard such as the TSE 300
   - with each other, by ranking them

6. Purely numerical comparisons of fund performance are inadequate as a guide to potential future performance. Length and consistency are essential considerations in evaluating the quality of a fund's track record.

INTRODUCTION

Having reviewed the basic characteristics of various asset classes, we turn our attention to examining the ways in which assets can benefit investors. Put simply, ***return*** is the profit (or loss) that can be realized from ownership of an asset. In this chapter we'll look at the different ways investments provide a return. We'll also consider some of the ways in which return is measured, outlining the important advantages and deficiencies of each method.

The Components of Return

Return is made up of two components.

- ***Income*** is the profit from an investment and is earned on a periodic basis. The income from stocks is the investor's share in the yearly profit of the company, and is paid in the form of dividends. The income from bonds is the stream of interest payments paid to the lender or bondholder.

- ***Capital appreciation*** is simply the increase in the market price of an asset over time. In the case of stocks, capital appreciation comes from increases in the share price. In the case of bonds, changes in the price are caused basically by changes in interest rates. Remember the teeter-totter: as interest rates decline, the price of a bond will rise, and vice versa.

Total Return

Total return is the sum of the income from the investment and any capital appreciation (or loss). For example, a stock that is bought at $10 and sold at $12 a year later and that pays a dividend of $1 gives a total return of $3 or 30 percent of the purchase price, as shown in Figure 4-1.

Figure 4-1. Calculation of Total Return

Sale price	$ 12.00	
Less: Purchase price	– $ 10.00	
Capital gain	$ 2.00	
Plus: Dividend	+ $ 1.00	
Return per year	$ 3.00	(30%)

The relative importance of income and capital appreciation will vary. In the U.S., over the period from 1926 to 1996, the average rate of total return from equities has been approximately 10.3 percent, of which about half is made up of dividend income and half from capital appreciation. The Canadian experience has been similar.

For bonds, the average total return in the U.S. over the same period has been approximately 5 percent, and the Canadian experience has been comparable. In both instances, this return has been driven almost entirely by prevailing interest rates.

Fluctuations in interest rates affect the total return on bonds in two ways. First, changes in interest rates will change the price of a bond. Some studies suggest that it is possible to increase the total return from a bond portfolio by 1 or 2 percent by actively trading the investments in the portfolio to maximize capital appreciation. In fact, capital appreciation was an important component of total return in bonds during the latter 1980s. Second, changes in interest rates affect the interest rate at which the periodic interest payments can be reinvested. The total return on an 8 percent bond will be 8 percent only if the interest payments can be reinvested at 8 percent. If interest rates were to decline to 6 percent, the total return on the bond would be lower.

Cash does not appreciate. The return from cash and cash-equivalent investments comes entirely from interest income, which will, of course, vary with current interest rates. Historically, the average rate of return on cash-equivalent investments has been about 3.6 percent.

The Return of Portfolios

Since portfolios comprise many individual investments, the total return of a portfolio equals the combined returns of the individual investments. The return of a portfolio depends on–

- allocation of assets
  This refers to the mix of different classes of assets. For example, a growth fund will invest primarily in equities, while an income fund will typically invest most of its assets in bonds. A balanced fund will invest some assets in equities and some in bonds.

- selection of securities

  Security selection refers to the choice of individual investments within an asset class. An aggressive growth fund usually invests in equities that derive all of their return from capital appreciation, while a more conservative growth fund often invests in equities that offer both dividends and capital appreciation.

The rate of return for mutual funds quoted in both newspapers and a fund's marketing material assumes the reinvestment of all income and distributions. One of the most common mistakes made by mutual fund investors—particularly those investing in funds that provide a steady income—is to forget that spending the earnings from the fund will cause the quoted return to differ from the return received by individuals who reinvest.

Measuring Returns

The rates of return reported for GICs, term deposits, or Canada Savings Bonds are *future* returns. An investor who purchases such an instrument knows in advance what the rate of return for the investment will be. In contrast, the future returns of a mutual fund are uncertain: the reported returns are *past* returns.

Simple Returns

The rate of return for periods of one year or less are ***simple returns***. They reflect the change in net asset value of the fund units over the preceding period, together with any dividends or distributions that have been paid. They are usually reported after the management expenses of the fund have been deducted, but do not reflect the effect of any sales charges.

Compound Returns

The most common way to evaluate investments that extend over more than one year is through compound annual returns. When the return on an investment is added to the original investment for reinvestment, the return is said to compound. Compound annual returns indicate the average performance of the investment when the effects of compounding are included.

Reporting returns in this way is attractive for a couple of reasons. The first is that compound returns can accurately reflect an investor's experience because—unlike simple returns—it adjusts for returns on the reinvested returns of the previous year. For this reason, securities regulators require mutual funds to indicate historical compound annual returns in conjunction with, or in addition to, any other performance data in their sales and marketing literature. The compound annual rate of return over one, three, five, and ten years must be reported, but two-year performance is also included by many funds. Funds also frequently include performance "since inception."

It is important to understand, though, that for compound returns to accurately reflect an investor's experience, the holding period must correspond to the reporting period. If the investor's holding period differs from the reporting period, there will almost certainly be a discrepancy between the reported performance and the investor's experience. For example, the experience of an investor who purchased a mutual fund in November 1987 will almost certainly differ from the reported performance of that mutual fund over the period beginning in August 1987. The reason is simple: the reported performance will include the effects of the market decline and "crash" in October 1987.

The other major attraction of compound annual returns is that they simplify the process of comparing the returns of investments with different time frames. Using compound annual returns, it is possible to compare a one-year investment with a return of 10 percent to a five-year investment with returns of 8, 12, 13, 5, and 9 percent. (The five-year compound return of this five-year investment is 9.36 percent.)

The chief drawback of compound annual returns is that they minimize the significance of variations in return. While the rates of return on GICs, certificates of deposit, and individual bonds are consistent (so long as these investments are held to maturity), the returns of mutual funds—even those that invest in bonds—vary. Mutual funds do not have a set rate of return. However, by reducing performance over several years to a single number, compound annual returns can create the dangerous impression that the returns of mutual funds are constant. This danger is exaggerated because compound returns figure prominently in funds' sales material, while the statutory disclaimer, "unit value and investment return may fluctuate," is reduced to fine print.

In fact, variations in return are important for a couple of reasons. The first is that inconsistency reduces the overall performance of the investment.

As the example in Table 4-2 illustrates, the most consistent rate of return maximizes the benefits of compounding. Although the average annual return of all the funds is the same (25 percent), the fund with the most consistent performance (Fund A) has the best compound return. The fund with the next most consistent performance (Fund D) returns the next best compound rate, and the fund with the least consistent performance (Fund B) has the lowest compound return.

Table 4-2. Consistency of Returns

Fund	Period #1 (%)	Period #2 (%)	Period#3 (%)	Period #4 (%)	Compound Annual Return (%)	Value of $1,000 Invested ($)
A	25	25	25	25	25.0	2,441
B	40	10	10	40	24.1	2,371
C	40	10	20	30	24.5	2,402
D	20	30	20	30	24.9	2,433

The other reason variations in return are important is that abnormal returns in one or two years can distort the compound annual return, skewing it so that it gives an impression of performance that is not warranted. The distorting effect of abnormal years on the compound annual return is often referred to as "end date bias," but, in fact, this distortion has nothing to do with the timing of the aberration. Rather, this effect is the same whether it occurs in the first year, in the last year, or in any intervening year. Identifying the problem as end date bias merely reveals the bias of observers who place disproportionate emphasis on more recent performance.

The danger with inconsistent returns is that far too many investors buy a fund after an unusually good year has skewed the compound annual return upward, or sell a fund after an unusually bad year has depressed the compound return. Indeed, it is the effect of the "one big year" that attracts them. At best, these investors find themselves disappointed when subsequent returns are substantially more modest. At worst, the illusion of consistency encourages investment in wholly unsuitable funds. The reality of inconsistent returns can spell real trouble for some investors, by precipitating a destructive, "buy high, sell low" cycle.

The performance of *CSA Goldfund* over the past 20 years starkly illustrates the risks of one big year. Table 4-3 sets out the annual returns of the fund and the TSE 300 from 1978 to 1996. If an investor had bought the fund in 1980, after the stunning performance (158.1 percent) of 1979, the subsequent five-year compound return (to the end of 1984) would have been only 3.34 percent, in spite of a second great year in 1980 (80.7 percent). With inflation over the same five years averaging about 9 percent, the investor's ***real rate of return*** would have been negative.

In 1982, the fund also had a good year. While the TSE 300 returned only 5.5 percent, *Goldfund*'s annual return was 41.8 percent, and its five-year compound return was 33.7 percent. If an investor had bought the fund in 1983, after the big year, the subsequent five-year compound return (to the end of 1987) would have been only 7.4 percent. Over the same period, the TSE 300 had a five-year compound return of 13.8 percent.

Consider a final example. In 1993, *Goldfund* had another stellar year. The return of the TSE 300 was 32.5 percent, with a five-year compound return of only 8.6 percent. *Goldfund*'s annual return was 115.4 percent, improving its five-year compound return from –9.9 percent 14.0 percent. If an investor had bought the fund in 1994, after the big year in 1993, the subsequent three-year compound return to the end of 1996 would have been –3.8 percent. That investor would have actually lost money. On top of that, the three-year compound return of the TSE 300 over the same three-year period was 13.6 percent.

Table 4-3. *CSA Goldfund* Annual Returns (1978–1996)

Year	TSE 300 (%)	Goldfund (%)
1978	29.7	5.2
1979	44.8	158.1
1980	30.1	80.7
1981	-10.2	-38.7
1982	5.5	41.8
1983	35.5	-5.1
1984	-2.4	-20.9
1985	25.1	16.1
1986	9.0	34.0
1987	5.9	22.6
1988	11.1	–29.7
1989	21.4	10.1
1990	–14.8	-2.7
1991	12.0	–11.3
1992	-1.4	-5.9
1993	32.5	115.4
1994	-0.2	-4.1
1995	14.5	-16.2
1996	28.3	14.0

Source: BellCharts; Financial Times

Year-over-Year Returns

One way to counter the difficulties with compound annual returns is to look at annual returns over a number of years. Table 4-4 shows the returns of the *Trimark Fund* and the *Bissett American Equity Fund*. The variations in returns are evident.

Table 4-4. Year-over-Year Returns (1987–1996)

Fund	1987 (%)	1988 (%)	1989 (%)	1990 (%)	1991 (%)	1992 (%)	1993 (%)	1994 (%)	1995 (%)	1996 (%)
Bisset American Equity	-13.90	15.30	16.50	-6,50	27.20	13.90	7.20	4.90	26.80	12.80
Trimark	-2.30	22.80	15.90	-9.90	28.30	29.00	31.60	14.90	16.70	14.70

Source: BellCharts

The drawback of year-over-year returns, of course, is that they do not provide any sense of a fund's overall performance. Although both funds clearly had a positive return in most years, it is difficult to determine accurately whether a fund's performance was good, bad, or average. As a result, fund comparisons are unreliable. Although both the Trimark fund and the Bissett fund had two losing years in the past ten and their best years were roughly comparable (31.6 percent in 1993 for Trimark; 27.2 percent in 1991 for Bissett), it is impossible to say on the basis of year-over-year data which fund had the better overall performance. (In fact, Trimark's 15.4 percent ten-year compound annual return easily outstrips Bissett's 9.7 percent.) These difficulties of comparison increase dramatically as the number of funds increases.

Adjusted Returns

There are three factors that reduce stated or ***nominal returns***:

- **inflation**

  Inflation is the erosion or reduction in the purchasing power of money. Over the past 25 years, the inflation rate has averaged about 5.25 percent per year, but it can vary widely depending on general economic circumstances.

  Inflation works like this: if an investment of $100.00 generates a nominal return of 10 percent per year, the investor will receive $110.00 at the end of the year. However, if inflation is 4 percent, the purchasing power of the original $100.00 is reduced by $4.00 to $96.00, and the profit of $10.00 is reduced by $0.40 to $9.60. At the end of the year, the "inflation-adjusted" or *real* purchasing power of $110.00 is therefore only $105.60 ($96.00 + $9.60). Practically speaking, the real rate of return can be calculated approximately by subtracting the inflation rate from the nominal rate of return (10 percent – 4 percent = 6 percent). It is important to remember that the rate of return reported by mutual funds is always the nominal rather than the real return.

- **taxation**
  Taxes also reduce nominal returns, but their effect is specific to the investor. In addition, some investment returns are taxed more heavily than others, as we'll see in Chapter 16.

- **sales charges**
  Mutual funds' published returns do not often reflect the impact of sales charges or other fees. Although many of the costs of a mutual fund investment are deducted before the return of the fund is calculated, sales charges are not always deducted. In many cases, sales charges diminish over time, so that they have no impact on long-term investments. In other circumstances, though, they will reduce the fund's real return.

Evaluating Returns

Simply knowing the rate of return is inadequate for the purposes of evaluating an investment. Investors also need to know–

- how well their investment compares to other investments
- what risks the investment entails

We'll look at the first question in the balance of this chapter and the second in Chapter 5.

Performance can be evaluated in a variety of ways.

- **comparisons to group averages**
  The average performance of a group of funds is a sort of "peer group" to which the performance of a particular fund can be compared. To be meaningful, this peer group must be suitable; just as a comparison of

apples and oranges is unhelpful, comparing a fund to an unrepresentative peer group is pointless. While obvious cases (such as the comparison of a bond fund to a group that includes both stocks and bonds) are usually avoided, there are less obvious examples. It is, for example, unreasonable to compare a fund that invests in real estate to a group of funds that invest in commodities, telecommunications stocks, or biotechnology companies.

In addition, averages can overstate the performance of a group. Since unsuccessful funds are often shut down or merged with more successful funds, the performance of the less successful fund is not reflected in the average.

- **comparisons to a benchmark**

A benchmark is simply an independent standard against which performance can be evaluated. The most common benchmarks are market indexes. An index is a statistical yardstick, and a market index is a theoretical portfolio of investments selected to represent the market as a whole. The Dow Jones Industrial Average (DJIA) and the TSE 300 are both market indexes. Comparisons to an index are therefore approximate comparisons to the broader market.

As with comparisons to averages, it is essential that the benchmark be reasonable. The composition of the benchmark is critical. It makes little sense to compare a mutual fund that invests in Canadian resources companies to the DJIA, which is made up of huge, industrial companies in the United States. Similarly, it is largely meaningless to compare a mutual fund that holds predominantly U.S.-based investments to the TSE 300, which reflects larger Canadian companies. Indeed, since a high proportion of the stocks in the TSE 300 are resources-based, this index is somewhat unsuitable as a benchmark for funds that invest heavily in advanced industrial or high-technology stocks.

Furthermore, comparisons to a benchmark index have an inherent fault. While the index incurs no administrative fees and is always fully invested, the same is not true of mutual funds. As a result, a fund can appear to underperform even an appropriate benchmark.

Another sort of benchmark is the rate of return required to meet an investor's expectations. This sort of benchmark permits an assessment of both the suitability of the mutual fund or other investment and the practicality of the expectation. The failure of an investment to meet expectations should cause an investor either to change the investment or to re-evaluate the expectation. We'll look at the process of defining financial expectations and needs in greater detail in Chapter 19.

- **ranking returns**

  To make more precise comparisons, funds can be ranked. In the simplest ranking system, the investment with the best performance is ranked number one, the investment with the next best performance is ranked number two, and so on. Ranking can also be used to evaluate both single-year and multiyear performance.

  The drawback in a simple ranking system is that the importance of small differences in performance can be exaggerated. With more than 170 "Canadian Equity" mutual funds, for example, the difference in five-year compound annual return between funds ranked number twenty-five and twenty-six is only 1/10 of 1 percent.

  To simplify the process of ranking, analysts often compare funds by ***quartile***. A quartile is 25 percent or one-quarter of all the ranked funds. The "top" or "first" quartile is simply the quarter of the group of funds having the highest returns. (Some analysts divide the funds into five groups, or ***quintiles***, which are each 20 percent of the total.) By reducing the rankings to just four or five groups, minor distinctions between funds can be conveniently ignored, and the process of measuring performance is greatly simplified.

The "Average Monthly Rank"

Recently, Duff Young and Riley Moynes devised a proprietary approach to comparing mutual funds which they call the "average monthly rank." This approach combines elements of compound annual return and year-over-year return. It equates the process of comparing funds to a decathlon, in which each month is a discrete contest and individual results are combined. The performance of funds is ranked each month: the fund with the best performance each month is ranked number one. The rankings for each fund are then averaged.

This approach makes sense to this point. But if we pursue the decathlon analogy further, big cracks appear. No one would argue, for instance, that an athlete who participated in only five of ten decathlon events could be appropriately compared with another who participated in all ten events. The catch is that funds have performance histories or track records of varying lengths; this approach works only if funds with track records of comparable length are compared. The longer histories of older funds must therefore be overlooked or ignored to match the shorter histories of newer funds.

To "standardize" the track records, Young and Moynes propose that a minimum track record of only three years is necessary. As a result, the *University Avenue Canadian Fund*, with a track record of just six years, is compared on an equal footing with the *Trimark Canadian Fund*, which has a sixteen-year performance record. The performance of the Trimark fund through the "crash" of 1987 is overlooked even though any prudent investor would want to know how well a fund performs in bad markets, and how quickly it recovers from a bad year.

Future Returns

The Importance of Track Records

Since the reported returns for mutual funds are past returns, the question "how good is the record?" has historically dominated mutual fund analysis. In fact, the important question is not the magnitude of past returns, but the prospect for future returns. The objective of evaluating performance is to identify funds that are most likely to meet the expectations of investors, and the emphasis should be on distinguishing performance that is the product of managerial skill from performance that is largely the result of luck. Unfortunately, the preoccupation with purely numerical comparisons misses the fundamental purpose of the analysis. By concentrating principally on identifying funds with the highest returns, investors overlook important qualitative factors behind the record.

Much of the academic analysis of mutual fund performance has been concerned with determining whether it is possible to outperform the broader market on a consistent basis. Proponents of ***efficient market theory*** contend that it is impossible to anticipate future investment prices, and that over time, returns in excess of those in the market as a whole cannot be sustained. In the language of statistics, the tendency of returns to gravitate toward an average is called "regression toward the mean."

John Bogle, chairman of the U.S.-based Vanguard Group of funds and one of the most forceful exponents of this view, argues that those who believe the markets can be beaten have "tortured the data" to support their conclusions. In his analysis of mutual fund performance, Bogle demonstrates that the probability of repeating top quartile performance from one ten-year period to the next is just one in three—only marginally better than "mere chance." But while Bogle accuses others of torturing the data to justify their (opposing) conclusions, he is at least as guilty. The important issue isn't the likelihood of repeating top quartile performance, but rather whether a fund can sustain above-average or top half performance from one period to the next. In fact, even Bogle's own data suggest that success can be repeated. If the likelihood of maintaining top quartile performance is (marginally) better than "mere chance," it is clearly much more likely that top half performance can be repeated.

He does, however, observe some connection between bottom quartile performance in the two periods. According to Bogle, while the evidence for repeating winners is meagre, the evidence for repeating losers is strong. This position is completely unreasonable, for if the funds that start at the bottom stay at the bottom, how do funds that start at the top gravitate toward the bottom? What is left to make the top?

The fact is that the careers of legendary investors such as Warren Buffet and mutual fund managers like Sir John Templeton and Peter Lynch provide indisputable evidence that it is possible to outperform the markets consistently. Lynch, for example, outperformed the S&P 500 index every year of his 14-year tenure as manager of the *Fidelity Magellan Fund*. The important issue is not whether the track records of these individuals is the product of mere luck, but rather, in evaluating past performance, what standards are most helpful in identifying funds with the greatest likelihood of future success.

How Long is Long Enough?

The relative worth of long- and short-term track records can be debated endlessly. On the one hand, long-term historical patterns exhibit remarkable stability. They may, however, minimize the significance of more recent developments that indicate changes in the long-term pattern. On the other hand, short-term performance may best indicate the effect of current circumstances, but may also magnify the significance of aberrations that are unlikely to be relevant in the future.

Our view is that longer track records are a better indicator of future performance, and that a track record of at least five years is essential, while a record of ten years is preferable. We base our view on a number of factors.

- Academic studies of mutual fund performance indicate that the relationship between past and future performance of mutual funds is strongest for longer periods. Some studies suggest, in fact, that the relationship between future performance and performance for the preceding single year is negative. In other words, funds with the best one-year records are more likely to perform poorly over the next year than funds with poor one-year records.

- As we'll see in Chapters 5 and 6, investment risk almost always decreases with the length of time the investment is held. Since mutual funds are intended for the most part as long-term investments, longer track records give a more accurate indication of a fund's true risk profile.

- Longer track records permit investors to evaluate the performance of a fund through a complete market cycle. It is particularly important to understand how well (or poorly) the manager performs in declining markets. Because the 1987 market "crash" occurred prior to the current surge of interest in mutual funds, few investors have experienced the effects of an important market decline, and fewer fund managers have demonstrated that they are capable of coping with the consequences of a significant downturn. Rising markets often mask the true risk of aggressive investment approaches. Aggressive strategies, which often produce very high returns during rising markets, are also prone to substantial losses in declining markets. To put it simply, it is a lot easier to make money when the markets are rising than when markets are falling and investors are redeeming their investments. Given the length of the current run-up in the markets, our view is that a track record of ten years is necessary to evaluate a manager's potential.

- Longer track records moderate the effects that unusually good or bad short-term performance can have on a fund's track record. Even over ten-year periods, unusual short-term results can skew a fund's overall performance, but their effect on performance measured over two, three, and five years is much more pronounced.

- Longer track records compensate for the effects of a manager's particular investment "style." As we'll see in Chapter 14, every manager's style produces better results in some market conditions than others. Over the short term, these differences in style can create a distorted impression of overall performance, but over the long term, differences in performance attributable to the manager's style are far less significant.

Consistency

The other characteristic that is helpful in identifying funds with the potential for success is the consistency of the track record. As we saw earlier, consistency maximizes return. Equally important, it implies a pattern that is far less likely to be due to mere chance, and that is accordingly more likely to be repeated in the future. One or two really unusual years can distort the compound annual returns of a fund, giving an impression of performance that is not truly warranted.

We've devised a very simple technique to evaluate the consistency of a fund's track record and to correct for the effect of "one big year" in compound annual returns. To determine a fund's return consistency, we recalculate ten-year compound return, eliminating the best and worst years from the calculation. The reasoning behind this technique is that removing the performance peaks and troughs from the track record reveals a fund's long-term level of return. Our view is that this underlying level of return is the most accurate indicator of potential. The more consistent the performance of a fund, the smaller the effect this sort of correction will have. For those who are interested, the basis and mathematical equations of the technique are set out in Appendix G.

The Limits of Past Performance

While track records can be helpful in evaluating the future prospects of an investment, they must be viewed in context. The track record of a bond fund, for example, will reflect the history of interest rates. When interest rates are high, high returns in bond funds are to be expected, but it is unrealistic to think that those same high returns can be sustained in a period of low interest rates. As we'll see in later chapters, one of the characteristics of the best mutual funds is the manager's ability to produce superior returns in a variety of market conditions. It is therefore important in evaluating even long-term track records to consider the context in which the data was compiled.

CHAPTER FIVE

RISK

EXECUTIVE SUMMARY

This chapter provides an introduction to the identification and measurement of financial risk.

1. The idea of a "riskless" investment is a myth.

2. Some risks are shared by all investments in a particular class, while other risks are unique to individual investments.

3. There are two important ways to characterize total financial risk:
   - the potential for loss
   - the volatility of return

4. Risk as the potential for loss seems straightforward but is difficult to measure. Loss can be understood a number of different ways. In addition, the risk of loss depends to a great extent on the length of time for which the investment is held.

5. Volatility is the fluctuation in an investment's return from period to period. Since volatility is easy to measure, it is most often used by academics as the measure of total financial risk. It is important because it creates a risk of loss in the forced sale of an investment. Very often, however, it bears very little relationship to an investment's potential for loss.

6. Investors can have very different views of the potential risks of a particular investment. Recognizing the potential for anxiety that an investment creates is critically important. An investor's level of anxiety will depend both on psychological motivations and on factors such as investment experience and income level.

INTRODUCTION

Many investors believe that it is possible to invest without risk. These people point to the guaranteed returns of term deposits, GICs, annuities, and government-backed bonds. Unfortunately, the reality is quite different. Investing inescapably involves risk, and the idea that an investment is "riskless" because it provides a fixed rate of return is a dangerous myth. Investments with a constant rate of return may seem secure, but they also have their risks. Skeptics need look back only 15 years, to the early 1980s, to appreciate the ravaging effects of high inflation on the purchasing power of money. And while this may suggest to some that investing is a fool's game, *not* investing involves even greater risks to our financial well-being.

In this chapter, we'll try to get a handle on what risk is. We'll look first at different types of risk. We'll then consider various ways to evaluate risk. In the next chapter, we'll look at some approaches to managing risk.

Types of Risk

There are a variety of financial risks. Some risks are shared by all investments in a particular asset class. All bonds, for example, are subject to the risk that an increase in interest rates will reduce bond prices. Other risks are peculiar to specific investments. For example, the risk that government-guaranteed bonds will default on their obligation to pay interest is nil, while the risk that high-yield (junk) bonds will default is greater.

Some of the more important financial risks are listed below.

Market Risk

Market risk relates to financial markets as a whole. Markets exhibit cyclical patterns. In ***bull markets*** investments as a whole do well; in ***bear markets*** investments in general do poorly. This is true of both stock and bond markets.

Inflation Risk

Inflation risk is the potential erosion of purchasing power. Just as the growth of an investment through compounding return can be phenomenal, the effect of compounding on inflation can be devastating. Given a moderate inflation rate of 5 percent per year, for example, the purchasing power of $1,000 in 20 years will be only $377!

Currency Risk

Currency risk or ***exchange rate risk*** is the susceptibility of investments to fluctuations in the relative value of currencies. Reduction (devaluation) in the value of a foreign currency relative to the Canadian dollar will have the effect of lowering the return of the investment. For example, the devaluation of the Mexican peso in January 1995 had the effect of reducing the value of mutual funds holding Mexican-based investments. Currency risk is not confined to investments in foreign markets. For example, a devaluation in the currency of a foreign manufacturer selling into Canada will reduce the price of the imported product, thereby creating a threat to domestic producers.

Single-Issue Risk

Often called ***security risk***, this is the risk associated with "putting all one's eggs in one basket." Investors who own the shares of only one company are entirely dependent on the success of that company. Every investment is subject to a unique combination of risks. The performance of a manufacturing company with a single large customer, for example, would suffer substantially from the loss of that customer. Investors who own shares in only this company may therefore be extremely vulnerable. Similarly, mutual funds with substantial holdings in a few securities (or even market sectors) are vulnerable to the possibility that these securities or sectors will do poorly.

Interest Rate Sensitivity

The degree to which the value of an investment varies with changes in prevailing interest rates is called ***interest rate sensitivity***. As we discussed in the previous chapter, the value of debt securities moves in opposition to interest rates: as rates rise, the price of the security will fall. The size of price changes depends on the term of the investment. The sensitivity of equity investments to changes in interest rates depends on the nature of the investment: utilities usually have greater interest rate sensitivity than industrial enterprises because the price of utilities is driven largely by their dividend yield. The dividend yield of utilities will become increasingly less attractive as interest rates rise, and the share price of most utilities will therefore fall to improve the dividend yield. Bond funds, and funds that invest in dividend-paying securities, will be particularly susceptible to this sort of risk.

Liquidity Risk

Liquidity refers to the ease with which an investor can buy or sell an investment. An illiquid investment involves greater risk than an actively traded investment because a seller may be forced to discount the sale price to conclude a transaction. Part of the difficulty with more complex derivatives is that the market for such instruments can be very illiquid.

Reinvestment Risk

Reinvestment risk reflects the possibility that an investment's current rate of return will not be available when the investment is changed or renewed. For example, in 1989 and 1990, government of Canada treasury bills (T-bills) paid interest of approximately 13 percent. An investment of $100,000 would have returned an annual income of about $13,000. By the end of 1993, the return on T-bills had fallen to around 4 percent, and the same investment would have yielded a mere $4,000. For those dependent on the annual income of such investments, this decline created a very serious risk problem. ***Call risk*** is a variant of reinvestment risk. It identifies the possibility that a bond may be redeemed early by the issuer and that investors may be unable to secure the same return on any alternative investment.

Credit Risk or Default Risk

Credit risk or ***default risk*** reflects the possibility that a debt investment will fail to pay interest or the principal amount at maturity.

Political Risk

While the other risks listed relate directly to economic activity, political risk identifies some factors that indirectly affect return. Political risks include the possibility of expropriations or nationalization of assets, or the imposition of foreign exchange controls on the profits of an offshore business by the host country. Political risk is extremely important for mutual funds that invest in foreign markets.

Evaluating Risks

The various individual risks to which an investment is subject can be summarized as–

- potential for loss
- uncertainty
- anxiety

Risk as Loss

For most people, financial risk is the potential for losing money. Choosing poor investments results in loss. The worst case is an investment that turns out to have no prospect of being profitable. A share in a mining company owning property that is discovered to have no exploitable minerals (such as BRE-X) is a good example. No matter how long an investor holds such an investment, an ore body that can be mined will not materialize. Since the value of a mining investment is dependent on exploiting an ore body, a mine without ore has no value. Similarly, a bond that defaults on its interest payments represents a complete loss of income.

Other investments may provide such a marginal return that almost any alternative would be an improvement. The value of the alternatives an investor forgoes is called ***opportunity cost.*** For example, if shares in ACME Manufacturing have returned only 1 percent per year over the past decade, investors would have been better off stashing their capital in a bank savings account. Although the investors may have more at the end of ten years than they did at the outset, they have still "lost" the value they could have had by making an alternative investment.

Many investors believe that a loss occurs only when an investment is sold for less than its purchase price. This belief is wrong. Taxes, for example, reduce real return. If the nominal (or stated) return on an investment is 10 percent, a tax rate of 50 percent will reduce the real rate of return to only 5 percent. We'll look at the impact of taxes in greater detail in Chapter 16.

Inflation also reduces nominal returns. If the nominal return on a GIC is 9 percent while inflation is 5 percent, the real return of the GIC is only 4 percent. Figure 5-1 illustrates why this is so.

Figure 5-1. Effect of Inflation on Nominal Returns

Initial investment	$ 1,000	
Add: Return @ 9%	+ $ 90	
Nominal value of investment at end of year	$ 1,090	
Inflation @ 5%		
Less: $1,090 x 0.05	– $ 54	(approx.)
Real value of investment at end of year	$ 1,036	
Real return (pretax)	3.6%	

The combination of taxes and inflation can have a major impact on real return because taxes are levied on the nominal return rather than the inflation-adjusted return, as shown in Figure 5-2. In the example, the actual or real return is less than zero—that is, there is a loss of purchasing power despite the fact that the dollar amount of the investment has increased.

Conversely, income-yielding investments may provide a real return even when they are sold at a nominal loss. For example, a fund that is bought at $10 per unit, that generates $1 of real after-tax income per year, and that is sold after three years at $9 per unit has produced a real after-tax return of $2 per unit despite the fact that it was sold for less than the purchase price.

Figure 5-2. Combined Effect of Taxes and Inflation on Nominal Returns

Initial investment	$ 1,000
Add: Return @ 9%	+ $ 90
Nominal value of investment at end of year	$ 1,090
Taxes @ 50% ($90 x 0.5)	– $ 45
Inflation @ 5% ($1.090 x 0.05)	– $ 54
Real value of investment at end of year	$ 991
Real return (after tax)	– 0.9%

The time frame of an investment is also extremely important in evaluating the risk of loss. The price of investments fluctuates, and an investment may result in a loss if held for one period of time, but not if held for a different length of time. If, for example, investor Jones purchases units of ACME Mutual Fund at $10 and the unit price subsequently declines to $9, there is only a potential loss. Jones does not suffer a loss unless he sells the units at the lower price. If Jones waits, the price may eventually increase.

Risk as Uncertainty: The Concept of Volatility

While the potential for loss is the important issue for investors, it is very hard to measure. As a result, academic analysis of risk has tended to focus on the uncertainty of return that is caused by fluctuations in the price of investments. The greater the price fluctuations of an investment, the greater the uncertainty about its future price and future returns.

The fluctuation in an investment's price is called volatility. The conventional view is that the higher the volatility of an investment, the greater its risk. For investments with large price fluctuations, such as stocks, the actual return in any given year may vary anywhere from –5 to +25 percent, although the anticipated return is +10 percent. Such assets are said to be "risky" because the range of possible returns is large. In contrast, investments such as T-bills, which do not fluctuate significantly in price, will have an actual return that is very close to their anticipated return. These investments are sometimes described as "riskless" because the actual future return can be established quite precisely. Investments such as bonds may have an anticipated return of only 5 percent, but an possible return for any given year that varies only from zero to 10 percent. Because the range of uncertainty about these investments is narrower, they are said to be less risky than stocks, but riskier than T-bills.

The great appeal of volatility is that it is easy to measure. Academics have devised two basic ways to measure it. ***Beta*** reflects the extent to which the returns of an investment fluctuate in comparison to the fluctuations in the returns of the general market, which represents a kind of "peer group." ***Standard deviation*** reflects the extent to which the returns of an investment fluctuate in comparison to its own average return. Of the two, standard deviation is somewhat less technical, and it is quoted by a number of newspapers as an indicator of the "risk" of a mutual fund investment. The average Canadian bond fund, for example, has a three-year standard deviation of 1.71, which means that the actual monthly return will usually be within 1.71 percent of the average monthly return. In contrast, the average Canadian stock fund has a standard deviation of 3.28, which means that the actual monthly return will usually be within 3.28 percent of the average monthly return. Since the range of price fluctuations in the bond fund is smaller than the range of price fluctuations in the stock fund, the bond fund is conventionally regarded as "less risky."

Volatility can be important. In circumstances where an investor may be compelled to sell, higher volatility can indicate a greater potential risk of loss. In general, however, the volatility of an investment is an unreliable indicator of an investment's actual risk. To understand how this is so, consider the following example. At the end of 1991, the *Cundill Security Fund* had a standard deviation of 3.20, which was somewhat less than the current average and considerably less than that of the *Trimark Canadian Fund*, which had a standard deviation of 4.45. Investors relying on the funds' relative volatility to choose the "less risky" fund would therefore have chosen the *Cundill* fund. In fact, that would have been the wrong choice. Over the subsequent five years, to the end of 1996, the two funds performed as shown in Table 5-3.

Table 5-3. Annual Returns for *Trimark Canadian Fund* and *Cundill Security Fund* (1992–1996)

Year	Return (%)	
	Trimark	***Cundill***
1992	6.6	–12.2
1993	37.8	39.9
1994	2.5	14.1
1995	10.5	20.2
1996	26.0	20.2
5-year compound return	16.1	13.2

Source: BellCharts

There were greater swings in the returns of the *Cundill* fund, which, in fact, lost money in 1992, while the *Trimark* fund did not have a losing year.

For those who are interested, a more detailed discussion of volatility is provided in Appendix H. As we'll see in the next chapter, the shortcomings of volatility as an indicator of financial risk have important implications for the way in which risk is managed. Our view is that portfolio management based primarily on the concept of volatility is fundamentally misguided.

A Note on Anxiety

Investors react very differently to the potential risks of an investment. Most people view investments with which they are comfortable as "safe," while they regard those that cause them to worry as "risky." The potential for anxiety that an investment creates is extremely important because investors are more likely to make irrational decisions—with negative consequences—regarding investments that cause excessive anxiety. Many people are uncomfortable investing in stocks because they mistakenly see the stock market as a zero-sum game, in which there are many "losers" for every "winner," even though the long-term returns from stocks are almost twice those from bonds. Similarly, many investors are extremely uneasy about volatility. As a result, they panic and sell investments simply because the price has temporarily decreased, although their professed intention is long-term investment.

The degree or level of stress that an investor experiences is the product of both objective factors and psychological motivations. The objective factors that affect the investor's capacity for risk include–

- investment horizon
- net worth
- income level
- stability of income
- need for liquidity
- investment experience

These factors are canvassed in Appendix I.

Psychological considerations affect the way in which situations and circumstances are perceived. Many investors would feel extremely nervous about making speculative investments without a substantial financial "cushion" to protect them in the event of a loss, while others would find such circumstances exhilarating.

Taken together, these psychological and objective considerations are often referred to as an investor's ***risk tolerance***. It is a relatively simple matter to identify the factors that contribute to an investor's anxiety, yet an accurate assessment of their overall effect is anything but simple. Each investor's combination of objective and psychological considerations is unique, making the development of a standard difficult. As a result, the techniques for gauging their overall effect on individual investors are inevitably inexact.

CHAPTER SIX

MANAGING RISK

EXECUTIVE SUMMARY

This chapter is about approaches to the management of risk. It describes why the conventional view of risk management is inadequate, and outlines an alternative.

1. There are three fundamental elements in risk management:
   - diversification of the investment portfolio
   - time horizon of the investor
   - risk aversion of the investor

2. The conventional view of risk management is called modern portfolio theory. It is based on the mistaken idea that volatility and financial risk are equivalent. The chief tool of modern portfolio theory is the process of asset allocation, in which different types of assets are combined in portfolios in an attempt to reduce volatility.

3. While asset allocation is extremely popular, it doesn't work in the long term. The volatility of investments decreases as the length of the investment increases, but asset allocations are made on the basis of short-term volatility. Because assets with short-term volatility have lower long-term returns, asset allocation actually increases long-term risk by overemphasizing investments with lower long-term returns.

4. The most successful long-term investors understand financial risk as the potential for loss. Over the long term, a diversified portfolio of equities (stocks) provides by far the best protection against loss.

5. To manage short-term risk, the most appropriate approach is to choose investments with maturities that match one's liabilities. The returns from such investments, although not always as great as those from equities, are far more reliable, and the risk of loss is much lower.

INTRODUCTION

In this chapter we examine approaches to managing risk. We start by examining the important factors in risk management. We then consider two approaches or systems of risk management. We look first at the conventional approach and highlight its limitations. Then we describe an alternative view of risk management that is based on a long-term perspective. This approach is used by truly successful long-term investors such as Warren Buffet, Sir John Templeton, Peter Lynch, and Robert Krembil.

The Elements of Risk Management

There are three important elements in risk management:

- **diversification**
  The concept of diversification is at the heart of risk management. Simply put, it means "don't put all your eggs in one basket." Diversification works to reduce financial risk by spreading it across a number of different investments.

- **time horizon**
  Time horizon refers to the period of time available in which to make an investment.

- **aversion to risk**
  Investing inevitably involves a trade-off between risk and return, and investors have to determine for themselves what combination of the two is appropriate.

The Conventional Approach to Risk Management

Modern Portfolio Theory and Asset Allocation

The conventional view of risk management is called ***modern portfolio theory***. It is a series of investment principles based on the idea that financial risk is volatility. Risk is managed by regulating a portfolio's volatility.

According to this theory, diversification is achieved by spreading investments across different asset classes using a process called asset allocation. Asset allocation has two related meanings. ***Tactical asset allocation*** or ***market timing*** is based on the belief that it is possible to increase returns by modifying a portfolio's asset mix in order to capitalize on anticipated changes in the markets. This is attractive in theory, but the academic and practical evidence demonstrates that market timing does not work. Modern portfolio theory relies on ***strategic asset allocation***, which is based on the fact that different types of assets have different levels of return and volatility. In general terms, assets providing higher returns are accompanied by higher short-term volatility. By diversifying a portfolio using different types of assets in different proportions, a manager can control the portfolio's overall return and volatility. A bond portfolio, for example, may provide an annual return of 4.8 percent with a standard deviation (volatility) of 8.6 percent. By investing 4 percent of the portfolio in stocks and 16 percent in T-bills, the portfolio manager can theoretically achieve the same return with a standard deviation of only 7.1 percent. Alternatively, by investing 30.5 percent of the portfolio in stocks and 0.5 percent in T-bills, the manager can theoretically achieve a return of almost 6.5 percent without increasing volatility.

In modern portfolio theory, the particular mix of assets in a portfolio is determined by the investor's ***time horizon*** and risk tolerance. The time horizon is the length of time available to investors in which to meet their financial objectives. Investors with a shorter horizon will require higher returns from their portfolios to achieve objectives than will investors with longer horizons. For example, an investor contributing $5,000 per year who wants to accumulate $1 million over the next 30 years requires an annual return of 11 percent while an investor contributing $5,000 per year who wants to accumulate $1 million over the next 20 years requires an annual return of 21 percent.

Risk tolerance is an investor's capacity to handle investment risks. In modern portfolio theory, risk tolerance is determined by both objective factors (such as level of current income and the need for liquidity) and by subjective factors (such as the investor's level of sophistication and psychological profile). An investor with a low risk tolerance will choose a portfolio mix that has low volatility and forego some return. An investor with a higher risk tolerance will choose a portfolio that has greater potential returns but also greater volatility. A fuller examination of the components of risk tolerance is provided in Appendix I.

The fundamental appeal of asset allocation is that it seems so precise. If an investor wants a return of 6.5 percent, asset allocation can theoretically determine what proportion of stocks, bonds, and cash-equivalent investments will provide that return with the lowest volatility. Table 6-1 illustrates this precision. Each of the portfolios in Table 6-1 provides an expected return of 6.5 percent, but the volatility varies widely.

Table 6-1. Effect of Asset Mix on Portfolio Volatility

	Portfolio					
	#1 (%)	#2 (%)	#3 (%)	#4 (%)	#5 (%)	#6 (%)
Stocks	36.00	32.00	31.00	40.00	42.00	43.50
Bonds	40.00	63.00	69.00	19.00	7.00	0.00
T-bills	24.00	5.00	0.00	41.00	51.00	56.50
Volatility (Standard Deviation)	8.40	8.50	8.70	9.10	9.70	10.20

Conversely, a portfolio with a standard deviation of 9.75 percent can generate returns ranging from 6.3 to 7.0 percent depending on the asset mix.

The appeal of asset allocation is reinforced by two factors. The first is that it seems simple. An investor merely determines what level of return is required, and then "mixes and matches" different asset classes to arrive at the allocation that provides the required return at the lowest possible level of risk. The second factor is that some academic research on portfolio performance appears to corroborate the overwhelming importance of asset allocation. A 1986 study of 91 pension funds by Gary Brinson, Randolph Hood, and Gilbert Beebower that appeared in *Financial Analysts Journal* is widely if mistakenly understood to have concluded that more than 90 percent of a portfolio's performance is attributable to its asset allocation.

A careful reading of the study reveals, however, that this conclusion is not warranted. The study's actual conclusion is that altering a portfolio's asset allocation from its long-term average allocation accounts for more than 90 percent of the resulting variation in return—a far more modest assertion.

The fact is that asset allocation doesn't work for two principal reasons. First, asset allocation has a short-term bias. Volatility is typically measured as the variation in monthly returns from a three- or five-year average monthly return. In reality, though, volatility is time-frame dependent. As the length of the holding period increases, the volatility of investments decreases. Figure 6-1 illustrates this effect. The upper curve indicates the maximum possible returns; the lower curve, the minimum possible returns. The area between the two curves represents the range of possible returns, both positive and negative (to a probability of 95 percent). The dashed line between the two curves indicates the anticipated long-term average return. As the time horizon of the investment increases, the range of anticipated returns shrinks.

Figure 6-1. Annualized Returns over Time

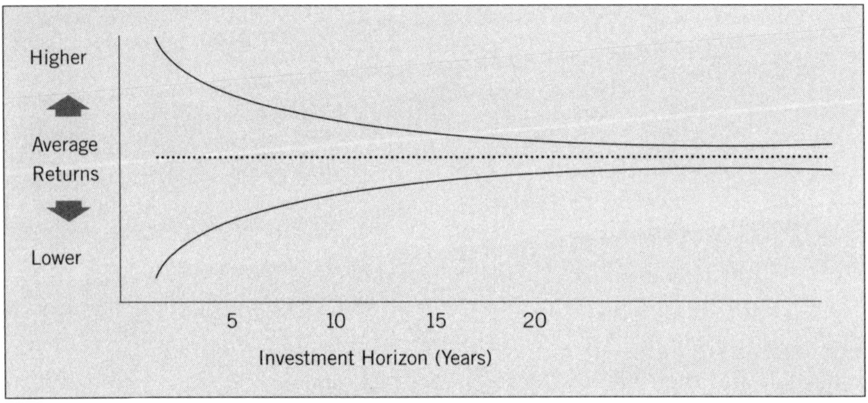

The difficulty is that asset allocations are made on the basis of short-term volatility. Focusing on differences in short-term volatility therefore leads to the mistaken view that diversification is best achieved by spreading risk across asset classes. However, since volatility decreases with time, it is unnecessary to offset the high volatility of one asset class with the low volatility of other asset classes. Increasing the time horizon nullifies the benefit of asset allocation. Indeed, asset allocation is actually counterproductive. Assets with low short-term volatility (such as bonds) also have lower long-term returns. Incorporating assets with low short-term volatility in a portfolio therefore increases risk by lowering the long-term returns of the portfolio.

The other reason asset allocation doesn't work is that it is not nearly as precise as its proponents imply. When asset allocators identify a projected rate of return for a portfolio, what they really mean is that the anticipated rate of return will be somewhere around the specified rate, most of the time. If, for example, the anticipated annual rate of return for a portfolio is 6.5 percent, with a standard deviation of 8.6, the reality is that there is a two-in-three chance that the return will be between –2.1 and 15.1 percent in any given year. There is a one-in-six chance that the return will be below –2.1 percent.

The following example illustrates how this is important. Suppose investor Jones is retired and calculates she needs an income of $30,000 per year. She receives a pension of only $17,000, but she has saved $200,000. If she can get a return of 6.5 percent on her capital, she will not have to alter her lifestyle. Asset allocation can structure a portfolio with an anticipated annual return of 6.5 percent and a standard deviation of "only" 8.6. But what happens when the actual return in the first year of retirement is only 3 percent? Jones's investment income is only $6,000, so she's $7,000 short. The hard reality is that there is an enormous difference between identifying the best allocation in hindsight and choosing the best allocation in advance, and the fact that asset allocation can explain performance does not make it possible to predict the asset allocation that will provide the best returns in the future.

Those who want a fuller description of modern portfolio theory and asset allocation will find a more detailed critique in Appendix J.

Asset Allocation and Mutual Funds

Asset allocation figures prominently in marketing mutual funds. The apparent simplicity and precision of asset allocation are enormously appealing and have proved extremely useful in attracting new investors. It is, however, critically important to distinguish between investment and promotional considerations. The vast majority of the asset allocation programs offered by fund groups compel participants to commit all their resources to a single fund group. These programs are therefore extremely effective in increasing the assets of the fund group, but limit the ability of investors to seek out the most suitable funds. Similarly, an increasing number of fund groups are extending the principle of asset allocation to the area of investment strategies by offering funds with different investment approaches among which investments can be spread. But while increasing the number of investment approaches is presented as a technique for improving diversification, there is no evidence that it actually reduces risk.

The Long-Term Approach to Risk Management

The most successful long-term investors understand financial risk in a completely different way than those who subscribe to modern portfolio theory. For individuals like Sir John Templeton, Peter Lynch, and Robert Krembil, financial risk is the potential for loss rather than mere price volatility. Managing this risk involves four elements:

Time Horizon

The key to reducing the potential for loss is to recognize that the suitability of an investment depends on the time horizon, and to "match" investments to a time horizon. For time periods greater than five years, equities (stocks) are always the most suitable investment. We saw in Figure 6-1 (page 88) that volatility is time-frame dependent and that the volatility of investments declines as the holding period increases. In fact, the volatility of stocks decreases most dramatically, and for holding periods greater than 20 years, the volatility of stocks is less than the volatility of bonds.

In addition, it is important to remember that the average historical returns for stocks are more than twice those for bonds (10.3 percent versus 4.8 percent). The higher returns from stocks provide additional assurance that investors will have enough money in the future to meet their needs.

A number of academics have argued that this so-called "time diversification" is illusory because, although the likelihood of loss decreases over the long term, the size of the potential loss increases as the time period increases. Theoretically, time does nothing to reduce the risk of loss. However, Jeremy Siegel of the Wharton School at the University of Pennsylvania has recently demonstrated in his 1994 book, *Stocks for the Long Run*, that, over the past two hundred years, the risk of loss has always declined with the length of the holding period. Over 20-year periods since 1800, the real annual return on a stock portfolio has ranged from a high of 12.6 percent to a low of 1.0 percent. In other words, over the past 200 years, a 20-year investment in a diversified stock portfolio has never lost money. In contrast, the real annual return on bonds over 20-year holding periods since 1800 has ranged from 8.8 to –3.1 percent.

It is worth noting that this data includes the time periods encompassing the depression of the 1930s. Recent data is even more compelling. Since 1945, even a five-year investment in stocks has never lost money. In short, then, a diversified stock portfolio provides by far the best long-term protection against the risk of loss.

For time periods of less than five years, there is a true risk of loss in equity investments. Advocates of asset allocation contend that the solution to the problem is to reduce volatility by varying the asset allocation of the portfolio. The typical allocation is heavy on bonds and light on equities because bonds have lower short-term volatility. As we've seen, though, lower volatility provides no protection against the risk of loss. Furthermore, all the investor's resources are reduced to the level of the lowest common denominator because the entire portfolio must reflect the investor's low tolerance for volatility.

On the other hand, if sufficient assets are set aside to provide a stable return for three to five years, the balance of the portfolio need not be constrained by concerns about short-term volatility. Our view is that the solution is to invest in securities with a maturity date that corresponds to the investor's needs. Regardless of the volatility of such an investment, the principal amount of the investment is repaid at maturity. If, for example, the proceeds of the investments are intended as the down payment on a house, an investment that matures just prior to closing provides the best assurance that the required funds will be available.

Mutual funds are generally unsuitable for these sorts of investments because they are perpetual investments, with no maturity date. The value of even a fund that invests exclusively in bonds can be depressed when the capital is required. To the end of January 1994, for example, the one-year return for the average Canadian bond fund was 17.3 percent, and the three-year return was 14.0 percent. An investor needing funds one year later would, however, be devastated: the return over the following year, to the end of January 1995, was –7.3 percent. Even an investor needing the funds three years later would be unpleasantly surprised: the three-year compound return from February 1994 to the end of January 1997 was a mere 6.2 percent.

In such cases, individual bond issues or MBSs are preferable because they have a guaranteed yield to maturity and a specific maturity date. In early February 1994, for example, the yield to maturity for both one-year Canadian government bonds and non-prepayable MBSs maturing February 1995 was approximately 4.35 percent, and the yield to maturity on 3-year Canadas was about 5.1 percent. The yield to maturity on corporate bonds was better still: three-year Bank of Nova Scotia bonds maturing in February 1997 yielded nearly 5.8 percent.

Diversification

The best long-term investors reject the idea that diversification requires asset allocation. According to Sir John Templeton, the risk of loss is reduced by investing not in bonds, but in a broad range of stocks.

The performance of a portfolio with investments concentrated in a limited number of market segments or sectors will be more highly dependent upon the prospects for those sectors. If expectations about a sector's prospects are correct, the portfolio will do well: if not, the performance of the portfolio will suffer. The more concentrated the portfolio, the greater the potential for "one big year" and the higher an investor's risk of loss.

In contrast, broadly-based portfolios are much less susceptible to the dangers of "one big year." Unless the investor or portfolio manager has an unerring capacity to choose poor quality investments, exposure to a wide range of sectors and industries ensures that the portfolio as a whole will not "tank." And, while the returns of a broadly diversified portfolio are rarely best over short time frames, they are typically more consistent. As we've seen, consistency contributes to long-term performance.

Although broad diversification is essential, excessive diversification is counterproductive. A portfolio that holds all the securities in the market is completely diversified, but the returns of such a portfolio will simply mirror market returns. A portfolio therefore needs enough investments to achieve diversification without constraining its capacity for superior performance. Numerous studies have demonstrated that in advanced industrial markets, portfolios of as few as 15 different investments can dramatically reduce the risk of loss. Portfolios investing in less developed markets are exposed to additional risks, and more extensive diversification is consequently appropriate in such situations.

Security Selection

Given the tension between superior returns and the broadest possible diversification, the ability to do good security analysis is absolutely critical. Modern portfolio theory underestimates the importance of security selection because it mistakenly exaggerates the importance of asset allocation. To appreciate the true importance of security selection in portfolio performance, it is necessary to adjust or "correct" for the effect of asset allocation. The process by which this is done is called ***attribution analysis***. In simple terms, it works by comparing the performance of a "real" portfolio to that of a "benchmark" portfolio, in which security selection plays no part. If, for instance, the portfolio we want to evaluate is made up of–

- 15 percent bonds
- 35 percent domestic large-cap stocks
- 20 percent domestic small-cap stocks
- 20 percent global equity
- 5 percent real estate
- 5 percent cash

then the benchmark would be a similarly weighted portfolio using a different index for each category. For the domestic large-cap component, we might use the TSE 300; for the bonds, the ScotiaMcLeod Universe Bond Index, and so on. We would then compare the performance of the real portfolio to that of the benchmark portfolio to determine how much, if any, extra return is attributable to the selection of particular securities.

In fact, security selection turns out to be much more important than the proponents of asset allocation allow. In a 1991 study, reported in *Canadian Investment Review*, of Canadian pension fund performance, Colin Carlton and John Osborn found that security selection was at least as important as asset allocation in explaining portfolio performance.

The chief reason advocates of asset allocation minimize the importance of security selection is that it is *extremely* difficult to make successful selections. Since it is much easier, and certainly flashier, to manipulate asset allocations, the obvious solution to the complexities of successful security selection is simply not to do it. However, security selection is far more effective than asset allocation. The proof is that there are portfolio managers who do it consistently. Using the tools of fundamental analysis, investors like Templeton, Lynch, and Krembil have been able to achieve long-term returns that consistently outperform both asset allocation systems and the broader market. In Chapter 14, we'll look at some of the characteristics of portfolio managers who are successful stock pickers, and at the various criteria that may be helpful in identifying those managers who are likely to be successful in the future.

Comfort Level

Although an equity investment may be the surest way to avoid the risk of loss, it is not always the most suitable investment. For some investors, the anxiety of investing in equities makes such a choice risky. The short-term volatility of stocks is unnerving for many investors and can precipitate a sale at an inopportune time. Without question, the worst mistake an investor can make is selling prematurely. Unfortunately, too many investors do just that because they have not properly assessed the anxiety an equity investment will create.

Comfort level is only one aspect of risk tolerance because it is not related to objective considerations such as income level and need for liquidity. An investor's comfort level is an indicator of psychological tolerance for risk. Investors who get nervous when the price of an investment exhibits substantial short-term instability should stick to less volatile investments, regardless of financial circumstances. In our view, standard deviation is much more useful as a guide to how uncomfortable an investment might make an investor than as a device for measuring the riskiness of the investment.

One of the considerations that is rarely weighed in choosing investments is the convenience associated with an investment. Investors who are quite comfortable with the risk level of an investment often still find themselves dissatisfied because of the time and effort it takes to monitor the investment. In evaluating one's psychological profile, the comfort that comes from ease of management is just as important as that from lack of worry. If your portfolio demands too much time, it is perhaps wisest to modify the portfolio.

It is important to recognize that moderating the short-term volatility of a stock portfolio by incorporating bonds, T-bills, and MBSs does not make the portfolio "efficient" and reduce risk. Indeed, quite the opposite is true. Similarly, a balanced fund is not efficient simply because it maximizes convenience. Such portfolios represent a compromise between the true efficiency of an equity portfolio and an investor's individual comfort level.

It is also important to bear in mind that comfort levels are very personal. The level that is suitable for your friend or neighbour may not be suitable for you. Indeed, one of the chief drawbacks of the ***asset allocation funds*** or asset allocation services offered by many mutual fund groups is precisely that they are fundamentally impersonal and generic. It is completely unrealistic to expect that such a service will fully meet specific personal needs.

PART TWO
TYPES OF FUNDS

Classifying Funds

Having outlined some of the basic investment concepts in Part 1, we turn our attention in Part 2 to describing different types of mutual funds. With more than 1,500 funds available, the variety is enormous, and understanding their features is essential. Classifying funds does several things. First, it helps to organize the list of funds. Second, it also simplifies the process of evaluating and choosing funds. Third, it eliminates unproductive "apples and oranges" comparisons.

Funds can be classified by a number of features. These include–

- asset type
- geography
- risk level
- objective

Each of these classifications emphasizes different fund characteristics. However, the process of evaluating and choosing funds depends on comparisons, and comparisons are useful only if they focus attention on a fund's truly significant characteristics. We believe it is important to be clear about why we adopt a particular approach. Unfortunately, the classifications used in the popular media are often based on a combination of criteria and can be confusing.

The most common classifications are based on asset classes. The appeal of this approach is that it requires little effort. For the most part, asset classes are easy to identify, and it is a simple matter to categorize a fund according to the largest asset class in its portfolio. Unfortunately, the simplest approaches are not necessarily the best. Focusing primarily on asset classes can obscure more important characteristics, and result in dissimilar funds being mistakenly compared. For example, the *Globe and Mail* classifies both the *Trimark Fund* and the *Templeton International Stock Fund* as "international equity" funds, but the *Trimark Fund* has historically invested primarily in the American economy, while the investment mandate of the *Templeton International Stock Fund* allows investment in any market *but* the U.S. (and Canadian) market. Similarly, the *Financial Post* classifies both the *Mackenzie Financial Industrial Bond Fund* and the *CI Canadian Bond Fund* as "bond and income" funds. Although both invest in Canadian bonds, the *CI* fund typically invests largely in bonds with less than ten years to maturity, while the *Mackenzie* fund usually invests primarily in bonds with more than ten years to maturity.

The problems with classification are compounded substantially by the fact that there is no consistency in the way funds are classified. For example, the *Financial Post* has a separate category for "resource equity" funds, while the *Globe and Mail* includes them with "precious metals." The *Globe and Mail* includes "real estate" funds with funds that specialize in particular market sectors, while the *Financial Post* deals with real estate funds in a separate category. BellCharts, a computer database for mutual funds, lumps together mortgage and shorter-term bond funds, while the *Globe and Mail* and the *Financial Post* deal with these types separately. The *Globe and Mail* combines "Canadian balanced" funds and "Canadian asset allocation" funds, while the *Financial Post* separates them. Strangely, the *Financial Post* differentiates between "Canadian balanced" and "international balanced" funds, but combines all "asset allocation" funds in a single category.

The difficulty with this confusion is that a fund's classification has a significant effect on its performance relative to other funds. If, for example, "real estate" funds are classified with other sector funds (such as "high-technology" funds), the returns of even the strongest real estate fund may seem mediocre when the high-technology sector is strong. Conversely, when the high-tech sector is weak, even marginal performance by real estate funds can seem relatively strong.

Classifying by Objective

Our view is that classifying funds by objective is an overlooked approach. By focusing on objectives, investors can most easily identify funds that suit their needs.

There are three fundamental investment objectives:

- safety of capital or principal
- provision of income
- growth of capital

A fourth objective—liquidity—is sometimes included.

In general, funds that seek safety of capital invest in cash and cash-equivalent securities, while funds that pursue capital appreciation, or growth, invest in equities. Funds that generally stress income invest in short- and medium-term bonds, preferred shares, and mortgages.

Objectives can be combined in a single fund, but they are often incompatible. One objective is usually paramount even in balanced funds, which have the dual objectives of growth and income. Chapter 10 is devoted to balanced funds. Emphasizing one objective typically limits pursuit of the others. However, by concentrating on objectives rather than asset classes or geography, investors can more easily identify which objective is paramount, so that they can be sure of making the most suitable choice.

The chief drawback of basing fund categories on objectives is that objectives are rarely self-evident. Considering the name of a fund, for example, is usually a particularly poor way to determine objectives. For example, the *Mackenzie Financial Industrial Income Fund* and the *Royal Trust Advantage Growth Fund* are actually balanced funds. Similarly in December 1996, Canadian investments made up more than 62 percent of the *Cambridge Global Fund*'s portfolio, although Canada accounts for only about 3 percent of the world's total capital markets.

The prospectus is also rarely a good indicator. The descriptions of objectives in prospectuses are almost always too vague to be useful, and can sometimes be misleading. The now notorious U.S.-based *Piper Jaffray Institutional Income Portfolio* is a good example. This fund appealed to many highly risk averse investors because its prospectus indicated that the fund's investment mandate was limited to investments in government-backed securities. The prospectus did not disclose that this mandate encompassed extremely risky derivatives based on government-guaranteed bonds.

In addition, the prospectus is required to identify only the fund's current objectives, and these may be quite different from those on which the fund's track record is based. For example, although the *BPI American Small Companies Fund* was started in June 1988, it was managed as a Canadian emerging growth fund prior to April 1991. And, although changes in a fund's fundamental investment objectives must be approved by unitholders, there is no requirement that prior objectives be disclosed to prospective investors.

Thus, an accurate determination of a fund's objectives requires disciplined evaluation. It involves examining the basic characteristics of the fund and the investment approach used by the current manager. It is not difficult, but it does require a degree of commitment.

A Note on Geographic Categories

While classifications based on objectives are most useful, some geographic distinctions are important because of their tax implications. Domestic funds invest predominantly in Canadian securities and are often eligible for favourable tax treatment. Foreign or international funds invest outside Canada. Global funds invest in both domestic and foreign markets. All of the investment objectives are met in each of these geographical categories, but tax considerations will have a bearing on an individual's choices. Chapters 16 and 17 cover many of these tax issues.

A Note on Offshore Funds

Although there are well over 6,000 mutual funds in the United States alone, and thousands more in Britain and other developed countries, Canadian law permits the sale of investments only where the prospectus has been approved by a securities commission. For most foreign fund companies, the necessity of obtaining approval from the various provincial securities commissions cannot be justified by the relatively small size of the potential market. As a result, Canadian brokers and dealers are authorized to sell offshore funds only by private placements to investors willing to invest a minimum $150,000 in a single fund. Canadian-based securities regulators can provide no recourse for ordinary investors who attempt to circumvent these restrictions.

A Note on the Currency Denomination of a Fund

It is important not to confuse the currency in which a fund reports its results with the actual performance of the fund. The performance of a fund is driven by the investments that it holds, regardless of geographical location. The currency in which the fund is denominated is merely a reporting mechanism and has no bearing on performance.

An exaggerated example illustrates the irrelevance of the currency in which the value of the fund is reported. *No Name Fund* holds only U.S. investments. Over one year, it had a return of zero, and the value of the Canadian dollar declined 50 percent relative to the U.S. dollar. If the fund's net asset value was U.S. $10.00 at the beginning of the year, it would be U.S. $10.00 at the end of the year. In Canadian dollars, the net asset value of the fund would have increased from $13.50 to $27.00, but $27.00 would still be worth only U.S. $10.00, and the return of the fund would still be zero.

For those who have U.S. dollars and anticipate a future need for U.S. dollars, the option of making an investment in U.S. dollars is a convenience that eliminates currency exchange costs. Those who incur regular expenses in U.S. dollars can also benefit from the service. For example, Canadians who spend winters in Florida can use mutual funds denominated in U.S. dollars in conjunction with the systematic withdrawal plans offered by mutual funds to create an income in U.S. dollars, and thereby avoid the inconvenience of converting Canadian dollars in the United States, where exchange rates may be less favourable. Of course, this convenience of conducting business in U.S. dollars has no effect on the performance of the investment.

CHAPTER SEVEN

GROWTH FUNDS

EXECUTIVE SUMMARY

In this chapter, we examine the basic types and characteristics of growth funds.

1. The fundamental objective of growth funds is capital appreciation.

2. Growth funds invest primarily in equities.

3. Growth funds have a wide variety of investment mandates. Some funds are largely restricted to the domestic market, while others invest in foreign markets. Some funds invest in a broad range of equities, while others focus on equities with particular characteristics, such as resources stocks or smaller companies.

4. In general, funds with broader investment mandates involve less risk of loss and are less volatile than funds with more narrowly focused mandates.

5. Growth funds are unsuitable for short- and medium-term investing and are unreliable as a source of stable income.

6. Investing in foreign funds may improve returns and lower risk by increasing the level of diversification.

Growth funds constitute the largest single category of funds. Of the 1,477 funds covered by BellCharts at the end of 1996, 776 are growth funds of one variety or another. Growth funds are also by far the most diverse: the investment styles of growth funds run the gamut from highly aggressive to remarkably sedate.

The primary objective of growth funds is capital appreciation. They may provide income, but it is incidental and usually irregular.

Growth funds invest primarily in equities, but they invest in other assets as well, including–

- bonds
- real estate
- futures

Types of Growth Funds

While growth funds share the basic objective of capital appreciation, they have a broad variety of ***investment mandates***. The investment mandate of a fund identifies what kinds of assets the fund will invest in.

Large-Cap Funds

These funds are sometimes referred to as "plain vanilla" funds. They invest mostly in large-capitalization (or blue chip) companies, but the portfolio can include medium- and small-cap companies.

Given time, the risk of loss in a large-cap fund is virtually nil. However, the safety of such funds does not necessarily preclude superior performance. The conventional wisdom is that, because market indexes such as the TSE 300 and the S&P 500 are based on ***large-capitalization stocks***, the performance of large-cap or mainstream funds will often simply mirror the market. In fact, this is nonsense. The U.S.-based *Fidelity Magellan Fund*, with $50 billion in assets, has generally outperformed the long-term returns of the S&P 500 although recent performance has slipped somewhat. To the end of 1996, 22 broad-based Canadian equity funds outperformed the ten-year compound annual return of the TSE 300.

Small-Cap Funds

As the name implies, ***small-cap funds*** predominantly invest in companies with smaller capitalization. What constitutes a small-cap stock is a matter of considerable debate. In the United States, companies with a capitalization of less than $1 billion are now characterized as small caps, but in Canada, $250 million is generally regarded as the limit. The rationale for investing in such companies is that their long-term growth prospects are better than those of large-cap stocks. The tendency of small-cap stocks to outperform large-cap stocks is called the ***small stock effect*** and exists in most stock markets.

Small-cap stocks are, however, riskier than large-cap stocks. Although large-cap and small-cap stocks are each overvalued relative to the other at different times, the extremes in small-cap stocks are often greater. Over shorter time horizons, the probability of losing money is greater in small-cap stocks than in large-cap stocks. The volatility of small-cap stocks is also substantially greater than that of large-cap stocks and may make small-cap stocks an inappropriate choice for investors who are uncomfortable with substantial fluctuations in price.

Many small-cap funds have more in common with ***venture capital funds*** than mainstream stock funds. Venture capital funds provide investment capital to businesses that are unable to obtain financing from more conventional sources such as banks or by issuing bonds or shares. These businesses are typically either in the very early stages of growth or in some financial difficulty. Because the potential for failure in these sorts of businesses is substantial, venture capital funds are risky investments.

Another part of the reason small-cap funds are riskier is that they are less diversified than large-cap funds. There is enormous diversity in large-cap stocks. Market capitalizations on the S&P 500, for example, range from less than $100 million to more than $140 billion. In contrast, small-cap stocks represent a much narrower "slice" of the broader market.

Sector Funds

Sector funds and ***specialty funds*** invest in particular industries within the economy. Resources funds, energy funds, high-technology funds and financial services funds are examples of sector funds. Although the short-term returns of sector funds are often phenomenal, these funds are inherently less diversified than other growth funds. As a result, these funds are typically substantially more risky than other growth funds. The differences between sector funds and conventional growth funds are covered in greater detail in Chapter 12.

Theme Funds

Theme funds are distinguished by their use of nonconventional criteria for investment. These criteria are extremely diverse. For example, the *Dynamic Global Green Fund* is based on criteria of environmental sensitivity. The *Ethical Group of Funds* invest in companies that promote both environmental and human rights. The *Talvest New Economy Fund* invests in various "leading edge" companies, such as those involved with computers, health sciences, and telecommunications. Finally, ***labour-sponsored funds***, which are a kind of venture capital fund, are noteworthy largely because of the significant tax advantages they enjoy. While some of these funds post adequate returns, their performance for the most part is unremarkable.

Aggressive Growth Funds

These funds invest in companies with potential for dramatic capital appreciation. Bill Anderson, the portfolio manager of the *20/20 Aggressive Equity Fund*, for example, looks for the financial equivalent of "home runs" rather than "singles" because "a few home runs are all you need." Similarly, "special situations" often offer the potential for very strong growth. The *Altamira North American Recovery Fund* invests in distressed companies and bail-out situations in anticipation of recovery, and the *Atlas Managed Futures Fund* invests in a variety of commodity and financial futures.

The potential for loss in aggressive growth funds is considerable. The portfolios of these sorts of funds constitute very focused or concentrated bets. Anderson holds only about 55 individual small-cap investments in the $375 million portfolio of *20/20 Aggressive Equity*. In contrast, the $330 million portfolio of the *Altamira Special Growth Fund*, which is a more conventional small-cap fund, includes about 150 different investments. Similarly, commodity futures, unlike resources stocks, are a leveraged pure play on the price of the commodity. The value of an investment in a resources company is affected by a whole host of factors, including management competence, the debt load of the company, and so on. In contrast, the only factor affecting the value of a commodity future is the market price of the underlying commodity. If the "bet" on the commodity price is wrong, returns will suffer dramatically. In addition, the risk that some of the investments in these portfolios will default is much greater than in mainstream growth funds.

Global Funds

As the name implies, these funds invest without restriction. Some invest primarily in large-cap stocks, whereas others focus on smaller-capitalization investments.

The enormous attraction of these funds is that they have the potential for the widest diversification. Rather than limiting choices to particular regions or countries, the objective of these funds identifies investments with strong potential for growth. While both the growth potential and volatility of funds focusing on smaller companies are greater than those of large-capitalization funds, the breadth of diversification still provides protection from the risk of loss.

Regional Funds

These funds invest in specific geographic regions such as Europe, Latin America, and the Asia Pacific region. Many of these regions hold potential for strong growth and provide an opportunity to diversify out of the Canadian economy to reduce the effects of cyclical markets.

There is enormous variety in the investment mandates of these funds, and the potential for loss depends on two factors:

- **the region in which the fund invests**
  Funds of regions in which financial markets are well developed are on the whole no more volatile than domestic funds. Funds emphasizing western Europe are a good example. Regions in which financial markets are less advanced or less open are somewhat riskier. Funds that focus on the established markets of the Asia Pacific Rim such as Taiwan, Hong Kong and Korea are representative. Regions with economies in which financial markets are only partially developed, such as Latin America and the "new" economies of Southeast Asia, have the greatest potential for loss. For example, in late 1994, the Mexican government abruptly devalued the peso. This move depressed the net asset values of Latin American funds by more than 30 percent.

The way in which the *region* is defined has a substantial bearing on the riskiness of the fund. "Asia Pacific" funds that include investments in the broadly diversified Japanese market are plainly less risky than "Asia Pacific" funds that invest in only the smaller economies of the region. Similarly, "Americas" funds that invest in only the emerging markets of Latin America are riskier than funds that invest in both Latin America and the advanced industrial markets of North America.

- **the companies in which the fund invests**
  As we explained above, the potential risk of loss is lower in funds that invest in broad-based, or large-cap, portfolios rather than in concentrated or small-cap portfolios. Even superficially similar funds can have very different investments. The *AGF European Growth Fund*, for example, focuses on small- and medium-cap securities, while the *Fidelity European Growth Fund* emphasizes large-cap investments.

Country Funds

Country funds invest in the markets of individual countries, and are even more specialized than regional funds. Strictly speaking, all domestic funds are country funds, but the term is usually reserved for funds that invest in a single foreign market.

- **U.S. equity funds**
  For a number of reasons, country funds that invest in the United States are by far the most important for Canadians. First, the United States is the largest capital market in the world, accounting for about 30 percent of global capitalization, while Canadian markets represent only about 3 percent. Second, the U.S. equity market is far more diversified. Although Canadian equity markets are well developed, they are clearly weighted towards resources-based securities. Third, the U.S. economy is less encumbered than the Canadian economy by public sector deficits, which tend over time to constrain growth.

  All these factors result in investment opportunities not available in Canada. Since 1990 the market cycles in Canada and the United States have generally diverged. While U.S. markets have been strong, Canadian markets have been relatively lacklustre. Even acknowledging that the

TSE 300 and the S&P 500 reflect different market structures, the ten-year total return for the S&P 500 to the end of 1996 was 15.1 percent, while the ten-year total return for the TSE 300 was only 10.1 percent. Some of this discrepancy is attributable to depreciation of the Canadian dollar relative to the U.S. dollar over this time frame, but much is attributable to the fundamental strength of the U.S. economy. For investors interested in the American equity market, there are currently about 90 funds available. These funds span the full range of types, from broad-based to sector funds.

- **other country funds**
  After the U.S. country funds, the most important country funds are those investing in Japan, whose economy is second in size only to that of the United States. There are currently more than a dozen Japanese funds available. Most Japanese funds tend to invest in large-cap companies.

  The risk of a country fund depends primarily on the diversification and maturity of the market. Both the U.S. and Japanese markets are mature and broadly diversified. Funds that attempt to exploit the growth potential of other individual economies, such as Korea or India, are extremely vulnerable to the risks of inadequate diversification.

Emerging Markets Funds

The term *emerging markets* signifies that the markets of these countries have not been fully integrated into the global economy. Emerging markets funds offer tremendous potential, but because their capital markets are generally poorly developed, investments in such funds are also subject to special hazards:

- Currency fluctuations can significantly affect the total return of the fund. This is not generally a problem in the Pacific Rim, where the local currencies are strong relative to the Canadian dollar. However, in Latin America and central Europe and Asia, falling currency values can negate otherwise respectable return.

  Many funds employ hedge strategies to minimize the risks of currency fluctuations, but care must be exercised to ensure that the hedging is reasonable. Hedge strategies using derivatives in the emerging market are more exposed to default risk than are hedges based on major currencies or markets because the markets of most emerging markets are less liquid. Some fund managers are of the view that a long-term perspective renders concerns about currency fluctuations irrelevant for stocks because the devaluation will give some sectors a comparative advantage. Export-oriented firms, for example, benefit from currency devaluation.

- Information on investments in emerging markets is typically more difficult to obtain. The accuracy of accounting and financial reporting is less reliable, and disclosure is often inadequate. In addition, many emerging markets are dominated by small groups that are naturally anxious to preserve their advantage.

- Investments in emerging markets are typically less liquid than in advanced economies because of administrative practices, including transaction costs and the time necessary to settle transactions; low market diversification; and low capitalization.

  These factors can make asset valuations difficult and limit the ability of the portfolio manager to realize returns.

Some growth funds attempt to reduce the volatility and risk of emerging markets by combining them with investments in developed countries. Trimark and Mackenzie Financial, for example, both offer "Americas" funds, which invest in companies of both developed and emerging markets.

Marketing Campaigns

As the number of funds has grown, more and more are differentiating themselves with marketing campaigns. Global Strategy, Mackenzie Financial, and Canada Trust, to name a few companies, offer "foreign" funds that are intended to provide the benefits of foreign investment without sacrificing "Canadian content" status for RRSPs. This objective is accomplished using derivatives and money market investments. Since the derivatives are highly leveraged, their return compensates for the (relatively) low return of the money market securities. This strategy may work, but in our view the use of derivative investments significantly increases the fund's riskiness.

Another marketing device employed by the AGF, CI, and GT Global fund groups is the consolidation of different regional and sector funds in a single "umbrella" fund. The objective in these schemes is to accommodate asset allocation programs by avoiding the usual tax implications of switching from one fund to another until an investor actually redeems out of the umbrella fund.

Yet another device attempts to achieve exposure to emerging markets without excessive risk by focusing on businesses in developed markets that are tied to growth in the emerging market. The *AGF China Focus Fund*, for example, invests in Canadian (and other) companies doing business in China, in addition to Chinese enterprises.

The Role of the Manager

The growth fund manager's most important role is to identify good investments. Chapter 13 discusses the more important approaches managers use to evaluate both securities and market conditions. Superior security and market analysis is very difficult to do consistently, and the manager's skill is critical to the long-term performance of a growth fund.

The manager must also regulate the liquidity of the portfolio by maintaining sufficient cash to meet requests for redemptions. If the assets of the fund were completely invested, it would be necessary to sell some of the investments in the portfolio to raise the cash for redemptions. In many of these forced sales, the full potential of the investment would not be realized; and the overall performance of the fund could suffer.

Some portfolio managers are mindful of the effect of short-term volatility on investor sentiment, and make an effort to manage the portfolio so that price gyrations are minimized. In the *Scotia Excelsior Canadian Growth Fund*, for example, about one-third of the stocks in the portfolio are chosen specifically because they moderate volatility and contribute liquidity. These stocks include banks and utilities. The other two-thirds are chosen for their potential superior return.

Investor Considerations

The diversity of growth funds makes generalizations about them difficult. Nevertheless, some basic observations are possible:

1. The defining characteristic of growth funds is their emphasis on capital appreciation. While investment mandates and policies vary enormously from fund to fund, the goal of capital appreciation is always paramount. For example, although there are profound differences between the *Atlas Large Cap Fund* (which invests primarily in companies on the TSE 300 and has low volatility) and the *Multiple Opportunities Fund* (which invests in Canadian small-cap companies and is extremely volatile), these funds share the fundamental objective of long-term capital growth.

2. Every fund performs better in some circumstances than in others:
   - ***Fair weather funds*** do best in bull (rising) markets and tend to underperform markedly in bear (declining) markets. They tend to focus on growth stocks, and be fully invested at all times.
   - ***Foul weather funds*** do best in bear markets and tend to underperform in bull markets. These funds typically hold portfolios heavy in blue chip stocks.
   - ***All weather funds*** perform equally well in bull and bear markets, but are not the top performers in either market. The portfolios of these funds usually concentrate on value stocks, or stocks with a high dividend yield, and the cash component of the portfolio tends to vary, increasing as the market rises and "bargains" become harder to find.

3. Growth funds are generally inappropriate for short- and medium-term investment goals. Growth funds are composed principally of equity investments, and since the short-term volatility of equities is greater than that for bonds, growth funds tend to be more volatile than bond funds. Growth funds are therefore suitable for investors who can be patient.

4. Growth funds are usually unreliable as a source of steady income. Most funds make distributions only once a year, and the size of the distribution is typically irregular since most funds make distributions only to the

extent necessary to eliminate the fund's tax liability. The liability for tax is largely dependent on the manager's investment approach, and it is generally impossible to project future distributions.

In many funds, systematic withdrawal plans can be used to replicate an income stream, provided investors recognize the limitations of such plans. In some years, the growth of the investment can easily cover the costs of the withdrawals, but there can be times when the fund's return is inadequate to cover the withdrawals. Prolonged withdrawals in excess of total return will result in encroachment on the investor's capital.

5. An investor's major positions should be in broadly diversified funds. More narrowly focused funds may offer greater short-term potential, but they entail greater risks as well as greater volatility. Narrowly focused funds should be used only as part of a more diversified portfolio.

6. Diversification out of Canadian equities is prudent. There are several reasons to take a global investment outlook:
   - Canadian capital markets make up only about 3 percent of the world total
   - Canadian markets are heavily weighted to resources
   - returns in some foreign markets are higher than in Canada

7. Excessive attention to management expense is misguided. The important issue is not the size of the management expense, but whether the manager adds value. Security analysis is often expensive, particularly in foreign markets, but the cost is often justified by superior returns. Similarly, if the higher costs of an active investment approach are offset by higher returns, the relative size of the expense is irrelevant. It is important to remember that mutual fund returns are reported after expenses are deducted.

CHAPTER EIGHT

INCOME FUNDS

EXECUTIVE SUMMARY

In this chapter we examine the basic types and characteristics of income funds.

1. The fundamental objective of income funds is to provide a current income. In addition, some income funds are suitable investments for meeting short- to medium-term objectives because they are less volatile and accordingly present less risk of a short-term loss.

2. Income funds invest in a variety of income-producing investments, including bonds, mortgages, and dividend-paying stocks.

3. Three basic features of a portfolio affect the character of an income fund:
   - average term to maturity
   - credit quality
   - exposure to stocks

4. Funds with very long average terms are usually quite volatile and therefore generally unsuitable for short-term objectives.

5. Control of costs is far more important in income funds than in growth funds.

INTRODUCTION

Income funds are intended to provide investors with a steady income flow while ensuring the safety of invested capital. Income funds offer many of the same features and advantages of GICs. They do this by assembling portfolios of income-producing securities. For the most part, these securities are interest- or dividend-bearing investments, but other types of securities with a stable income stream (such as royalty trusts) are also included in income funds.

Income funds do not typically exhibit the same degree of short-term volatility as equity funds, but the value of income funds can vary significantly. In fact, balancing a high income and stable net asset value is one of the most difficult problems for the managers of income funds.

Types of Funds

There are three basic types of income funds:

- bond funds
- mortgage-based funds
- dividend funds

Depending on the objectives and investment policies of a fund, its portfolio may consist of one type of security or a combination of types. We'll look at each type of fund in turn.

Bond Funds

A bond is a promise to repay a debt at some future time, and to pay interest on the debt until it is repaid. The most important factors that distinguish different bonds are the length of time until the debt is repaid (the ***term to maturity***) and the integrity of the borrower's promise to pay (the ***quality*** of the bond). ***Bond funds*** are also differentiated by the ***average term to maturity*** and the credit risk of the portfolio.

Short-Term Bond Funds (Income Funds)

These funds have average maturities of less than five years. They have relatively low short-term volatility and typically make monthly or quarterly distributions. On the other hand, the income stream from income funds is less certain. Because the investments in the portfolio have shorter maturities, they must be replaced more frequently. This makes the portfolio more vulnerable to fluctuations in interest rates. If interest rates rise, the investments in the portfolio can be replaced as they mature at higher yields, but if interest rates decline, the yield on replacement investments will also be lower.

Long-Term Bond Funds

These have average maturities longer than five years. Since the investments in the portfolio mature more slowly, they need to be replaced less frequently. As a result, the income stream from these funds is quite stable. However, they have considerable volatility, and many long-term bond funds make distributions only once per year.

The comparison of two Talvest funds in Table 8-1 neatly illustrates the differences between short- and long-term bond funds in income (return), safety of capital (volatility), average term, and average duration.

Table 8-1. Comparison of Fund Characteristics

FUND	OBJECTIVE	Average Term (yrs)	Average Duration (yrs)	Asset Mix (%)			3-Year Return (%)	3-Year Stand. Deviation
				<5 Years	>5 Years	Cash		
Talvest Bond	high-interest income / capital protection	8.74	5.38	23.20	79.10	4.50	13.90	20.60
Talvest Income	high-interest income / high capital protection	4.23	3.39	61.60	13.50	7.40	12.60	13.90

Source: Talvest quarterly portfolio reports, 04/93.

Since the *Talvest Income Fund* is much more heavily oriented to shorter-term investments than the *Talvest Bond Fund*, both the volatility and return of the income fund are accordingly lower.

Government Bond Funds

The essential feature of government bond funds is their high credit quality. Bonds issued by the federal and provincial governments are of very high quality, since default is (virtually) unthinkable. Bonds issued by municipal governments are usually of lesser quality because municipal governments have only a limited power to impose taxes with which to repay the debt.

The term to maturity of government bond funds can range from short to very long.

Corporate Bond Funds

These offer a higher yield than funds investing primarily in government bonds, but they have greater default risks. For those who think that investment grade rating is a guarantee of credit quality, it is important to remember that the debt rating of Olympia & York was excellent on the morning of its collapse.

High-Yield Bond Funds

Bond issues that are either unrated or rated below ***investment grade*** are often called junk bonds. These offer significantly higher yields than investment grade issues, but also entail significant higher default risk. Adequate diversification and portfolio management capable of evaluating the credit risk of these issues are absolutely essential.

Foreign Bond Funds

These funds invest in bond issues of foreign governments. The quality of these funds depends on the make-up of the portfolio. Issues from highly industrialized economies in, for example, the United States, Germany, and Japan are of high quality but issues from Latin American governments are of lower quality. In addition, although foreign bonds offer an opportunity to diversify out of the Canadian economy, they can entail currency risk. A devaluation in the denomination of the bond will reduce its return in Canadian dollars, regardless of the quality of the issuer.

Mortgage-Based Funds

A mortgage is simply a loan secured by real estate. Investments in the mortgage market can take the form of either direct loans to borrowers (a mortgage) or shares in MBSs. There are funds that invest in both types.

Mortgage Funds

A mutual fund that invests in mortgages buys them from mortgage lenders, and thereby acquires the right to receive the mortgage payments from borrowers. The vast majority of mortgage funds are offered by the mutual fund subsidiaries of banks, trust companies, and other traditional mortgage lenders, which provide the funds with a ready source of mortgages.

Mortgage funds most commonly invest in residential mortgages, although some funds include commercial and industrial mortgages in the portfolio. The most important reason for this is that many residential mortgages are guaranteed by the ***Central Mortgage and Housing Corporation* (*CMHC*)**. Since the CMHC is an agency of the federal government, this guarantee means the quality of these investments is very high. The yield on mortgages that are not guaranteed by the CMHC is usually slightly higher than the yield on CMHC mortgages, in recognition of their higher default risk. Sometimes, mortgages in the portfolios of bank-sponsored funds are guaranteed, not by the CMHC, but by the sponsoring bank.

Typically, the yield on mortgages is higher than for bonds, to compensate for some peculiar risks of mortgages. The ***prepayment privilege*** of some mortgages creates uncertainty as to the degree of reinvestment risk. While call risk is a feature of many bonds, the circumstances under which bonds can be called are clearly identifiable. ***Prepayment risk***, however, is driven by the motivations and circumstances of individual mortgageholders, and is much less predictable. In addition, the liquidity of mortgages is often lower than for bonds because every mortgage is different.

Mortgage-Backed Security Funds

These securities are created when a financial institution "pools" a number of government-guaranteed residential mortgages and sells "shares" of the pool to investors. MBSs offer comparable return and greater liquidity than a conventional mortgage investment. Most importantly, the mortgages from which the MBS is created are all guaranteed by the CMHC. They therefore present no credit or default risk. The income from non-prepayable MBSs is very stable and predictable, while the income from prepayable MBSs is somewhat less predictable because it is affected by prepayments by borrowers.

Dividend Funds

Dividend funds invest in preferred and common shares, which pay dividends. Their chief attraction is that dividend income receives preferential tax treatment relative to the interest income generated by a bond or mortgage-based fund. As a rule of thumb, the effective return on dividend income is equal to 1.35 times the yield. We'll look at why this is so in Chapter 16.

In addition, dividend-paying investments typically offer greater potential for capital appreciation, and should therefore provide better total returns than short-term bond (income) funds. To the end of 1996, the average five-year compound annual return for dividend funds was 11.7 percent, while the average five-year compound annual return for income funds was 7.4 percent.

A Cautionary Note

Since 1981, the total returns on bonds have actually exceeded those on stocks. While the TSE Total Return Index returned a compound annual rate of 11.2 percent over the 15 years to the end of 1996, the ScotiaMcLeod Universe Bond Index returned 13.5 percent.

Unfortunately, this strong performance has created a false sense of security in many investors about the potential benefits of fixed-income investing. The reality is that the high returns on fixed-income investments over the past 15 years are an anomaly, and it is virtually a mathematical certainty that returns over the next 15 to 20 years will not be so generous. Remember the teeter-totter. As interest rates decline, bond prices rise. Double-digit bond returns have been driven by a gradual 12 percent decline in interest rates from their historic highs in 1981. Since a further decline of 12 percent is impossible, so too are fixed-income returns that consistently outstrip stock returns. Indeed, bond returns are likely to come under increasing downward pressure, as the likelihood of rising interest rates grows.

This simple analysis has at least two implications. The first is that reliance on absolute past performance as a guide to anticipated future performance is unwise. Performance relative to a benchmark or average is a much more appropriate guide.

The second implication is that investors need to readjust their expectations about bond returns. Bonds have historically been valued for the stable income they provide, and investors who purchase fixed-income investments in anticipation of returns that rival those of stocks are almost certain to be disappointed.

The Role of the Manager

The most basic task for the portfolio manager of income funds is to balance the inevitable conflict between high income (which can involve considerable price volatility) and price stability (which typically reduces the income stream).

A second responsibility for most of these managers is to control the costs of the fund. When bonds (and mortgages) yield about 8 percent, management expenses of 1.5 percent will reduce the effective pretax return to 6.5 percent. Since there is far less variety in bonds than in stocks, the ability of the portfolio manager to add value by realizing capital appreciation is usually quite limited. As a result, higher expenses typically result in lower returns.

Most income fund managers are not required to conduct security and credit analysis, since most income funds invest only in issues rated investment grade or better. The managers of high-yield (or junk) funds, dividend funds, and some foreign funds are the exceptions. Furthermore, because credit and security analysis can add significant value, the expenses of these funds can be somewhat higher than those of other income funds.

Managers of income funds holding foreign debt investments also have to manage currency risk. Unlike equities, a decline in the value of the currency in which a foreign bond is denominated represents an irretrievable loss. Equities can often recover, since a currency devaluation may make the foreign company more competitive, but a bond cannot recoup the loss on the currency exchange through increased efficiency.

Investor Considerations

1. It is a myth that you cannot lose money if it is invested in bonds. There is the risk of default on corporate and foreign bonds. In addition, there is no assurance that the "fixed" return of bonds will protect against the effects of inflation. For investments with terms longer than 20 years, the volatility of bonds is slightly greater than that of stocks.

2. A bond is not the same as a bond fund. A bond has a specific maturity date, but a bond fund does not. A bond investor will get back the full amount of the investment on maturity (barring default) regardless of

changes in interest rates. In contrast, increases in interest rates can significantly reduce the net asset values of a bond fund.

3. Expense ratios are important in most income funds. Higher expenses can only be justified when they result in higher net returns. Since the potential for bond fund managers to add value is relatively limited, the need to control costs is correspondingly greater.

4. The frequency of distributions is important in income funds. This frequency varies widely. Some income funds make distributions monthly, while others make quarterly distributions, and others still make only semi-annual or even annual distributions. Long-term bond funds are generally unsuitable as income funds because, although the income they produce is relatively high, it is frequently paid only annually or semi-annually.

   As the availability of high-yield income investments has gradually declined with the general decline in interest rates, the returns on income funds have come under increasing pressure. Faced with the prospect of lower returns, investors have turned increasingly to funds that offer greater certainty by paying a regular "fixed" distribution. While the attraction of such funds is fairly obvious, they have a number of characteristics of which investors should be aware:

- When the returns of a fund are insufficient to meet its obligations, a portion of the periodic distribution is merely a repayment of the investor's capital. Mackenzie Financial's *Industrial Dividend Growth Fund*, for example, pays a fixed distribution of $0.60 per unit per year ($0.05 per month), but in 1996 (which was a very good year for investments) more than half the payout ($0.307) was merely a "return of capital." This can give some investors an inaccurate impression of the fund's performance.

- While the portfolio manager makes every effort to ensure the consistency of the pay-out, a distribution is not, and generally cannot be, guaranteed. The *Guardian Monthly Dividend Fund*, for example, was forced by the declining yields on its investments to reduce its "fixed" distribution from $0.06 to $0.05 in March 1996, and to $0.045 in October, as a result of the declining yields in its portfolio.

- In an effort to bolster yields, a number of these funds have modified their investment mandates to permit greater emphasis on low yielding stocks that exhibit long-term potential for significant capital appreciation. In November 1996, for example, Mackenzie Financial's *Industrial Income Fund* increased its allowable stock exposure from 30 percent to 35 percent. Other funds, like the *BPI High Income Fund* and the *GT Global Canada Fund (Income Class)*, have bolstered their yield by investing substantially in royalty trust units.

5. Government bond funds are no safer than individual government bonds. Individual government bonds are guaranteed, and a portfolio of government bonds does not provide any additional protection against credit risk. In contrast, ***corporate bond funds*** and high-yield (or junk) bond funds are safer than individual corporate or high-yield bonds because diversification and security selection based on professional security analysis provide a level of protection against default risk.

6. Strip bond funds are not income funds. These invest in zero coupon or strip bonds. The bonds are almost always government issues, and therefore of high quality, but because the value of interest payments is factored into the discounted price of the strip bond, the only income stream comes from capital gains made on the sale of investments in the portfolio. For the same reason, strip bonds and the funds based on them are very volatile. Investors buy these funds to exploit changes in interest rates in search of capital gains rather than to earn current income.

7. The portfolio of a dividend fund requires particular scrutiny. While a corporation is obliged to pay interest on its debts, it is not required to pay dividends, although it may have an excellent record of doing so. Depending on the financial health of the business, dividends can be reduced or even suspended to meet legal obligations. The dividends on preferred shares will be more certain than those on common shares, but neither type is assured.

   Investors who purchase dividend funds because of the preferential tax treatment accorded dividend income should ensure that the portfolio of the fund is in fact composed of dividend-paying investments. A fund with too many bonds and other interest-bearing investments may create unexpected tax liability.

Many commentators advise against holding dividend funds in tax-advantaged plans because the benefit of preferential tax treatment is lost, but this viewpoint does not acknowledge the other merits of these funds. Typically, dividend funds are less volatile than other equity funds, and this lower volatility may be more consistent with the investor's risk tolerance.

CHAPTER NINE

MONEY MARKET FUNDS

EXECUTIVE SUMMARY

In this chapter we examine the basic characteristics of money market funds.

1. The fundamental objective of money market funds is to protect invested capital. There is no possibility of capital appreciation with these funds, but they are useful for a variety of short-term purposes, as–
   - an alternative to bank savings accounts
   - a source of emergency funds
   - a place to "park" assets

2. The most important difference between types of money market funds is the term to maturity. Funds with an average term greater than 180 days are not permitted to use the word *money* or *cash* in their names.

3. The greater the average term to maturity, the greater the volatility of the fund.

4. There are two different pricing methods for money market funds:
   - mark to market
   - amortized cost

   In some circumstances, the amortized cost method can misstate the real value of the fund.

5. The control of costs is critical in money market funds.

The paramount objective of money market funds is to protect invested capital. While income funds generally tolerate some volatility for greater returns, money market funds invest only in short-term securities that do not compromise safety. These include government investments such as treasury bills and high-quality short-term corporate fixed-income securities.

Fund Characteristics

Term to Maturity

Money market funds invest in short-term debt obligations and cash equivalent securities such as banker's acceptances. As a result, the variety of money market funds is quite limited. Funds which use the word *cash* or *money* in their names are restricted to investments maturing in 13 months or less (25 months for government obligations) with a dollar-weighted term to maturity of 180 days or less. Funds that do not use the words *cash* or *money* are not subject to these restrictions, but nevertheless invest in short-term securities.

The important difference between money market funds is their average term to maturity. Funds with a longer average term to maturity have higher returns and higher volatility than funds with shorter average terms. The *Elliott & Page Money Fund,* for example, has a maximum average term of 180 days (although its usual or normal position is an average term of about 60 days). In contrast, the investment mandate of the *Spectrum United Canadian T-Bill Fund* restricts the fund's average term to a maximum of less than 91 days.

Because the investments have a short term, and are of high quality, these funds have very little volatility. At the same time, however, there is no real possibility for capital appreciation. All of the return from a money market fund is derived from ***current yield.*** In addition, money market funds have considerable reinvestment risk. While the net asset values of money market funds are stable, the long-term returns are not.

Computing Returns

The return from a money market fund comes entirely from interest income. Distributions are very frequent. Many money market funds make distributions weekly. However, size of the returns varies considerably, since the level of the fund's return is directly related to short-term interest rates. When interest rates are high, the return of the fund will also be high. If interest rates are low, the return of the fund will also be low.

Most money market funds publish two rates of return:

- indicated yield
  Indicated yield is the yield calculated from income accrued by the fund over the preceding seven days; it is expressed on an annualized basis. Fund companies are required by law to identify this measure of performance.

- effective yield
  The ***effective yield*** is calculated by compounding the indicated yield at the currently prevailing interest rate, and is therefore based on the assumption that the indicated yield will continue into the future. However, because the investments in a money market portfolio have short terms, it is unlikely that indicated yield will be constant. In periods of declining interest rate, effective yield will overstate the performance of the fund; when rates are rising, it will understate performance.

Pricing Method

As in the case of other funds, distributions are typically paid in the form of additional units. However, money market funds are often priced differently from other mutual funds. The net asset values of growth funds and income funds are priced on a ***mark-to-market*** basis, which varies with the values of the investments in the portfolio. As the values of the portfolio's investments increase, net asset values rise. Most money market funds, in contrast, are priced on the basis of ***amortized cost***. The net asset value is fixed (for example, at $10 or even $1), and fluctuations in the value of the investments in the portfolio are reflected in the yield of the fund. If the value of the fund's investments increases, the yield of the money market fund rises. Units are bought and sold at the fixed price plus accrued interest from the date of the last distribution.

While the amortized cost approach to valuing fund units reflects the importance of preserving capital, it can affect the reliability of the reported value. Particularly in funds with longer average terms to maturity, the amortized cost method can overstate net asset value if interest rates rise sharply and understate net asset value if rates drop abruptly.

The Role of the Manager

For the managers of money market funds, controlling costs is critical. Even more than in income funds, the range of different investments in these funds is limited, and variations in performance from one fund to the next are based on the ability of the manager to exploit very small differences in yields. In such circumstances, even slightly higher expenses will have a noticeable negative effect on net returns, and there is a direct relationship between high expenses and low returns.

Investor Considerations

1. Money market funds are useful for a number of short-term purposes.

   - **saving plans**
     Just as investors are assured of receiving the full amount of a GIC or term deposit at maturity, it is a virtual certainty that money market investors will get their money back. Money market funds offer at least two advantages over GICs and similar instruments as savings vehicles. First, money market funds generally offer a superior rate of return. The important distinction is that the return on money market funds, like that on other mutual funds, but unlike that on GICs and other vehicles, is not predetermined. When interest rates increase, the return on a money market fund will also increase; when interest rates are declining, the return on a money market fund will also shrink.

     The second advantage money market funds have over other savings instruments is that they are more liquid. Term deposits and GICs have specific maturity dates, with penalties for early redemption, but there is no "maturity" date for money market funds. They can be redeemed at any time for full value with no penalty.

- **emergency reserves**
  Money market funds can also be part of an individual's liquid assets, for use in emergencies.

- **temporary investment**
  Through the structure of mutual fund families, money market funds provide a temporary place to hold investment capital outside the stock or bond markets. In most cases, transferring assets from a growth or income fund to a money market fund within the same fund family incurs only a minimal charge. Converting long-term investments to medium- and short-term investments during cyclical highs, for example, enables investors to "lock in" or secure their investment gains. Money market funds offer a convenient and advantageous way to achieve these goals.

  Some investors exploit this sort of service in an attempt to boost returns by moving assets to money market funds to avoid cyclical downturns and switching out of the money market funds when the market rallies. Although the evidence convincingly indicates that "market timing" does not work, its seductive appeal persists. As a result, most fund families restrict the number of switches that investors may make without penalty.

2. It is impractical to choose a money market fund purely on its own merits. Because there is so little to differentiate most money market funds, it is more convenient for investors to use the money market fund offered by the fund group that manages their growth funds or income funds.

CHAPTER TEN

BALANCED FUNDS AND ASSET ALLOCATION FUNDS

EXECUTIVE SUMMARY

This chapter examines the important characteristics and uses of balanced funds and asset allocation funds.

1. Despite the differences in their names, there is no significant difference between balanced funds and strategic asset allocation funds. Both attempt to combine the objectives of growth and income.

2. Tactical asset allocation funds are funds in which the mix of assets in the portfolio is modified in response to anticipated changes in the market in an attempt to maximize returns.

3. Some balanced funds emphasize the objective of growth, while others stress the objective of income.

4. The investment mandates of some funds limit the proportion of the portfolio that may be invested in any single asset class, while other funds allow the portfolio manager complete discretion in allocating investments.

5. Balanced funds can offer a less volatile alternative to growth funds, but there is a price to be paid in reduced long-term returns.

6. Balanced funds also offer the convenience of a single investment.

INTRODUCTION

Balanced funds attempt to combine the objectives of growth funds and income funds. Simultaneously, they seek to provide the significant capital appreciation of growth funds with the stable income of income funds. To many investors, they seem to be the perfect investment, and this appeal is not lost on the marketing departments of fund sponsors, which often promote the convenience and simplicity of a balanced fund investment. Several balanced funds are promoted as "one-decision" investments. In fact, balanced funds necessarily represent a compromise, and as with all compromises, some benefit must be relinquished.

Balanced funds were conceived in the late 1930s and popularized in the 1950s. During the extended bull market of the 1960s, the performance of most balanced funds in the United States lagged behind that of growth funds as a result of the dampening effect of their bond component. However, in the 1980s, bond investments surged, and interest in balanced funds, and in their more modern cousins, asset allocation funds, was revived. While asset allocation funds are promoted as being more disciplined than balanced funds because they claim to rely on complex econometric models and computer-driven strategies, the essential feature of both balanced and asset allocation funds is the combination of growth and income investments in a single portfolio.

Types of Funds

Balanced funds can be distinguished in two important ways. The most important distinction is the "balance" that funds strike between the objectives of growth and income. Some funds, such as the *Trimark Select Balanced Fund*, clearly emphasize the objective of growth. A minimum of about 70 percent of the portfolio is invested in equities, and the income objective is merely to match the savings rate offered by the banks. In contrast, the objective of income is clearly paramount for the Mackenzie Financial's *Industrial Income Fund* (which is a balanced fund, despite its name). As a rule, no more than 30 percent of the portfolio will be invested in equities, and the fund pays a fixed quarterly dividend of $0.25 per unit (or $1.00 per unit per year).

Another way to distinguish between different balanced funds is to examine the degree to which the fund varies the proportions of different asset classes. Some funds impose maximum and minimum levels on the degree to which a fund may invest in any particular asset class, while other funds may in principle invest exclusively in one asset class. Some analysts argue that the investment mandates of balanced funds are limited, while those of strategic asset allocation funds are unrestricted, but this is incorrect. The *CI Balanced Fund*, for example, has no limits on the proportion of assets that may be invested in any asset class.

In any event, the extreme weightings contemplated by broad investment mandates of some funds are virtually never applied. The danger in taking extreme positions is that the returns of the fund will be markedly different from those of other funds. This can mean either that the fund will significantly outperform its "peers" or that it will significantly underperform its peers, depending on the way in which the market develops. In fact, portfolio managers, just like individual investors, are far more concerned about the consequences of being wrong than they are with being right. Furthermore, few managers are so utterly certain about market trends that they will ignore other opinions. As a result, few fund managers stray too far from the consensus.

Despite the similarity in names, tactical asset allocation funds are different than strategic asset allocation funds. The mix in the assets in the portfolios of strategic asset allocation funds (and balanced funds) is modified largely in response to fund managers' judgements about investors' overall needs. In tactical asset allocation funds, the asset mix of the portfolio is typically modified in response to anticipated changes in market conditions in an effort to maximize returns.

The Concept of Rebalancing

Over time, the proportion of growth and income investments in the portfolio will change. In part, this is the result of management decisions to vary the proportions in response to economic and market conditions. In addition, the portfolio itself is dynamic. The proportion of the different assets in the portfolio is constantly changing because different assets have different rates of return. When stock markets are rising and bond markets lag, the proportion of the fund in stocks will grow relative to the proportion in bonds. Conversely, when bond markets are strong and stock markets are weak, the bond component will increase in comparison to the stock component of the fund. While it is possible to allow the proportion of assets to change as the returns of the different investments vary, this passive approach is almost never employed in practice both because the cash flows of a mutual fund make it impractical and because a measure of active management is expected of investment funds. To maintain the desired proportions, the portfolio must be rebalanced from time to time. Rebalancing can be guided in one of three ways.

Rebalancing to Meet a Benchmark

Rebalancing can be driven by the requirement that performance meet a certain standard. For example, funds which attempt to provide a level of income tied to an external benchmark (such as the bank savings rates) will find it necessary to shift assets from growth investments to income investments when the income of the fund drops below the benchmark. Conversely, when the income greatly exceeds the benchmark, some assets in the portfolio will be shifted into equities.

Rebalancing to a Predetermined Percentage

Some portfolio managers will periodically rebalance to a neutral or target position. For example, the *Guardian International Balanced Fund* has a target of 50 percent equities and 50 percent bonds, while the *Dynamic Partners Fund* has a target of 65 percent equities and 35 percent bonds.

To control administrative costs, most funds rebalance only when the actual proportions diverge from the target proportions by a predetermined amount. The *Dynamic Partners Fund* is rebalanced when the value of either component changes by 3 percent. The *Elliott & Page Balanced Fund* is rebalanced when the portfolio mix diverges from the target by 5 percent.

Rebalancing to Anticipate Market Trends

Other balanced funds employ a more complicated approach to establish target proportions. Starting from a base, or neutral, position, managers adjust the proportions of assets in stocks and bonds to reflect their outlook for the stock and bond markets. If, for example, the neutral mix is 60 percent stocks and 40 percent bonds, a manager anticipating rising interest rates might reduce the target proportion of bonds to 25 or 30 percent. The manager would then rebalance the portfolio to meet these modified targets.

How a neutral position is determined is rarely specified. While few fund managers are likely to admit it, the proportions of assets are probably driven as much by marketing considerations as by any justifiable economic rationale.

A Note on Asset Allocation Services

Asset allocation services are programs offered by fund sponsors and financial services firms that spread an investor's assets among a variety of mutual funds. There are three distinct approaches:

Fund of Funds

These investments are most similar to balanced funds. They are mutual funds that invest in other mutual funds offered by the same fund group. The *Dynamic Managed Portfolio* is an example. In some cases, like the *Spectrum United Portfolio of Funds*, the portfolio includes both mutual funds and individual stock or bond selections. Some, like the *CI Sector Fund* and the *AGF International Group of Funds*, are structured to minimize some of the tax consequences of switches between individual funds, and all such funds are structured to prevent the duplication of management fees.

Allocation Services

AGF offers a program that shifts investments between three different mutual funds in an effort to enhance returns. There are no fees for the service, but every time the proportion invested in the various funds is changed, a switching fee is imposed. Apart from the cost, these switches can affect tax liability. Royal Mutual Funds, which offered an asset allocation service introduced by Royal Trust in 1991, has recently announced plans to discontinue the service, claiming that its customers are probably equally well off with one of the balanced funds offered by the group.

Comprehensive Asset Management Services

These are the most recent innovation. These vehicles permit investors to tailor the combination of mutual funds to suit their circumstances. Some programs, such as Midland Walwyn's COMPASS, permit the investor to determine both the number and the proportion of individual funds included in the portfolio. Other programs, such as Mackenzie Financial's STAR service, offer a range of predetermined portfolios from which investors must choose.

Proponents argue that these services offer a couple of benefits. The first is convenience: investors are spared the burden of having to decide how to allocate their resources to meet their objectives. This is a double-edged sword, since the investor also surrenders control over the allocation. In fact, all but the most sophisticated of these programs are fundamentally impersonal, and it is unlikely that these "off the shelf" approaches will fully satisfy the needs of individual investors.

The second benefit claimed for these services is that they improve the efficiency of portfolio management. Advocates of asset allocation argue that, by separating the functions of security selection and asset allocation, they can achieve superior results. However, there is no evidence that the performance of asset allocation services is better.

In our view, these programs are little more than new names for market-timing systems. Often, the marketing potential of these programs can be the most important factor in their appeal. There are a number of reasons why this is so.

- The vast majority of these services compel participants to commit *all* their resources to a single fund group. These programs are therefore extremely useful in increasing the assets of the fund group, but limit the ability of investors to seek out the most suitable funds across the spectrum of fund groups.

- The burgeoning number of mutual funds focused on various niche markets has been largely justified by the so-called "requirements" of asset allocation. A portfolio of stocks, bonds, and cash is now said to be outdated: a "modern" portfolio must include at least some of the following asset classes:
  a. domestic equities
    i. large-capitalization
    ii. small-capitalization
  b. foreign equities
    i. developed markets
    - United States
    - Europe
    - Japan

ii. emerging markets
  - Latin America
  - Far East

c. domestic government bonds
  i. long-term
  ii. medium-term
  iii. T-bills

d. domestic nongovernment bonds

e. foreign bonds

f. real estate
  i. domestic
  ii. foreign

g. commodities and financial futures

To the average investor, however, this proliferation of new asset classes is neither helpful nor productive: more than anything, it increases the asset base on which fund companies charge fees, and serves as a justification for professional asset allocation programs.

- An increasing number of fund sponsors are extending the concept of asset allocation to the area of investment strategies. Global Strategy and 20/20 Financial Group (now part of the AGF fund group), for example, both offer funds with multiple advisers sharing responsibility for the portfolio. In other cases, different funds in a group employ different management styles. Mackenzie Financial, for instance, offers one series of funds with ***top-down investing***, and another series based on ***bottom-up investing***. But while increasing the number of investment approaches is presented as a technique for improving diversification, there is no evidence that this strategy reduces risk, and our view is that it is essentially a marketing tool.

The Role of the Manager

Not surprisingly, the manager's role in a balanced fund combines the roles of the manager in growth funds and income funds, but the importance of identifying good investments usually predominates. It is almost always the stock portfolio that determines the total return of the fund. The bond portfolio provides an income, but because its contribution to the growth of the portfolio is usually small, decisions about its composition are relatively minor.

Investor Considerations

1. Investors should ensure that the fund's investment mandate is compatible with their needs. The relative importance of growth and income objectives should be carefully considered, but investors should not expect either the growth of a growth fund, or the income of an income fund.

   Although the prospectus is often unhelpful in this regard, there are other indirect ways of evaluating the relative importance of a fund's objectives. One way is to consider the reputation of the manager. For example, T.A.L. Investment Counsel, which manages the *Talvest Diversified Fund*, built its reputation largely on fixed-income management. In contrast, Trimark Investment Management, which runs the *Trimark Income Growth Fund*, is known best for equities management. Another way is to examine the fund's portfolio characteristics for several years. A fund that emphasizes growth will hold a greater proportion of equities, while a fund that stresses income will typically hold more bonds.

2. Balanced funds allow investors who are psychologically unprepared for the short-term volatility of growth funds to invest without forgoing all the long-term advantages of a growth investment. Because balanced portfolios include fixed-income investments, their short-term variability is usually lower than is typical of growth funds. At the same time, however, the potential for capital appreciation is better than is typical of income funds because the portfolio includes growth investments.

   It is sometimes suggested that investors who want a balanced portfolio should purchase separate growth and income funds. There are at least two rationales for this view:

   - There is a potential cost saving on the management fees in the bond portfolio.

- Investors can shop for the "best" growth manager and the "best" fixed-income manager.

This view, however, ignores both the convenience of "one-stop" shopping and the important psychological benefit of the lower volatility that balanced funds offer. The greater volatility of the growth fund component may cause the investor to sell growth funds prematurely or not invest at all.

CONCLUSION

While balanced funds and asset allocation funds may seem like the perfect investment, it is critical to remember that they represent a compromise between the goals of growth and current income. For investors who are uncomfortable with the short-term volatility of growth funds, balanced funds offer an opportunity to participate in the benefits of long-term growth. There is, however, a price for diminishing the anxiety of investing. Incorporating the stabilizing influence of fixed-income securities into the portfolio will eventually reduce performance, since equities always outperform fixed-income investments in the long term. Investors who are looking for a fund that provides an easy route to superior returns by loading up on each asset class during its cyclical upturn are almost certain to be disappointed. While there may well be a place for balanced funds in a personal investment program, they are no substitute for thinking about individual goals and circumstances.

CHAPTER ELEVEN

INDEX FUNDS

EXECUTIVE SUMMARY

This chapter examines the advantages and limitations of index funds.

1. Index funds mimic a market index such as the Dow Jones Industrial Average or the TSE 300.

2. The chief advantage of index funds is that they do not significantly underperform the market. However, they never outperform the market.

3. Because the portfolio is determined by the composition of the index, the portfolio manager's primary responsibility is to control costs. More than for any other type of fund, higher expenses will be reflected in lower returns, and expenses should be a significant factor in choosing an index fund.

4. Closet indexing is an objectionable investment strategy in which managers secretly mimic an index in their choice of funds. The purpose of this approach is to ensure that the fund does not seriously underperform other funds in its class. The danger is that the investor pays for active management, which is not provided.

INTRODUCTION

An index fund is, very simply, a fund that is based on an index. As we've seen, an index is a "yardstick," and a market index is a theoretical portfolio of securities representing a market. The TSE 300, for example, is a sample of 300 investments chosen to represent the TSE as a whole. All major exchanges have a variety of indexes.

The justification for index funds is based on the indisputable fact that it is very difficult to outperform the market index. The concept that the market cannot be "beaten" is one of the pillars of modern portfolio theory. It is attributable primarily to academic studies undertaken in the 1960s that showed that investment portfolio managers often underperformed common market indexes. However, this research is now more than 30 years old, and modern academic analysis largely repudiates this view.

Characteristics of Index Funds

The fundamental characteristic of index funds is that they are passively managed. This means that decisions about the most promising sectors and securities, and the timing of purchases or sales, are not required. The portfolio is determined entirely by the composition of the index, and is only modified if the index is changed. There are a large number of indexes, and there are now a large number of index funds. The best-known index is the U.S. Dow Jones Industrial Average, which is a selection of 30 corporations trading on the New York Stock Exchange. In the United States, the most widely used index is now probably the S&P 500, but there are literally dozens of others. There are also a multitude of foreign indexes and some global ones. The Europe, Australia and Far East (EAFE) index and the Morgan Stanley Capital International (MSCI) index are the best known.

In Canada, the TSE 300 is the best-known index. It is comprised of 300 stocks, divided into 43 distinct components which are grouped into 14 subindexes. There are three significant funds based on it. *The Great-West Life Equity Index Fund*, with $928 million in assets, was established in 1983. The Toronto-Dominion Bank's *Greenline Canadian Equity Index Fund*, with $258 million in assets, was established in 1985. The Bank of Montreal's *First Canadian Equity Index Fund*, with $265 million in assets, was established in 1988. In addition, the *NN Financial Canadian 35 Index Fund* is based on the TSE 35 Index, which represents the most widely traded companies on the Toronto Stock Exchange.

There are also indexes for bonds. In Canada, the most widely used bond index is the Scotia McLeod Universe Bond Index. However, while there are bond index funds in the United States, none is available in Canada.

Advantages of Index Funds

Since the returns of many actively managed funds do not match the broader market, the chief benefit of index funds is that they offer the assurance that they will not significantly underperform. In effect, index funds ensure that investors will not be left behind in the quest for financial security.

In addition, an index fund provides investors looking for exposure to particular markets or regions the assurance that the investment approach of the portfolio manager will not distort that exposure. The mandate of the *Fidelity Far East Fund*, for example, is to invest in all of Southeast Asia except Japan, but the actual investment approach of the manager over the past couple of years has been to concentrate the portfolio in Hong Kong–based investments. For investors wanting broad exposure to the Asia Pacific Rim, the current stance of the fund is inappropriate: an index fund would be more representative of the whole geographical area.

Limitations of Index Funds

Despite their intuitive appeal, index funds have several limitations.

- An index is not static. Typically, an index is reviewed annually and does change over time. Although a great deal of care goes into the selection of the index, it nevertheless represents a specific view of the overall market. For example, in the effort to be representative of the market, there is an inevitable tendency to include "newer" industries in an index. The "new" industries tend, however, to be more actively traded and often have higher p/e ratios than "older" industries. The consequence of modifying the index is therefore to increase the price of the index and distort the picture of the overall market.

- By relying on an index to define the portfolio, the fund manager has effectively delegated the selection of stocks to some other person or agency that may have goals quite different from those of investors. The securities in an index fund are intended to reflect the liquidity, capitalization, and volatility of the market, while the securities in an investment portfolio are intended to provide superior growth or stable income.

- There is no Canadian index that mirrors the market as a whole. Typically, bigger companies are disproportionately represented on most indexes. To put it simply, indexes such as the Dow Jones, the TSE 300, and the S&P 500 are biased in favour of large-capitalization companies. For example, BCE Inc., the parent company of Bell Canada, represents more than 3 percent of the TSE 300, although it constitutes far less of the broader market.

  This is a problem because large- and small-cap companies often do not exhibit similar market behaviour. There are times when small-cap stocks offer better returns than large-cap stocks. For example, small-cap stocks generally outperformed large-cap stocks from 1990 to 1993. At other times, the pattern is reversed. As a result, the index will appear to "outperform" the broader market when large-cap stocks are strong. Conversely, when small-cap stocks do particularly well, the index may lag behind the broader market.

- Despite the best intentions of the manager, it is impossible for the portfolio of an index fund to exactly mirror an index. The index is fully invested, but actual portfolios cannot be fully invested. A portion of assets must be in cash—either to meet redemptions or as a result of capital inflows. But holding cash will skew the performance of the index fund: in rising markets, the inclusion of cash will pull down the performance of the fund, while in falling markets it will bolster performance. Management expenses will also reduce the returns of an index fund relative to those of the index.

- Unlike an actively managed fund, the portfolio manager of an index fund cannot take steps to insulate the portfolio from market declines by modifying security selections or increasing the cash component of the portfolio.

The Role of the Manager

The manager's role in index funds is very different from that in other mutual funds. The performance of the fund is dictated by the index on which it is based, and there is no place for security analysis and active management to improve performance.

The manager has two basic tasks. The first is to match the index as closely as possible. There are three major approaches to indexing:

- replication
  In this approach, the portfolio is composed of the same securities as the index in the same proportions. The portfolio will behave (almost) exactly like the index it mirrors.

- optimization
  In this approach, the portfolio holds a representative sample of the securities in the index. By limiting the number of securities, managers attempt to minimize the costs of running the fund.

- sampling
  This approach is used for bond indexes that are difficult to duplicate cost-effectively. Bonds are divided into groups, and a selection of bonds from each group is chosen to make up the portfolio.

The manager's second task is to control the costs of the fund. An index itself has no costs, but a fund based on an index incurs the costs of buying securities with the invested funds and meeting the administrative needs of investors. Since the index does change from time to time, there are also costs associated with the periodic sale of securities. In addition, an index fund must keep a (small) portion of the portfolio in cash to meet the ongoing demand for redemptions, and this can distort the performance of the fund in comparison to the index. As a result of these costs, the performance of an index fund is inevitably worse than the performance of the index on which it is based. Moreover, because there is no active management, the costs of managing the fund cannot be offset against superior returns.

As a result, the control of costs is critical in index funds. Figure 11-1 starkly illustrates the effect of expenses on returns by comparing the relative growth in value of one dollar invested in the TSE 300 and two index funds based on it from 1987 to 1996. Because the index itself has no expenses, its growth exceeds that of either the *Great-West Life Equity Index Fund* or Toronto-Dominion's *Greenline Canadian Index Fund*. The higher the fund's expenses, the lower the fund's returns. The returns of the Great West Life fund, which has an expense ratio of 2.64 percent, are consequently lower than the returns of the TD Greenline fund, which has an expense ratio of only 1.11 percent.

A Note on Closet Indexing

For managers to ensure that a fund's performance does not fall below that of its competitors, buying the index is a simple and convenient solution. Because indexing is passive, it adds very little value and there is therefore no justification for substantial management fee. In "closet indexing," the indexing strategy is undisclosed, enabling the manager to charge fees that are appropriate to active management.

Closet indexing should be avoided for two reasons. First, there is no point in paying fees for active management that is not provided. Second, there is no assurance the practice of mimicking the market will be sustained. Because the strategy is undisclosed, the manager can change it any time.

Figure 11-1. Management Expense Ratios in Index Funds

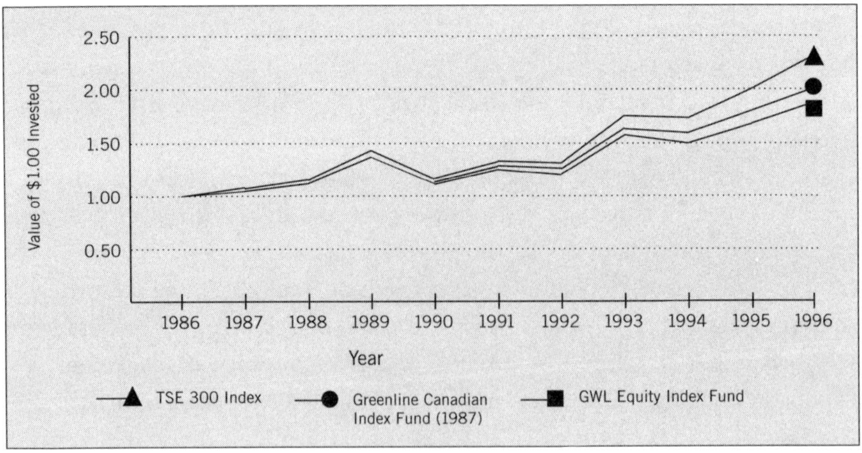

Source: BellCharts

Investor Considerations

- Investors who want an index fund should ensure that the fund is truly passively managed. Some funds purport to be index funds but actually attempt to "tweak" the index to boost returns.

- Investors should ensure that the costs of the fund are as low as possible. Differences in cost are the only meaningful distinction between index funds.

A FINAL NOTE

Index funds essentially abdicate the goal of outperforming the market in favour of (nearly) matching it. They are, like all "single-decision" systems largely a mechanical substitute for thought. Although it is true that many actively managed funds underperform the market and that the process of picking superior performers requires considerable effort, these two facts do not lead to the conclusion that index funds are best and that a strategy of indexing is the safest approach.

CHAPTER TWELVE

SECTOR FUNDS

EXECUTIVE SUMMARY

This chapter examines the advantages and limitations of sector funds.

1. Sector funds are growth funds that invest in particular sectors of the economy.

2. Although the format of the mutual fund provides some diversification, sector funds are poorly diversified.

3. The performance of sector funds is extremely uneven. While they do very well when the sector enjoys strong growth, they can perform very poorly when the sector is weak.

4. The cyclical character of their performance means that they are highly volatile. This can be a problem for investors who are uncomfortable with significant fluctuations in price.

5. Sector funds are also highly susceptible to the risk that the portfolio manager will attempt to time the market in an effort to avoid poor returns during cyclical lows in the sector.

6. Sector funds are inappropriate for novice investors and should in any event constitute only a small part of an investor's portfolio.

INTRODUCTION

Sector funds are a particular form of growth fund. We deal with them separately because the differences between them and other growth funds are at least as significant as the similarities.

Sector funds had their first incarnation in the latter 1930s and 1940s. They were based on the fact that different sectors of the economy do well at different points in the business cycles of economic expansion and contraction. The intention was for investors to hop from one sector to another as each reached its cyclical peak, and to thereby exploit volatility, benefiting from "upside" volatility while avoiding negative "downside" volatility. The trick of knowing when to switch, however, proved too difficult to master. Investors typically bought into a sector as it reached its peak and sold following a decline. These funds faded in popularity in the 1950s but re-emerged in the early 1980s in conjunction with the rise of asset allocation programs.

Characteristics of Sector Funds

General Observations

Sector funds provide an opportunity to invest in a small portion or single segment of the economy. Given the predominance of resources industries in the Canadian economy, it is not surprising that the majority of Canadian sector funds are natural resources funds (particularly energy and precious metals funds). However, funds also specialize in the financial services industries and in high-technology industries, particularly telecommunications, biotechnology, and health sciences.

Other funds specialize in real estate. The recession that began in 1990 and the peculiar rules for valuing real estate investments combined to severely reduce the performance (and appeal) of these funds, and many were converted to REITs. Only a few "true" real estate mutual funds remain, and not all are available to the general public.

Advantages

There are two reasons why investing in particular sectors might be desirable.

Positive Outlook for the Sector

It is well recognized that market strength is cyclical and that different segments of the market do well at different times. The opportunity to capitalize on periods of strong growth is obviously attractive.

Tax Benefits

Some sectors are accorded preferential tax treatment. Real estate investments, for example, are eligible for ***capital cost allowance***, which is compensation for the wear and tear on property. The oil and gas sector is also accorded significant tax concessions that can enhance the performance of funds investing in these securities. In many cases, these special tax provisions are exploited through investments that are similar in some ways to mutual funds, such as REITs and royalty trusts.

Benefits of Mutual Fund Format

Mutual funds offer a number of advantages for investing in specific sectors:

- The mutual fund format attempts to eliminate the risk of bad stock selection while maintaining the benefit of exposure to specific sectors. ***Single issue risk***, which reflects the possibility that an investment in only one company will prove to be a poor choice, can be eliminated by investing in a diversified portfolio.

- The mutual fund format provides the opportunity for specialized professional management. While all mutual funds offer professional management, sector funds permit the portfolio manager to develop expertise in specific sectors; this knowledge will in principle translate into greater skill in evaluating financial circumstances and identifying opportunities.

- The mutual fund format makes it possible to include in tax-deferred plans certain assets that are otherwise not eligible. For example, direct investments in gold bullion and real estate are ineligible for RRSPs. However, by investing in an eligible mutual fund that includes these ineligible assets in the portfolio, individuals can benefit indirectly.

Limitations

While sector funds offer some advantages, they also involve significant risks.

Limited Diversification

Almost by definition, the diversification of the individual sectors is limited because all the investments in the sector are more or less equally subject to the same risks. In Chapter 6, we noted that limited diversification can result in erratic performance characterized by periods of abnormally strong (or weak) returns. We also observed that investors frequently invest after a "big year," significantly increasing their potential for loss.

Management Risks

There are a couple of different risks here. First, any attempt by the manager to take a "defensive" position by switching to cash investments before a market downturn is subject to the obvious risk that the manager will miss the turning points. Staying in the sector too long or failing to get back into the sector soon enough diminishes returns. Ibbottson Associates has calculated that the return of American investors who missed the ten best days of the market between 1983 and 1992 would have declined from 16.2 percent to 11.6 percent, and the return of those who missed the forty best days would have dropped to only 3.6 percent—well below the inflation rate over the same period. In a diversified portfolio, the relationship between the cyclical price movements of different investments is relatively weak. In the specialized portfolio of a sector fund, however, cyclical price movements of the investments coincide, increasing the risk of "missing the market." Attempts to predict changes in the direction of the market is really market timing, and market timing doesn't work. A fuller discussion of market timing's deficiencies can be found in Appendix J.

In fact, many managers are reluctant to undertake a dramatic shift into cash during market down turns because they cannot take the risk of holding excessive cash when the market upturn comes. As a result, many fund managers make only limited changes to the portfolio. Since the diversification of these funds is limited, the price fluctuations of the investments in the portfolio are largely unmoderated, and volatility is consequently quite great.

There is also an increased risk that the manager of a sector fund will be a "closet indexer." Any fund manager is under constant pressure to ensure that the performance of the fund does not fall below that of its competitors by simply buying the investments that comprise the index. In sector funds particularly, the number of investments suitable for mutual funds is often relatively limited, and a strategy of buying the securities in the relevant sub-index can frequently be difficult to detect. As a result, it is tempting for the manager of a sector fund to engage in a surreptitious strategy of indexing, charging standard management fees while adding only minimal value to the portfolio.

High Volatility

The high volatility of sector funds can cause unmanageable stress. To the end of 1996, the average monthly standard deviation of the 15 sector or specialty funds with a ten-year record was 5.55 percent. In contrast, the average monthly standard deviation of the 81 large-cap Canadian equity funds was only 3.75 percent. The severity of potential price declines in sector funds easily exceeds the comfort level of most investors, and can precipitate a sale of the investment at the low point in the sector's cycle.

Sector-Specific Risks

A number of sectors have risks that are unrelated to the lack of diversification. Real estate, for example, is valued largely by appraisal: it is not until investments are actually sold that the market value of such investments can be ascertained. It is therefore possible for a large discrepancy to develop between the appraised value and the (ultimate) market value, and these discrepancies can seriously affect returns. If, for example, an investor buys units in a real estate fund that holds an asset appraised at $10 million but subsequently sold for only $8 million, the net asset value of the fund will decline sharply.

The Role of the Manager

The manager's primary task is to choose a portfolio of investments that derives maximum benefit from the market strength of the sector. It is important to recognize that asset mix, security selection, and buy-and-sell strategies are minor determinants of performance compared to the relative strength of the sector itself. When the sector is "hot," a sector fund will perform well regardless of these other factors. When the sector is "cold," the most conscientious and skillful attention to these factors will not make the fund a star.

Some managers also attempt to insulate the portfolio from market downturns. It is almost certain that if a sector outperforms the market at some times, it will underperform at other times. The most common "defensive" technique is to move assets out of the sector. The difficulty is that these attempts to predict market fluctuations are almost always unsuccessful in the long term, and the consequence of missing the turnaround can often be severe.

Investor Considerations

Investors should bear the following points in mind when considering sector funds.

1. Sector funds are a poor choice for novice or small investors. Their high volatility can be worrisome, and they are inappropriate as the major holding in a portfolio.

2. Most investors should avoid excessive concentration in any individual investment. The same principle of moderation should be applied to investing in sector funds, given their similarities to individual securities.

3. Sector funds may be attractive to investors who want to fill niches in a personal portfolio.

4. While sector funds have often provided impressive short-term returns, they perform best for a relatively brief period in the market cycle. For investors who choose securities on the basis of short–term records, sector funds can be a recipe for disaster, since the likelihood of buying into deteriorating returns is sizeable.

PART THREE
MANAGERS, TAXES, AND COSTS

In our view, managers and taxes receive too little attention when investors choose funds. For all intents and purposes, the manager *is* the fund. When investors choose a stock or a bond, they consider the characteristics of the investment, but choosing a mutual fund is different. In the evaluation of mutual funds, the manager's overall investment approach is far more important than the composition of the portfolio. However, examining the manager's approach is not simply a question of "profiling" the individual who makes on investment decisions. It involves a thorough consideration of the manager's strategy and the organizational framework in which investment decisions are made.

Taxes are also critically important because prudent investors want to keep as much of what they earn as possible. The composition of the fund's portfolio is only one of a number of factors that affect the investor's tax liability. The fund manager's approach and the investor's own investment program also have significant tax consequences but are often ignored. While the generalizations in a book can never be a substitute for professional advice, they can help to highlight issues that may require further scrutiny.

Costs, on the other hand, receive *too much* attention. Comparisons of fund costs detract from the truly important considerations, such as management quality. Our purpose in addressing the subject is not to add to a sterile debate, but to dispel the myths about costs so that attention can be focused on choosing the most suitable funds rather than the cheapest.

CHAPTER THIRTEEN

INVESTMENT APPROACHES

EXECUTIVE SUMMARY

This chapter examines the investment approaches that fund managers use to achieve the objectives of a fund.

1. Investment approaches are either passive or active:
   - Passive approaches attempt merely to replicate the returns of the broader market.
   - Active approaches attempt to obtain returns greater than those of the broader market.

2. Active approaches can be considered from a variety of perspectives:
   - security selection strategies
   - sell strategies
   - trading strategies
   - management style

3. In our view, the best approaches take a long-term perspective based on fundamental analysis.

INTRODUCTION

The quality of a mutual fund depends on its manager. The manager's most important responsibility is to oversee the fund's investment portfolio. Indeed, the term *manager* is commonly used to mean *portfolio manager*.

The set of strategies and techniques used by the portfolio manager to achieve the objectives of a mutual fund constitute an investment approach. In this chapter, we examine various investment approaches. In the next chapter, we'll look at other important considerations in choosing a good manager.

Investment Approaches for Stocks

Investment approaches are either passive or active. ***Passive investing*** attempts merely to replicate the returns of the market by holding a representative cross-section of investments from that market. As we saw in Chapter 11, indexing is a passive approach because it creates a portfolio that matches a market index. ***Active investing***, in contrast, attempts to achieve returns above those of the broader market. Active investing encompasses strategies for selecting, trading, and selling investments.

Strategies for Selecting Investments

There are a variety of ways in which portfolio managers choose investments.

Top-Down Investing

Top-down investing is based on the assumption that particular industry groups or sectors will show above-average performance at different stages in a market or economic cycle. It begins with a consideration of general economic and political conditions and seeks to identify emerging trends in interest rates and the stock markets. It then attempts to identify the sectors that are likely to do well in the anticipated economic climate. Finally, it tries to determine the particular companies that offer the best prospects within the preferred sectors.

A number of top-down managers now identify their investment strategy as ***sector rotation*** to distinguish themselves from managers who use a "classic" top-down strategy. We see very little difference between the two approaches, although some might argue that the period of time over which sector rotation predicts emerging trends is shorter than that of a "classic" top-down strategy. Alex Christ, the portfolio manager of the flagship *Mackenzie Financial Industrial Growth Fund*, for example, takes a much longer perspective than John Zechner, the portfolio manager of the *CI Canadian Growth Fund*, who is an acknowledged sector rotator. In addition, a few managers identify their investment strategy as tactical asset allocation. As we saw in Chapter 6, this is the active attempt to increase returns by predicting changes in the markets and modifying the mix of assets in an investment portfolio to capitalize on those changes. The managers of the *Dynamic Partners Fund* and some funds in the stable of 20/20 Financial Group (now merged with AGF) employ this strategy. In our view, all these strategies involve a degree of market timing. And, as we saw in Chapter 6, market timing doesn't work very well.

Bottom-Up Investing

This approach is the opposite of top-down investing. A bottom-up manager looks at individual companies, evaluating them by estimating their projected performance through the business cycle. A portfolio of investments is gradually assembled from the mass of companies considered. This approach constantly reviews the universe of possible investments, revising the portfolio as current investments cease to be attractive and new investments are identified. Bottom-up investing looks for sound companies regardless of sector or business cycle and does not depend on market timing.

Value investing is a bottom-up strategy that was pioneered by Benjamin Graham and David Dodd in the 1930s. The essence of this strategy is the identification of investments in which "real" or "intrinsic" value exceeds the market price. As we saw in Chapter 2, the "true" value of stocks is determined from an analysis of the financial statements of the company and an estimation of future prospects for the business. Value investors look for companies with low debt, or high cash flow, or those with low p/e ratios. Peter Cundill, the manager of the *Cundill Value Fund* and the *Cundill Security Fund*, is a value investor who describes his strategy as "trying to buy a dollar bill for fifty cents."

Growth investing is a bottom-up equity strategy that focuses on a company's potential for superior long-term growth in earnings, with the expectation that the price of the investment will rise as a result. While value investing places a premium on choosing investments that are undervalued on a balance sheet, growth investing does not preclude investments that are accurately valued provided there is potential for long-term growth in earnings. As a result, small companies are often particularly appealing for growth investors. The now almost legendary Peter Lynch, who ran the hugely successful *Fidelity Magellan Fund* in the United States, is primarily a growth investor.

A number of managers blend elements of growth and value investing in an approach that is sometimes called GARP—growth at a reasonable price. The equity managers of the Trimark group are prominent GARP investors.

Not all the investment choices of a bottom-up investor pay off, of course. The managers at Templeton, for example, acknowledge that about one-third of their investment choices do not turn out as projected. In particular, Templeton recognizes that its managers often purchase a stock too soon and sell too early. The hope is that the success of the winners will more than offset the losses of the dogs, but it can sometimes take the markets considerable time to recognize the value of these investments, and this can result in short-term intervals during which these funds underperform their competitors.

Theme Investing

Theme investing occupies the middle ground between top-down and bottom-up strategies. In contrast to top-down investing, theme investing does not look at trends in stock markets. It does, however, consider emerging market developments as a focus for investment choices. The *Spectrum United Canadian Growth Fund*, managed by Kiki Delaney, employs this strategy. Beginning with long-term "themes" that currently include "government debt," free trade and global competitiveness, and the environment, she attempts to identify companies that will enjoy superior growth as a result of developments in these large-scale themes.

Momentum Investing

While growth, value, and theme investing clearly emphasize different criteria, all are grounded solidly in fundamental analysis. In contrast, ***momentum investing*** is heavily based on technical analysis, which relies on trading statistics to identify price trends. Richard Driehaus, who manages AGF's *20/20 Aggressive Growth Fund*, is a momentum investor whose motto is "Buy

High, Sell Higher". This approach also considers tools such as earnings reports, looking for results that exceed expectations, stimulating other investors to buy and thereby initiate a trend. A manager using this strategy assumes that once a trend is established, it will continue, and therefore attempts to structure the portfolio to "ride" the trend. Driehaus will not buy simply because prices are low, even if the fundamental indicators are good.

In our view, momentum investing is unreliable. Like top-down investing and sector rotation, it depends ultimately on timing for its success. Because it is driven by trends, there is a sort of herd mentality to the strategy, and investors themselves fuel the trend, with some investors inevitably paying inflated prices. When the trend finally slows, momentum investors all want to sell at the same time, and those who time their exit poorly can get badly burned. Nevertheless, Driehaus has achieved superior long-term results using this strategy.

Sell Strategies

Active managers also use different sell strategies. Most managers use a variety of criteria that must be met before an investment can be sold. Investment approaches based on fundamental analysis, for example, rely on criteria such as:

- achievement of target price
- availability of significantly cheaper alternative investments of similar quality
- deterioration of factors such as cash flows, debt ratios and dividend yields
- incorrect price projections

Managers who rely on technical analysis look for changes in trends that signal price declines. They use criteria such as:

- "double top" or "down triangle" chart patterns
- volume patterns indicating more sales than purchases at a given price

Still other managers take a broader view of the market, relying on market indicators and general economic data such as:

- consumer and producer price indexes
- manufacturing capacity utilization ratios
- employment statistics

Trading Strategies

Active investment approaches also differ in their trading strategies. Some managers employ a strategy of buying and selling investments frequently in an attempt to make profits from short-term price fluctuations.

Other managers pursue a "buy-and-hold" approach, in which investments are held for a considerable time in an attempt to achieve substantial gains. Management at Trimark employs this approach: at least one of the investments currently in the portfolio of the *Trimark Canadian Fund* has been held since the fund was established in 1981.

A manager's trading strategy is closely related to the investment horizon. The investment horizon is the period of time over which a manager attempts to forecast the performance of potential investments to assess their merit.

Shorter investment horizons are much more prevalent than longer horizons. The majority of portfolio managers have an investment horizon of 12 to 18 months. Portfolio managers who take a view of four to five years are much less common. The principal reason is that many mutual fund investors place disproportionate emphasis on short-term performance. Portfolio managers are therefore under considerable pressure to achieve impressive short-term returns to attract and retain investors. However, while investment strategies based on long horizons rarely have outstanding short-term performance, the approach is usually justified over the long term. The *Trimark Fund*, for example, rarely has the highest performance over a single year, but its five-year performance is consistently in the top quartile. In contrast, while strategies based on short investment horizons and active trading often produce remarkable short-term returns, they are typically far less consistent over the long term. In 1993, for example, Jonathan Baird's short-term approach for the *Dynamic Canadian Growth Fund* achieved stunning returns of 100.2 percent, far exceeding the category average of 34.6 percent. In 1994, however, the fund's return of –8.3 percent underperformed the category average of –3.5 percent, and in 1995, the fund's return of 4.2 percent was almost 10 percent below the category average of 14.0 percent. In our view, long-term strategies are superior because they reinforce the investment discipline of the manager. We'll look at the importance of discipline in the next chapter.

There are also additional costs associated with active and short-term strategies. The frequency with which investments are traded is called ***port-***

folio turnover. In an active trading strategy, portfolio turnover is quite high. The turnover of Frank Mersch's *Altamira Equity Fund*, for example, often exceeds 200 percent, which means that on average he trades every investment in the portfolio twice each year. In contrast, the portfolio turnover of the *Trimark Canadian Fund* is about 20 to 25 percent, indicating that an individual investment is held on average for four to five years. As we'll see in Chapter 15, portfolio turnover can have significant tax implications for funds held outside tax-sheltered plans.

Investment Style

The investment style of a portfolio manager is the tendency to invest in a pattern. Just as a fishing enthusiast has a favourite spot, a portfolio manager has distinct preferences for certain types of investments. For example, the portfolio manager for the *AIC Advantage Fund* prefers financial services companies. This does not mean that the portfolio will hold only financial services stocks: it means only that the tendency of management at AIC is to include these stocks in the portfolio.

Other managers such as Robert Krembil at Trimark, have a preference for emerging technologies. This does not mean that the Trimark funds are always composed exclusively of technology investments, but only that the Trimark portfolios will usually include a significant proportion of these technology investments.

Different kinds of stocks do best at different stages in the market cycle. As a result, different styles will also do well at different times. Understanding this tendency helps in evaluating the performance of the manager because it is then possible to distinguish performance that results from the manager's style from performance that results from the manager's active investment choices. For example, the *AIC Advantage Fund* achieved an annual return of 66.5 percent in 1996, outperforming the average Canadian equity fund by 31.5 percent. Although we might initially conclude that its manager had exercised considerable skill, the TSE 300 "financial services" sub-index returned 55.8 percent in 1996. To a considerable extent, it is the manager's style that has fuelled the fund's performance, while the contribution of the manager's particular investment choices has been far more modest.

Fixed-Income Investment Approaches

As with stocks, investment approaches for fixed-income portfolios may be either passive or active. Indexing, which we described in Chapter 11, is a passive approach. ***Laddering*** is another passive approach in which the portfolio manager assembles investments with a range of maturities. As the investments mature, they are reinvested to maintain a constant average maturity.

There are three basic active approaches to fixed-income portfolio management:

Interest Rate Anticipation

An approach that is based on forecasting interest rates is called ***interest rate anticipation***. This strategy is a kind of debt counterpart to a top-down strategy. Beginning with an analysis of general economic conditions, the manager draws conclusions about emerging trends in interest rates and invests to take advantage of those trends. The average maturity of a portfolio will be increased when interest rates are expected to decrease, and reduced when a rise in interest rates is anticipated. "Pure" interest rate anticipators do not perform credit analysis and invest only in bonds with the highest credit ratings. ***Yield curve*** anticipation is a more sophisticated variant that attempts to exploit differences in the yields of bonds with different maturities.

Value Investing

As in equity investing, value investing in bonds involves the attempt to identify particular bond issues that are undervalued compared to other issues. By purchasing an undervalued issue, the portfolio manager hopes to capitalize on the appreciating price of the cheaper bond as the yield spread narrows.

There are different ways in which value can be exploited. Sector rotation involves varying the weighting or proportion of different types of bonds in the portfolio, without compromising the fund's credit quality. Depending on the portfolio manager's analysis of various fundamental factors and the outlook for supply and demand, provincial bonds will at certain times seem undervalued relative to federally issued bonds or corporate bonds. At other times, federal issues will seem undervalued. Credit analysis is a longer-term approach based on the evaluation of a bond issuer's characteristics. For example, credit analysis may suggest that the credit characteristics of a bond issuer justify a credit rating higher than that assigned by rating agencies. Credit analysis is particularly important in high-yield or junk bond investing.

Spread Trading

Spread trading seeks specific undervalued bonds through an examination of historical relationships and patterns. If, for example, supply considerations, such as a new issue, cause yields to be high relative to historical norms for a particular retail company compared to other bonds of comparable credit, the portfolio manager will sell the more expensive bond and buy the cheaper one.

Figure 13-1 illustrates schematically the elements in fixed-income management and the relationship between the three basic approaches. The elements on the left-hand side are emphasized by interest rate anticipators, while the elements on the right-hand side are emphasized by value investors. Spread traders emphasize the elements that fall below the horizontal dashed line.

Figure 13-1. Fixed Income Management Process

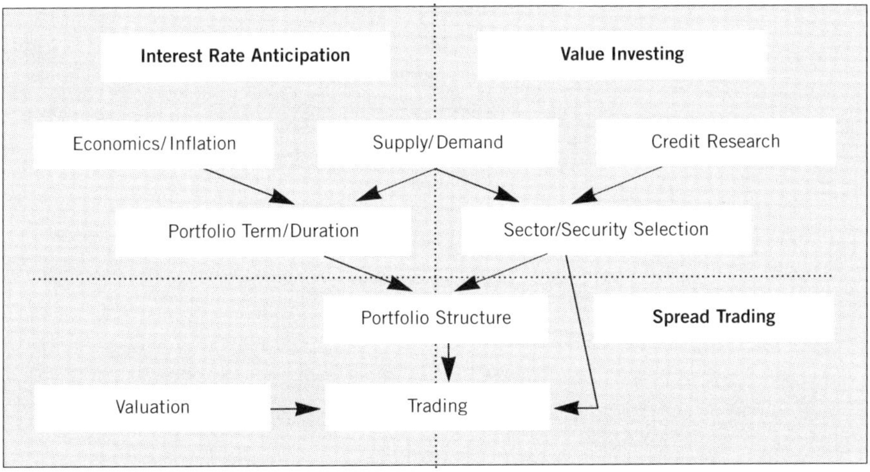

Most fixed-income managers actually employ a combination of approaches. ***Core investing***, for example, is a "quasi-passive" approach, in which the fund's average maturity or duration is modified within very narrow limits around a benchmark, and returns are enhanced through sector rotation, spread trading, and (in some cases) credit analysis.

Our view is that strategies that emphasize value investing are preferable to those in which interest rate anticipation predominates, for a couple of reasons:

- Predicting interest rates is very hard to do consistently. A 1985 study of the interest rate forecasts of one hundred pension fund managers found that predictions were correct less than half the time (see Figure 13-2).

Figure 13-2. Success in Predicting Interest Rates

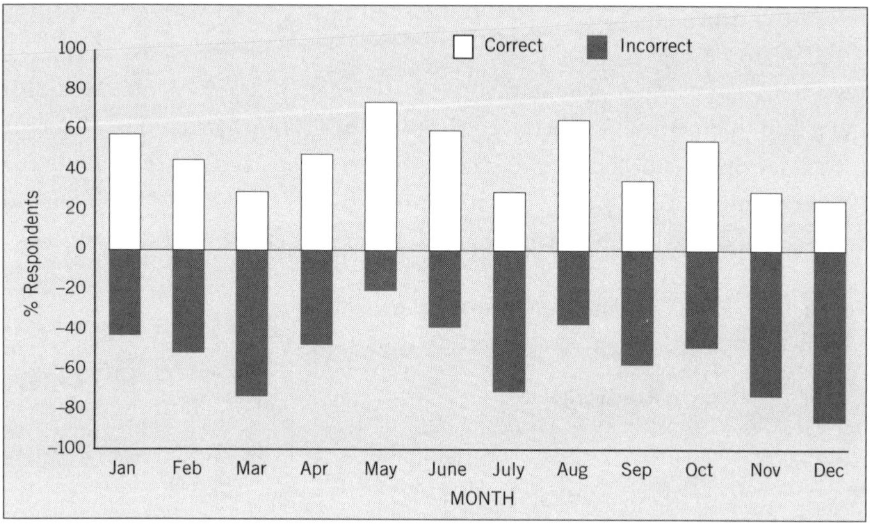

Source: Citicorp Economics Dept / Economic Week, 02.88

- Interest rate anticipation is essentially a form of market timing. In contrast, value investing, and credit analysis in particular, are rooted in fundamental analysis.

- Interest rate anticipators tend to be very accurate or very inaccurate on their market calls. As a result, these managers are more likely either to outperform or to underperform the market by a broad margin.

Cautionary Notes

Investment approaches are not always easy to identify, for a variety of reasons.

- Some portfolio managers use a variety of approaches. Sometimes this is because the fund has multiple objectives. Balanced funds are an example.

- Many managers are reluctant to divulge detailed information about their investment approach. A number of portfolio managers use proprietary techniques to identify suitable investments and are concerned that comprehensive disclosure may compromise their advantage.

- There is sometimes a discrepancy between the stated approach and the actual approach. Some managers, for example, use closet indexing. Another strategy that is often not acknowledged is market timing. Despite its increasing lack of credibility, many portfolio managers employ this strategy, believing it can work if it is done "right."

- Marketing considerations often cloud the issue. Some descriptive terms (such as *value*, *fundamental*, *growth*, *conservative*, and *long-term*) have particular investor appeal. Fund sponsors understandably want to describe their management approach as favourably as possible, but the accuracy of these positively charged terms is sometimes questionable. Talvest, for example, purports to employ both asset allocation and value-based bottom-up stock picking in its approach for the *Talvest Global Asset Allocation Fund*. Similarly, Goodman & Co., which manages the Dynamic group of funds, describes itself as a "value investor." In fact, the investment approach of the *Dynamic Income Fund* emphasizes interest rate anticipation, and the prospectus of the *Dynamic Canadian Growth Fund* describes its managers and investment approach as follows: "We consider ourselves value managers... relying on sector and intrinsic value analysis.... We continue to like both [oil and gas, and forest products] sectors, but stock selection is very important." It is clear that elements of sector rotation play an important part in this approach.

Sometimes, the attempt to use positively charged terms simply results in confusion. Investors Group, for example, describes the *Investors Asset Allocation Fund* as "a quantitatively driven risk averter."

CHAPTER FOURTEEN

CHARACTERISTICS OF GOOD MANAGEMENT

EXECUTIVE SUMMARY

This chapter examines factors to consider in identifying a good manager.

1. There are a variety of considerations in evaluating the management of a mutual fund. Although some considerations are more important than others, all must be balanced and weighed in each case.

2. The manager should have a substantial track record for managing funds with similar investment mandates.

3. The manager should be disciplined. Managers who abandon their investment approach in the pursuit of superior short-term returns lack discipline.

4. The manager should have a strong capacity for independent research.

5. There should be a substantial likelihood that management will not change dramatically. Frequent changes in management personnel call into question the manager's track record, and undermine the management's investment discipline.

6. It is preferable that those responsible for portfolio management have an equity interest in the fund's management company. Portfolio managers who provide services on a contractual basis may be less committed to an investment discipline and more apt to pursue high short-term returns because they can be terminated more easily.

7. The best decision-making approaches are based on the idea of managers working as a team.

8. In general, funds that place excessive emphasis on "star" managers should be avoided.

9. The manager should provide superior customer service.

INTRODUCTION

In the last chapter, we examined various investment approaches that portfolio managers use to achieve the objectives of a mutual fund. In this chapter, we look at factors that are important in identifying good managers.

Management's Track Record

The portfolio manager of a mutual fund must have a substantial track record. The track record of a fund managed by one individual is meaningless if that individual is new to the fund and the record was established by a previous manager.

In our view, the manager's track record should meet the following requirements:

- **It should have a minimum length of five years.**
  Over this length of time, the effects of aberrations in performance resulting from the portfolio manager's particular style are usually negligible.

- **It should encompass a full market cycle.**
  Most mutual fund investors have no experience with a bear market, since most of the surge of interest in mutual funds came after 1990, during the longest bull market this century. By examining a manager's performance over a full market cycle, investors are afforded an opportunity to see how successfully a manager's investment approach protects against market downturns.

- **It should reflect experience with similar investment mandates.**
  It is essential that a manager's record relate to funds with comparable investment mandates. Success in managing a small, resources-based fund, for example, cannot be relied upon as evidence of anticipated performance in managing a large, broad-based fund. A manager's previous experience is only relevant if it relates to a fund with similar objectives and portfolio characteristics. For example, until mid-1997,

the track record of Gerry Coleman and Jerry Javasky at the five-year old *Ivy Canadian Fund* could reasonably have been bolstered by examining their previous track record at the old *United Canadian Growth Fund*, because the investment mandates of the funds were so similar. With the departure of Gerry Coleman to CI in May, 1997, the portfolio management arrangement at the Ivy fund changed, and accordingly the relevance of the United fund's track record to the evaluation of the Ivy fund became more uncertain.

Unfortunately, some funds use inappropriate comparisons to bolster the credibility of the portfolio manager's track record. One technique is to draw on a portfolio manager's previous experience in managing other types of investment funds such as pension funds or closed-end mutual funds. In fact, the management of an open-end mutual fund is significantly different from the management of other types of funds. Unlike in pension funds and closed-end funds, the cash flows in open-end funds are unpredictable. In pension funds, cash flows can be anticipated. The benefits that a pension plan must pay can be determined relatively precisely on the basis of actuarial assumptions, and because the pay-outs from a pension plan are predictable, the income required to meet those obligations can also be determined with relative precision. In the case of closed-end funds, there is neither cash flowing in, nor a demand for redemptions: cash flow comes entirely from the income and sale of investments. In a mutual fund, in contrast, the rate of both new investment and redemptions is much less certain. The process of portfolio management is therefore complicated by the need to absorb these cash flows without impairing the performance of the fund.

In addition, investors typically have much higher short-term expectations of mutual funds. While the beneficiaries of pension funds are "locked in" to a long-term perspective, mutual fund investors can redeem their investments if they are dissatisfied. This creates a pressure to perform that is not imposed on pension fund managers and that has consequences for the way in which the fund is managed.

In short, it is misleading to conclude that a manager who has exhibited success in managing a pension fund or a closed-end fund will have similar success with (open-end) mutual funds.

Another method for creating a management record is the technique of ***back testing***. Back testing establishes the merit of a particular investment strategy by applying the strategy retroactively to determine what the previous performance would have been if the strategy had been used. This technique is particularly popular in buttressing the credibility of asset allocation funds and services, which are often based on formal models of market behaviour. By demonstrating that the allocations dictated by the model would have produced superior results, the model's designers attempt to show that the assumptions on which the model is based are appropriate, and that a strategy based on the model will therefore produce superior results in the future.

There are, however, at least two difficulties with this technique. First, the model that is being tested is itself based on historical data, and it should therefore come as no surprise that such models perform very well in back tests—after all, the designers are merely confirming the data on which the model was based. Second, the rationale for back testing assumes a similarity in circumstances between the past and the present; this similarity is usually unjustified. It is interesting to note that none of the global or Latin American asset allocation models based on back-tested models successfully anticipated or adjusted for the débâcle of the 1995 Mexican currency devaluation.

Management's Discipline

Discipline means that the manager's approach to investing is applied consistently through varying economic and market conditions. Although most fund managers claim to pursue a "disciplined" investment approach, discipline is in fact very hard to maintain. A recent study based on data supplied by the U.S. mutual fund research company Morningstar Inc. found that more than one-third of U.S. equity funds had changed their investment approach in the preceding year.

The pressure to perform is intense. Managers are subject to constant comparison with their competitors, and in many cases, they are entrusted with the life savings of thousands of unitholders. As a result, they are always susceptible to the urge to second-guess their approach and the choices they make for their portfolios. Yet it is precisely the ability to resist these pressures that leads to success. Frank Mersch, who manages the *Altamira Equity Fund*, says that mistakes occur when portfolio managers abandon their investment discipline.

Discipline can be achieved in very different ways. Although the approaches of Trimark and Templeton, for example, are very different, both have highly disciplined management. The Templeton organization uses a comprehensive series of criteria to screen or filter the broad selection of investments. This approach is highly systematic and quite uncompromising. In contrast, Trimark uses a much less rigid approach that is based on exploiting the information and expertise it has developed in evaluating previous opportunities. For example, Trimark managers relied on expertise they developed in the entertainment business, in the evaluation of Sony and Paramount, and in the fermentation industry, in the evaluation of Novo Nordisk (a Swedish biotechnology business), and identified untapped potential in Seagrams, which had both entertainment and beverage components.

Discipline does not preclude changes in the investment approach. The portfolio managers at the *Fidelity Magellan Fund* have had very different investment approaches, but each has applied an approach in a disciplined way. However, change should be infrequent. Frequent changes may mean that there is no discipline.

Managers who are truly disciplined have an independent perspective and are prepared to take positions that diverge from the consensus when appropriate, even when this move attracts short-term criticism. Some managers pride themselves on their ***contrarian*** approach—that is, taking a position simply because it opposes the consensus view—but the most successful managers are not doctrinaire. As Robert Krembil says: "Sometimes that freight train coming down the tracks really is a freight train, and you don't want to get in front of it just because you want to be different from the crowd."

Independent Research

The ability to acquire and use information effectively is a key determinant of good management. All funds rely on outside sources—such as brokerage houses and market research reports—for at least some of their information. The best managers, however, do a significant amount of their own research. Fidelity's reputation for access to, and exploitation of, information is famous, but fund companies such as Templeton and Trimark are also well known for the quality and detail of their investigation.

There are a couple of reasons why independent research is important. One reason is that research undertaken by brokerages and other conventional sources may be less than objective. While there is inevitably a degree of judgement in financial forecasting, it must be recognized that the projections for some investments may be based on highly optimistic and questionable assumptions that may be motivated by obligations to corporate finance or syndicate clients rather than institutional or retail clients. Independent research is also important because it increases the available investment choices. Portfolio managers cannot outperform the competition unless they invest differently, but most institutional research follows a limited universe of investments. By restricting its portfolio to those investments covered by institutional research departments, portfolio managers dramatically reduce the likelihood that their investments will be different. In addition, a commitment to independent research provides managers with not only a unique perspective for investment decisions, but also a shared sense that what they do at these funds is special.

Management's Stability

Stability refers to the extent and degree to which management changes over time. Good management does not change dramatically or abruptly. If the personnel who manage the fund are constantly changing, both the track record and the discipline of management are suspect.

In some funds, stability of management is obvious. Where the fund is the creation of the portfolio manager, management is usually stable. Peter Cundill, for example, has been the portfolio manager of *Cundill Value Fund* and *Cundill Security Fund* since he created them in 1975, and Alex Christ has been the portfolio manager of the Mackenzie Financial's *Industrial Growth Fund* since its inception in 1967.

In cases where management has changed, other factors need to be considered. One consideration is the seniority of those who have left. At Trimark, for example, there have been a number of changes in personnel over the past several years, but Robert Krembil, who founded the funds in 1981, continues to be the "lead" manager of the flagship equity funds, and the various changes in management have not had any appreciable effect on either the investment approach or the performance of the funds.

The situation at Trimark contrasts starkly with Krembil's previous fund at Bolton Tremblay. After Krembil stopped managing the *Taurus Fund* in 1981, the fund floundered for several years under a succession of managers, and performance deteriorated substantially. The fund was eventually merged with the *BT Landmark American Fund* and finally swallowed by the *BPI American Equity Value Fund.*

Changes in management of the Cambridge group of funds produced a similar decline in performance. Tony Massie had been the driving force behind the *Cambridge Growth Fund*, but he left in 1992 to manage equity portfolios for Global Strategy. He was replaced by Raoul Taskok, whose investment approach was entirely different and significantly more aggressive. With the exception of 1993, subsequent performance of the fund has been mediocre: the fund ranked in the fourth quartile in 1994, 1995, and 1996.

Another consideration is the depth of the organization. Some managers are capable of developing and promoting new talent. Fidelity, for example, has an informal apprenticeship program in which recruits start as analysts and graduate first to small sector funds and then to larger broad-based funds as their skill and experience develop. During this process, they assimilate the investment approach and discipline of the organization. The three managers of the *Fidelity Magellan Fund* who succeeded Peter Lynch, for example, had worked as analysts for Lynch before being assigned their own funds, and while there are clear differences in the investment approaches of the successors, all maintained a discipline that was reflected in superior long-term performance of the fund.

Similarly, Sir John Templeton, who founded the Templeton group of funds, no longer takes a day-to-day role in the management of the funds, but many of the current managers have substantial track records with the company. Although there have been some recent defections from the management team, particularly to the company running the new Hansberger group of funds (Thomas Hansberger is a former partner of Sir John Templeton), senior management remains. Mark Holowesko, Mark Mobius, and Don Reed are all protégés of Sir John Templeton and are firmly committed to the investment approach he pioneered.

In Canada, the now defunct Confederation Life was widely recognized for the quality of the portfolio managers that it trained and developed.

Management's Association with the Fund

In general, the fund's investment portfolio can be managed in one of two ways. It can be administered internally, by staff who are an integral unit of the fund's management. Fund groups such as Trimark or Templeton use this in-house approach. Alternatively, the portfolio may be administered externally by advisers who contract their services to the fund. Fund groups such as CI, 20/20 Financial and Spectrum United have adopted this "hired gun" arrangement.

The chief rationale for the use of external advisers is that it provides fund investors with access to the best available talent. The management of 20/20 Financial, for example, explained its use of contract advisers as follows in its 1994 semi-annual report:

> We don't believe having salaried managers on staff, in one or two locations, sharing a common corporate culture and reporting to management committees, is the most effective way to run an investment fund. Major pension funds and wealthy individuals... seek out and hire the world's best managers, the same way sports teams become winners by handpicking the top free agents.

In fact, the performance of funds managed internally and externally is almost indistinguishable. Of the 68 conventional Canadian equity funds with a ten-year track record as of December 31, 1996, 52 were advised in-house, and 16 were managed externally. The average ten-year compound return of the 16 externally advised funds was 9.55 percent, while that of the 52 funds advised in-house was 9.44 percent.

In a small number of cases, funds have used both in-house and external advisers during the ten-year period under review. The *Spectrum United Canadian Equity Fund*, for example, was advised in-house by Gerry Coleman and Jerry Javasky until 1992, when responsibility for portfolio advice was contracted to Kiki Delaney. That sort of qualification aside, however, it is reasonably clear that the difference in performance between the in-house funds and the contract funds is relatively insignificant, and that contracting portfolio advice to outside advisers does not materially improve performance.

Relative performance is not, however, the only consideration in evaluating a fund's management. As we explained above, one of the most important characteristics of good management is its stability. If a fund's portfolio advisers are constantly changing, its past performance is unreliable as a guide to future performance.

In our view, there is a much smaller likelihood that there will be dramatic or abrupt changes in personnel when the portfolio is advised internally. In many cases, those responsible for portfolio investment were founders of the fund or fund group. Robert Krembil of Trimark, Peter Cundill of the Cundill group, Robert Farquharson of AGF, Alex Christ of Mackenzie Financial, and Ned Goodman of Dynamic are all examples of portfolio managers who created their own funds. Even if the short-term performance of their funds lags, it is unlikely that there will be wholesale changes in the investment group.

The same cannot be said of funds that employ external portfolio advisers. It is, quite simply, easier to sever a contractual relationship than it is to remove personnel who are an integral part of the fund's organization. As a result, it is far more likely that relatively short-term underperformance will precipitate a change in advisers. The philosophy of 20/20 Financial, for example, was to "attract top performers and keep them *only so long as they deliver results* [emphasis added]."

The difficulty with this attitude is that it fails to allow for the cyclical character of portfolio management. Every portfolio manager has periods of weakness and strength, but it is frequently possible to distinguish between cyclical variations and a more substantial deterioration in performance only by taking a long-term perspective. The relative ease with which an external adviser can be replaced does not encourage such a long-term outlook and may result in the removal of the portfolio adviser just as a fund's performance is about to improve. Even more damaging is the fact that the portfolio adviser assuming responsibility is often chosen because of recent strong performance at some other fund. Almost inevitably, this superior performance fades. The consequence is that the fund's lagging performance is prolonged rather than shortened. In 1994, for example, Ultravest Investment Counsellors' Chuck Roth replaced Connor, Clark & Lunn in managing the *20/20 Canadian Growth Fund* (now the *AGF Canadian Growth Fund*). Roth's performance in 1994 and 1995 was mediocre, and when AGF took over the 20/20 Financial Group in May 1996, Roth was replaced by Veronika Hirsch. However, Roth continued to manage the *Colonia Special Growth Fund*, which earned 69.8 percent in 1996. In contrast, Hirsch left AGF three months after she was assigned to the fund, and was replaced by two junior portfolio managers. The *20/20 Canadian Growth Fund* posted fourth-quartile returns in 1996 with a return of 16.1 percent compared to 28.3 percent for the TSE 300.

It should be noted that the mandate of the *Colonia Special Growth Fund* is to achieve long-term capital appreciation through investment in small-capitalization companies, while the mandate of both the *20/20 Canadian Growth Fund* and the *AGF Canadian Equity Fund* is to invest in medium-to-large Canadian companies with prospects for superior long-term capital growth. However, the portfolio of Hirsch's AGF fund was biased strongly in favour of speculative resources investments (such as Bre-X, Diamond Fields and Goldcorp) while the portfolio of Roth's 20/20 fund more faithfully reflected the fund mandate (with investments such as Alcan, Bombardier and Imasco). The comparison on which the decision to replace Roth was based was therefore unreasonable: a comparison with his Colonia fund's 1995 performance (23.7 percent) would have been more appropriate.

Marketing considerations contribute to this instability. In an effort to capitalize on the enormous interest in mutual funds, many fund groups have greatly increased the number of funds they offer over the past few years. The result has been intense competition for investors' dollars, and in the quest for ways to differentiate funds, the use of external advisers has been exploited to enhance a fund's cachet. Funds invariably describe the reputation of their external portfolio advisers as "exceptional," and the relationship between the fund and the adviser as "special." However only a very few advisers are truly superior, and that special relationship lasts only as long as the adviser's performance is robust. In September 1993, for example, Global Strategy described AsiaInvest, one of the advisers for the "multi-adviser" *Asia Fund*, as follows:

> ... a young, performance-driven boutique set up and run by locals in Hong Kong. Walter Wu, who is the key investment guy ... was named top fund manager of the year last year [1992] both by the consultants Micropal, and the influential Asian daily, the *South China Morning Post*.... [AsiaInvest managers] are among the *best managers in the world* [emphasis added].

Yet, despite this glowing description, Global Strategy unceremoniously dumped AsiaInvest only 18 months later, in March 1995, citing mediocre performance and replacing it with Schroder Capital Management Ltd., which Global Strategy described as "one of the strongest investment managers in the world."

A fund's comparatively low level of commitment to external advisers is often matched by the attitude of those advisers. Some general studies of management behaviour suggest that external managers are less committed to the long-term success of an organization than internal managers. Managers who do not have a stake in the organization may be more likely to pursue strategies that put their own interests ahead of the organization's interests. In the context of mutual funds, this may mean that external portfolio managers, who are more susceptible to abrupt removal, are more likely to pursue strategies emphasizing short-term performance in an effort to bolster their own positions and reputations. Internal portfolio advisers, with a vested interest in the viability of the fund, are more likely to pursue approaches that maximize long-term performance.

The lack of long-term commitment from external portfolio managers is most starkly reflected in the phenomenon of the "star" manager. In characterizing its portfolio adviser as a star, a fund enables unsophisticated investors to put a name and face to portfolio decisions, and differentiates itself from the competition. The difficulty is that external portfolio advisers, like free agents in professional sport, may have little loyalty to the funds they advise. In a little more than two years, for example, Jonathan Baird has shifted his allegiance not once but twice. In September 1995, he moved from the Dynamic group to the University Avenue group. Only one year later, he announced plans to assume management of a new fund to be offered by the CI group, and to devote himself exclusively to CI once his contract with the University Avenue group expired. Similarly, Veronika Hirsch moved with great fanfare from the Prudential group to the AGF group in September 1995, only to accept an offer from Fidelity a mere ten months later.

External advisers also have to contend with potential conflicts of interest. An external adviser typically has several funds as "clients," and some investment choices will often be suitable for more than one client. There is a potential for conflicts about allocation when such investments are available in only very limited quantities. The prospectus of funds employing external advisers often devotes considerable attention to explaining the way in which potential conflicts will be resolved, but the external adviser is frequently required to strike a compromise that is less than ideal.

Recently, a number of funds have developed a sort of hybrid position between internal and external portfolio advisers, in which the fund managers hold equity positions in the firms that provide portfolio advice to the fund. Trimark, for example, has recently taken an ownership position in Lloyd George Management, which provides portfolio advice to the *Trimark Indo-Pacific Fund.*

By using external portfolio advisers, the management of a fund acquires immediate access to expertise on distant regions; this expertise would be slow and difficult to develop internally. However, by creating institutional rather than merely contractual links between the adviser and the fund manager, these fund companies are strengthening the lines of communication with the internal advisers of other funds in the group. While it will unquestionably be more difficult to terminate such an adviser if the relationship does not work, the equity interest signifies that a long-term relationship is anticipated.

Management's Approach to Decision Making

The way in which portfolio investment decisions are made is very important. Four broad approaches can be distinguished.

The Individual Approach

For certain funds, a single person controls the decision-making process. Very often, these individuals rely on associates who accumulate and organize information, but the associates are clearly subordinate. It is the dominant individual who actually makes the investment decisions.

Two points are particularly important about management by individuals. The first is that nobody works in a vacuum, and in this sort of management arrangement it is impossible to determine the precise value of the contribution that subordinates make. Jonathan Baird, for example, claimed the credit for the track record of the *Dynamic Canadian Growth Fund* following his departure from the company in the summer of 1995, but Jonathan Goodman (who had been a part of the Dynamic organization through Baird's tenure and who assumed responsibility for the fund after Baird left) claimed that the fund had always been managed by a team, with all the members contributing investment ideas.

The second important point is that if the investment approach of a fund is determined by a single individual, the discipline and stability of fund management can be extremely uncertain.

The Committee Approach

For other funds, investment decisions are made by a committee. Elliott & Page, for example, uses a four-person "policy group" to determine asset and sector allocations. Several benefits are claimed for this approach. One claim is that it provides a broader range of expertise on which to base investment decisions. But, while it is certainly true that the base of expertise is more clearly identified, it is far from clear that committees have greater access to expertise than do individual managers.

Another claim is that collective management allows for the infusion of "new blood" into the organization. While any organization must evolve if it is to continue to be viable, there is certainly no assurance that the new ideas and perspectives will be consistent with the established investment approach or discipline of the fund.

A third claim is that committee management provides a mechanism for built-in succession and thus for long-term stability. This may be true in isolated instances, but in general it is unlikely, since the committee structure does not naturally lend itself to the development of a shared outlook. In an organization in which each member has a "vote," each decision is a separate compromise of interests rather than an expression of underlying consensus.

The Team Approach

The essence of the team approach is that decisions are made by consensus. In many teams, there is a lead manager who focuses the decision-making process and is ultimately responsible for implementing the decisions but the attitude is very much primus inter pares—first among equals. The portfolio managements of Trimark and Templeton typify this approach.

Like the committee approach, the team approach broadens the managers' expertise and allows for the introduction of new ideas. However, a number of features distinguish the team approach. First, a shared investment discipline is essential to consensus-based decisions. Second, the success of the organization is inseparably linked to the success of the team—performance cannot be attributed to one single individual. Third, the team is often responsible for managing a group of funds.

Appearances can be deceiving. Claims of team management are very common, but a true team perspective is rare. It is important to distinguish management structures that truly foster discipline and stability from those that are contrived merely to give the appearance of continuity. There is a risk that management is organized collectively to disguise frequent personnel changes behind a mantle of stability, and thereby prevent the exodus of fee-paying investors.

The Multiple-Adviser Approach

This approach is borrowed from the management of pension funds. The portfolio is divided into pieces, and each piece is separately managed. Various funds in the Global Strategy group and the AGF group employ this approach. The rationale for this management structure is the diversification of investment strategies. As we mentioned earlier, no strategy is best in all circumstances, and performance resulting from an individual strategy is usually somewhat cyclical. The multi-adviser approach attempts to minimize the consequences of this cyclical pattern.

While the scheme has undeniable marketing appeal, its investment merit is less obvious. Over the long term, cyclical variations in performance as a result of a particular investment strategy become far less important. At the same time, however, this approach cannot contribute to long-term discipline because the absence of a shared investment approach is deliberate. In fact, the performance of multimanaged funds is often disappointing. Research on the U.S. experience indicates that the performance of these funds regularly lags behind the average. Partly, this is because the effects of a single approach are diluted by the effects of others. Partly, it is because the tenure of the portfolio managers of these funds tends to be shorter.

A Note on Star Managers

In the past few years, the profiles of some fund managers have become increasingly public. Pressure from the media, and the need for funds to distinguish themselves from the competition have combined to create the "cult" of the star manager. The mutual fund universe now seems to be full of "stars" such as John Zechner, at the CI group; Frank Mersch at Altamira; Jonathan Baird, previously at Dynamic, then University Avenue, at the date of publication at CI; Veronika Hirsch, first at AGF and then at Fidelity.

There certainly are star managers. Peter Lynch is unquestionably a star. Sir John Templeton is a star. Their long-term track records are undeniable. However, there are not nearly as many stars in the firmament of mutual funds as the fund companies would have investors believe.

From a marketing perspective, the star manager approach is usually an unqualified success. Unfortunately, star status is all too often conferred on the basis of a relatively short track record that is usually established in a bull market. While Kiki Delaney's performance at the *Spectrum United Canadian Growth Fund* has been reasonably good, she has been portfolio manager there only since 1992. Her previous experience was as an analyst at Guardian Capital and Gluskin Sheff, where she worked under Ira Gluskin. Similarly, Jonathan Baird's overall performance at the *Dynamic Canadian Growth Fund* was well above average, but his tenure there began only in 1991, and his performance was below average in both 1994 and 1995.

In addition, marketing the star all too often draws attention away from the basis for the reputation. It is generally recognized, for example, that Frank Mersch's record at Altamira was achieved for a relatively small fund as a result of a few highly successful speculative investments, but this record is unreliable as a guide to the likelihood of his success in managing a fund approaching $2 billion. Similarly, Veronika Hirsch's star status was achieved as a result of highly concentrated investments in a small natural resources fund, but it was marketed as an indicator of future success in managing a big, broad-based fund.

In short, most stars do not shine as brightly as investors are led to believe. It is extremely important to examine the star carefully, to ensure that you are buying true value.

Administrative Capabilities

While issues of administration are not particularly exciting, they are nevertheless extremely important. According to Arthur Labatt, the president of the Trimark group of funds, more people redeem funds as a result of dissatisfaction with the administration of a fund than for any other reason, and the conclusions of a 1994 study by Dalbar Inc. reinforce this view. Dalbar's study found that the single most important issue for investors was not performance, but the quality and clarity of account statements.

There are a variety of different administrative responsibilities, services including the provision of transfer services (the maintenance of shareholder data and the processing of unit purchases, reinvestments, distributions, and redemptions), the administration of accumulation purchase plans, the operation of RRSP and other tax-deferral accounts, the processing of periodic withdrawals and fund switches, and the preparation of statements and reports to unitholders.

Funds that are part of a fund group often emphasize the convenience of their administrative features, including–

- standardized accounting and reporting
- uncomplicated (and economical) switches between funds
- cost efficiencies resulting from shared order processing functions

In our view, however, focusing attention on the availability of features such as discounted switching fees mistakenly reinforces the idea that frequent changes are appropriate. In addition, the convenience of investing in a single fund group and receiving standardized statements is often illusory, since such an approach also limits an investor's choices to the funds offered by the group.

Management that provides clear, informative, and timely statements is clearly desirable. It is important to bear in mind, however, that the fundamental merit of a fund manager is determined by the ability to meet the fund's investment objectives. Excessive emphasis on "bells and whistles" can detract from the real issue. It is also important to remember that exceptional customer service cannot relieve investors of the ultimate responsibility for overseeing their personal portfolios.

A FINAL NOTE

It is important to understand that, although we clearly feel that some considerations are more significant than others, the relative importance of the considerations will vary across funds. In every case, the significance of each factor must be balanced against the others. In some cases, for example, the manager's discipline and association with the fund will be less important than the track record. Less frequently, the manager's association with the fund will outweigh concerns about a track record.

CHAPTER FIFTEEN

PORTFOLIO CHARACTERISTICS

EXECUTIVE SUMMARY

This chapter examines the portfolio characteristics to consider in evaluating a fund.

1. In identifying suitable funds, a number of portfolio characteristics are important. For stock portfolios, these characteristics include–
   - average market capitalization of the investments
   - portfolio quality
   - number of investments
   - portfolio concentration
   - cash component

   For fixed-income portfolios, the average maturity and duration of the portfolio are also important

2. Portfolios with smaller average market capitalization are typically more volatile than those with larger average capitalizations. In addition, average market capitalizations provide insights into a fund's actual investment mandate and approach.

3. In general terms, funds with fewer individual holdings are more likely to demonstrate a disciplined investment approach.

4. The greater the degree of portfolio concentration, the higher the probability of loss.

5. In bond funds, average maturity provides an excellent indicator of volatility.

6. Portfolio turnover may be indicative of both the manager's investment approach, and the tax efficiency of the fund.

7. The market behaviour of derivatives often differs from that of other types of investments, and investors should carefully examine the use of derivatives in any portfolio.

8. The importance of fund size is a myth. Fund size alone has no effect on performance. It is true, however, that rapid asset growth may adversely affect performance.

INTRODUCTION

While portfolio management is the single most important consideration in identifying mutual funds with the greatest likelihood of superior future performance, a number of portfolio characteristics are also important. Some are important because they provide insights into the investment approach employed by the portfolio manager. Others are important because they affect the fund's risk profile.

Portfolio Structure

Portfolio structure encompasses a number of characteristics.

Average Market Capitalization

As we saw in Chapter 3, market capitalization is a measure of the size of a corporation and is determined by multiplying the number of shares by the price per share. Blue chip stocks are shares of large, well-established companies, which generally have market capitalizations of at least $500 million. The shares of newer companies with smaller market capitalizations (less than $500 million) are typically referred to as small-cap stocks. Average market capitalization simply refers to the capitalization of the average holding of a fund.

Average market capitalization is important for at least two related reasons. First, it gives some indication of a fund's risk profile. Generally speaking, the performance of funds with smaller average market capitalizations will be more erratic than that of funds with larger average capitalizations. Although the long-term performance of U.S. small-cap stocks slightly exceeds that of large-cap stocks since the end of World War II, the bulk of this long-term performance has been driven by massive outperformance in the relatively brief period between 1975 and 1983. Excluding this "boom," small-cap stocks have underperformed large-cap stocks by 25 percent. Even for investors with a long-term horizon, it is clear that success in small-cap investing depends substantially on good timing.

Average market capitalization can also be a useful gauge of a fund's investment approach. For example, small-cap stocks are more likely to be growth stocks than value stocks, so a fund with an average market capitalization that is relatively low and a "value" approach to investing should raise questions.

BellCharts, as well as the *Globe and Mail* and the *Financial Post*, classify Canadian equity funds by average market capitalization, but investors should be wary of such classifications. The *Globe*, for example, classifies the *Cundill Security Fund* as "large-cap" while the *Financial Post* classifies it as "small/mid-cap."

Portfolio Quality

Although average market capitalization provides some sense of portfolio quality, the kinds of investments the portfolio manager makes are also important. Funds that are composed predominantly of more speculative issues may offer the potential for higher returns, but they also carry a greater risk of loss. In September 1996, for example, the *AGF Canadian Equity Fund*'s largest investment (at 5.1 percent) was in Bre-X Minerals. At the time, Bre-X was clearly a large-capitalization company, with a market capitalization of $4.7 billion. However, regardless of one's view of the events of early 1997, Bre-X was never anything more than a junior mining company. It had no operating mine and, indeed, no enforceable right to mine its property. Notwithstanding its enormous market capitalization, it was a highly speculative investment, and its weighting in the portfolio should have attracted attention.

In contrast, the largest investment of the *Mackenzie Financial Ivy Canadian Fund* at the end of September 1996 was the Royal Bank (at 4.9 percent). Similarly, the largest investment of the *Trimark Canadian Fund* in September 1996 was the Toronto-Dominion Bank (at 6.2 percent).

Quality is also important in bond funds. Particularly when interest rates are low, there is considerable pressure on bond fund managers to boost yields, but the simplest way to increase yields is to lower the credit quality of the portfolio's investments. This, of course, has implications for the fund's risk profile, since decreasing credit quality increases default risk. It is critical that the managers of funds that invest in lower-quality bonds have expertise in credit and security analysis to deal with this increased risk.

Number of Investments

Although the absolute size of a fund affects the number of investments in the portfolio to some degree, the number of investments nevertheless varies considerably. Some portfolio managers hold a lot of small investments, none of which constitutes more than a small fraction of the total. For example, there are typically more than 200 separate investments in the *Altamira Equity Fund*'s $2.4 billion portfolio. Other managers tightly limit the number of positions. *Mackenzie Financial Ivy Canadian Fund* usually holds fewer than 35 individual positions, although its portfolio is roughly the same size as that of the Altamira fund.

In our view, limiting the number of individual investments in stock portfolios offers a couple of advantages. First, it helps to ensure that only the best investments are included. If investments can be added to the portfolio without displacing others, it is less likely that the evaluation of either the potential new investments or the existing composition of the portfolio will be as rigorous. Second, a portfolio with fewer individual investments permits the fund managers to do the more intensive research that discloses hidden value and that is crucial for superior long-term performance.

It is a myth that small-cap funds require larger numbers of investments to compensate for their greater risk. Richard Dreihaus, who uses a momentum strategy in managing small- and mid-cap funds in both Canada and the United States, has a solid long-term track record despite the fact that he holds a relatively small number of investments in his portfolios.

Limiting the number of investments is also important in controlling the costs of bond portfolios. Given that the primary determinants of bond prices are the relationships between interest rates, maturity rates, and coupon rates, multiple investments in bonds with similar maturities and yields to maturity merely increase the costs of managing the portfolio without contributing significantly to performance. As a result, few bond fund managers hold more than 50 positions in their portfolios. Indeed, the *Dynamic Government Income Fund* holds only two bonds in its portfolio. In global bond funds, a greater number of positions may be appropriate since the manager must also manage currency rate fluctuations.

Portfolio Concentration

A third important characteristic is the distribution of the portfolio's investments. Some managers hold a broad range of investments in their portfolios, while others make much more concentrated "bets" on particular sectors or businesses. For example, the *Trimark Canadian Fund* and the *AIC Advantage Fund* have similar investment objectives and approaches. However, the portfolio compositions of the two funds are profoundly different. The two charts in Figure 15-1 compare the portfolio breakdowns of the two funds at the end of 1996. The weighting of each fund is shown in black, while the weighting of the TSE 300 is shown in grey. While the portfolio of the *Trimark Canadian Fund* is distributed reasonably broadly across the sectors in the TSE 300, the concentration of the *AIC Advantage Fund* in the financial services sector is extremely pronounced.

Figure 15-1. Portfolio Composition – **(A)** *AIC Advantage Fund* 12/96

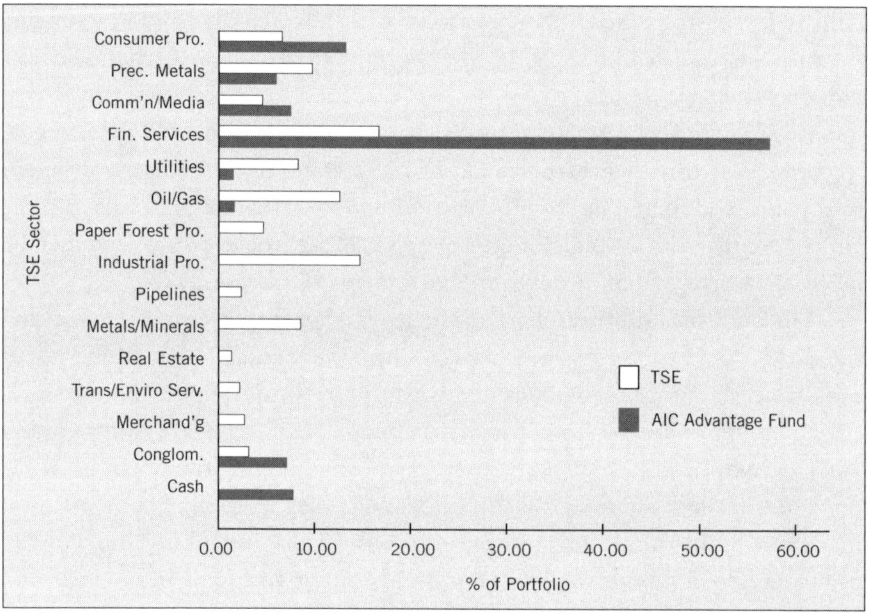

Source: Quarterly Report, 12/96

(B). *Trimark Canadian Fund* 12/96

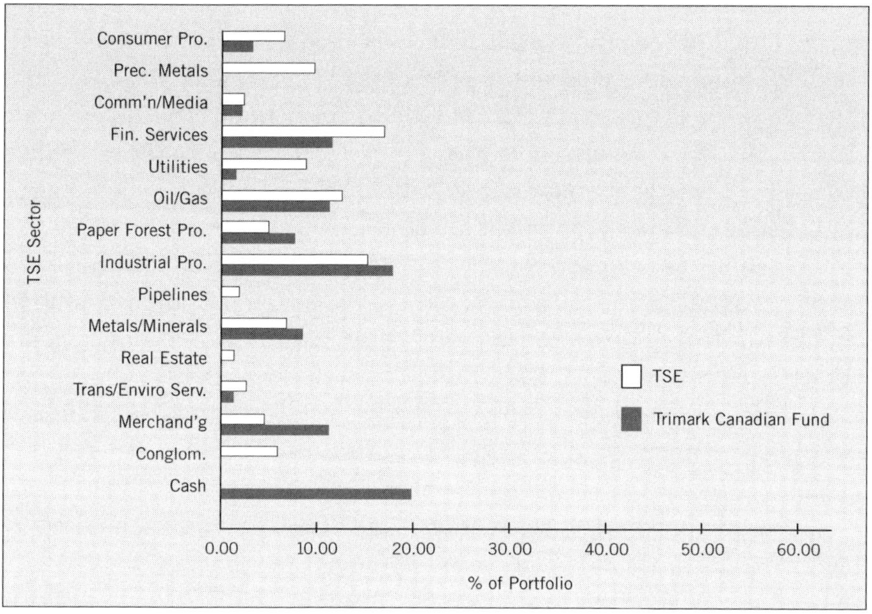

Source: Quarterly Report, 12/96

Portfolio concentration is important for a couple of reasons. It can provide useful information about the fund's risk profile. Generally speaking, the greater the concentration of the portfolio, the riskier the fund. For example, the risk of loss in sector funds, which have portfolios that are consistently concentrated in specific themes or industry groups, is substantially greater than in broad-based funds.

Portfolio concentration can also provide insights into the portfolio manager's investment approach. Wide swings in portfolio weightings may indicate a strategy of sector rotation. Similarly, portfolio weightings that closely approximate those of a fund's benchmark index may suggest that the portfolio manager is practising closet indexing. Managers that practise closet indexing should be avoided. Investors who believe indexing is an appropriate investment approach will be far better served by a true index fund.

Portfolio concentration is also relevant in bond portfolios. If the most important changes in weighting occur between bonds with different maturities, the management may have adopted the investment approach of interest rate anticipation. If these changes in weighting occur between sectors (federal, provincial, and corporate), the manager may be putting emphasis on sector rotation.

It is not always easy to evaluate portfolio composition. In some cases, the funds simply do not provide a breakdown. Trimark and AIC, for example, merely list the securities they hold in their quarterly reports. In other cases, evaluation is hindered because funds use a variety of different classifications. Sometimes, these classifications reflect the fund's investment approach. Funds using top-down investment approaches, for example, are more likely to use categories such as "cyclicals," "interest-sensitive," and "capital goods." Frequently, however, the classifications are a confusing mixture of TSE groupings and peculiar categories. The *AGF Canadian Equity Fund*, for example, has separate "health care" and "resources services" categories in addition to the conventional TSE groupings, although each investment in these categories is a constituent investment of a TSE 300 subindex.

Occasionally, these unconventional categories are misleading. Figure 15-2 shows the portfolio composition of the *AIC Advantage Fund*, as presented in its 1996 fourth-quarter report. Although the chart indicates that "financial services" and "mutual fund management" investments comprise, respectively, 33 and 29 percent of the portfolio, the TSE "financial services" subindex actually includes mutual fund management companies. The effect of separating them is to substantially understate the actual concentration in the portfolio.

Figure 15-2. Portfolio Composition – AIC Advantage Fund

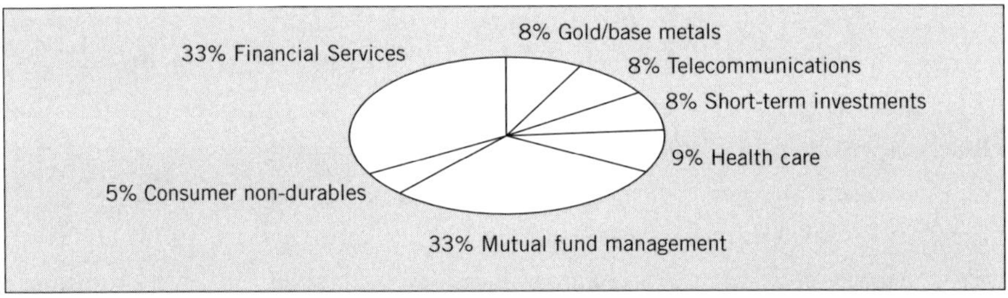

Source: Quarterly Report, 12/96

In fixed-income portfolios, some funds classify the portfolio by sector (federal, provincial, municipal, and corporate), while others classify by maturity (long, medium, and short).

A further check on the portfolio's concentration is to examine the proportion of total assets that are invested in the fund's largest positions. Both the *Altamira Equity Fund* and the *Trimark Canadian Fund*, for example, have slightly more than 30 percent of fund assets invested in their top ten holdings. The Trimark fund, however, has only 55 positions, while the Altamira fund has more than 200 positions.

Cash Component

All funds, regardless of type, hold a certain percentage of the portfolio in cash or other short-term investments. There are several reasons for this:

- It is impractical for the manager to invest funds immediately upon receipt. The amounts received from individual investors are generally too small either to purchase a meaningful new investment for the fund or to allot among the fund's current investments. Additionally, suitable investments are not always immediately available.

- A certain amount of cash must always be available to meet requests for redemptions. If the assets of the fund were completely invested, it would be necessary to sell some of the investments in the portfolio to raise the cash for redemptions, and such "forced" sales would in some instances be made at a loss, thereby negatively affecting the overall performance of the fund.

- Some fund managers actively adjust the amount of cash in the portfolio as part of their investment strategy.

Examining the portfolio's cash position can provide a number of insights. It may help to explain the performance of the fund relative to its peers. In bull markets, funds with a high cash position will typically perform less well than funds that are fully invested. Conversely, in bear markets, funds with a high cash position will generally perform better than their fully invested peers.

Analysis of the cash position may also help to illustrate the discipline of the investment approach. Portfolio managers clearly recognize that holding a substantial cash position during a bull market will almost inevitably cause the fund to underperform more fully invested peers. The willingness of a portfolio manager to hold cash in rising markets therefore suggests a true commitment to the management's investment approach. On the other hand, a cash position that varies in the absence of changing cash flows suggests an attempt by the portfolio manager to time the markets—definitely a danger sign.

Fixed-Income Portfolios

While the portfolio characteristics discussed above are generally relevant for both equity and fixed-income funds, considerations of average maturity and duration apply specifically to fixed-income funds. Average duration, in particular, provides a precise measure of the degree to which the value of a fixed-income fund will fluctuate. For every 1 percent change in interest rates, a fixed-income portfolio will change in value by a percentage equal to its duration. A fund with an average duration of three years, for example, will decrease in value by 3 percent for every 1 percent increase in three-year interest rates.

Clearly, funds which focus on bonds with shorter maturities and durations will fluctuate less in response to changes in interest rates than funds emphasizing bonds with longer maturities. For those who are unnerved by substantial price swings, short-term bond or income funds are typically more appropriate. There is a trade-off though: the income stream from shorter-term funds is less consistent. As investments in the portfolio mature, they must necessarily be replaced by investments with yields which correspond largely to prevailing interest rates. Since investments with shorter maturities must be replaced more frequently, they are more susceptible to changes in short-term rates. This vulnerability is reinforced by the fact that short-term rates typically change more than long-term rates.

Portfolio Turnover

Portfolio turnover is the frequency with which the investments in the portfolio are traded. The manager of a fund with low portfolio turnover may trade less than 10 percent of the portfolio's value annually, while the manager of a fund with very high portfolio turnover can trade more than 200 percent of the portfolio's value in a year.

Evaluating a fund's portfolio turnover offers several insights. For funds that are held outside tax-sheltered plans, portfolio turnover is an indicator of the fund's tax "efficiency." Generally speaking, the higher the portfolio turnover, the greater the tax liability the fund will attract. We'll look at this issue in more detail in Chapter 16.

Portfolio turnover is also a useful guide to a fund's investment approach. A fund with a long-term investment horizon typically has lower portfolio turnover than a fund with a shorter-term outlook. In stock funds, high portfolio turnover is usually associated with sector rotation and momentum investing. In bond funds, high turnover is typically associated with spread trading.

Despite its merits, portfolio turnover is consistently underutilized as a tool for portfolio evaluation. Few funds disseminate this information in their promotional material, and some actively resist disclosing it. Generally speaking, managers of funds with low portfolio turnover are more forthcoming, and investors should be suspicious of a manager who claims to have a long-term approach while refusing to quantify the fund's portfolio turnover.

One way to get a rough sense of a fund's portfolio turnover is to examine its annual brokerage costs. Brokerage costs in a fund with very high portfolio turnover will constitute a significantly greater percentage of total assets than those of a fund with low portfolio turnover. Brokerage costs of more than 0.5 percent of fund assets suggest relatively high portfolio turnover. In 1996, for example, the brokerage costs of the *Altamira Equity Fund* were more than 1 percent of fund assets, while the brokerage costs of the *Trimark Canadian Fund* were a very modest 0.07 percent of fund assets.

Derivatives

As we discussed in Chapter 3, there are several problems associated with the use of financial derivatives. They can be quite illiquid and are often difficult to value accurately. They often have undesirable, unanticipated tax consequences when held outside tax-sheltered plans. In addition, the market behaviour of derivatives often differs from that of other types of investments. While some uses for derivatives are quite conventional, the use of derivatives to enhance returns and circumvent foreign content restrictions is a relatively recent development. There is simply not enough information to properly evaluate how these investments will perform in periods of extreme market uncertainty. Investors should carefully examine the use of derivatives in the portfolio.

A Note on Fund Size

Although there is much debate about the significance of fund size, our view is that the size of the fund alone has very little bearing on a fund's prospects for future success.

Small Funds

Small funds are often said to be better than large funds because they allow the manager greater flexibility in choosing the portfolio's investments, thereby improving performance. Large funds must make larger investments than small funds. For a fund with a portfolio of $1 billion, a single investment of 5 percent equals $50 million, but for a fund with a portfolio of $100 million, a single investment of 5 percent equals only $5 million, and there are a lot more $5 million investments from which to choose. A large fund could buy more $5 million investments, but the greater number of investments in the portfolio would be much more difficult to manage. A larger fund must therefore "dilute" the discipline of its approach in order to find sufficient compatible investments.

In addition, small funds are often said to be able to adjust their portfolios more quickly to changing economic and business circumstances. The larger investments of large funds can sometimes limit the liquidity of the portfolio. Generally speaking, it is more difficult to sell a $50 million investment quickly than it is to sell a $5 million investment.

Those who believe that size matters often point to the fact that the performance of larger funds frequently appears to "track" the market more closely than that of smaller funds. The reason for this relationship has much more to do with the way in which the market index is constructed than with the size of a fund. The market index is composed primarily of the largest companies in the market. Thus, it is inevitable that the performance of large funds will appear to correspond to the performance of the index more closely than the performance of small funds because large-cap investments tend to make up a greater proportion of the portfolio in larger funds. While smaller funds have enjoyed superior short-term performance from time to time, their long-term performance is no better than that of larger funds. A study by mutual fund analysts at Midland Walwyn found that the average size of the bottom ten funds in the international equity group was less than $19 million, while the top ten funds in the category averaged $1.6 billion in assets. While small size may produce superior returns, it is more likely to result in significant underperformance.

The effectiveness of a fund's investment approach is, however, partially dependent on its size. It is probably true that small size is an advantage for portfolio managers who trade actively and invest in more speculative and illiquid issues, but for large-cap managers with long-term investment horizons, size is immaterial.

Another advantage sometimes claimed for small funds is that the manager has less career risk in taking positions at odds with the consensus. Since an investment approach that takes the consensus view is likely to produce only ordinary or average results, the lack of psychological barriers to unconventional investment approaches provides greater opportunity for superior performance. Yet, while this is true, it is equally true that the lack of psychological constraints on an investment approach can result in markedly inferior performance.

Recently, a number of funds have adopted a policy of limiting or "capping" the size of a fund by refusing new investors. The reason usually given is that by controlling the size of the fund, the portfolio manager will be better able to sustain superior performance. In funds with investment approaches based on speculative portfolios or heavy trading, capping the size of the fund makes some sense. It also makes sense in cases where the regulatory prohibition against holding more than 10 percent of an issue interferes with the fund's investment program. One example is the *Guardian Monthly Dividend Fund*, which was capped in October 1996 because the availability of preferred shares was declining. Another example is the *AIC Advantage Fund*. This fund has heavily weighted Mackenzie Financial Corp. for the past few years. The rate at which the fund was attracting investment through 1996 meant that the size of its positions would exceed 10 percent of Mackenzie's total issued capital. To avoid the requirement that Mackenzie's weighting in the portfolio be reduced, AIC's sponsors simply introduced a second fund, the *AIC Advantage II Fund*, thereby entitling them to hold a total of up to 20 percent of total issued capital. And indeed, AIC's total position in Mackenzie Financial was significantly higher than 10 percent in March 1997.

Frequently, however, the decision to cap a fund is motivated more by marketing considerations than by investment fundamentals. The fund manager typically introduces a new, smaller "clone" fund to satisfy disappointed investors, and almost invariably, the clone fund carries higher management costs than its prototype. Thus, the *AIC Advantage II Fund* has a management fee of 2.25 percent, while the *AIC Advantage Fund* has a management fee of only 2.00 percent.

Large Funds

There are also arguments favouring greater size. The advantage most frequently suggested is that larger funds are more efficient. Since many administrative costs are relatively fixed, the cost per unit is lower in larger funds than in smaller ones. Support for this argument seems to come from the United States, where fund expenses are generally lower. Since many U.S.-based fund organizations are very large by Canadian standards, the lower expenses are attributed to the size of the organization. In fact, there are a host of better reasons for the differences in expenses.

Larger organizations also often have a reputation for better research, and this makes some sense. Good research is expensive, and big outfits can more easily absorb the high costs. Trimark's Krembil says that, rather than impeding performance, the greater size of his organization provides the resources to do the intensive research on which its success is based. Enormous size allows Fidelity to maintain research offices in London, Tokyo, and Hong Kong. Similarly, Templeton's success in global investing is based to some extent on an unparalleled network of local analysts who supply the information on which the company's distinctive approach is based.

Larger size also contributes to the creativity and innovation of the organization, and these elements can have an important bearing on both the quality and application of research. With more than 200 funds, Fidelity has institutionalized the process of sharing ideas and information among its managers. At Trimark, Krembil says that the larger size of the flagship funds enables the organization to justify the employment of portfolio managers with specific expertise, which can then be applied in funds with more narrowly focused mandates. In return, these niche funds provide information that benefits the larger funds.

In addition, larger organizations often attract the most promising managers. There is greater opportunity to learn from successful senior managers and to build personal reputations, and there is usually a bigger pay-packet associated with management of a bigger fund.

While large size can be an advantage in some circumstances, a rapid increase in size is often a liability. Organizations that expand rapidly frequently lack the administrative systems necessary for effective management, and it is easy for the discipline of the investment approach to suffer. Peter Cundill, for example, attributes the only loss suffered by the 20-year-old *Cundill Value Fund* (in 1990) to a surge in new investment that induced him to relax his investment approach. The result was the acquisition of too many companies that did not fully meet his rigid value criteria. Similarly, there is some evidence that the rapid growth of the *Altamira Equity Fund* following its early successes constrained Frank Mersch's aggressive investment approach by compelling him to invest in larger, more liquid issues, which offered less potential for taking quick profits. It is also widely recognized that Altamira's rapid growth strained the administrative systems of the company, resulting in increased customer dissatisfaction and subsequent redemptions.

It is important to understand how an organization achieved its size. Organizations that have grown as a result of new sales driven by sophisticated marketing campaigns are far less impressive than those in which the expansion is attributable to the portfolio manager's investment acumen. Although the performance of the *AGF Canadian Equity Fund* to the end of August 1995 was well below average, with a one-year return of only 2.4 percent and ten-year returns of 5.1 percent (both below average), fund assets nevertheless nearly doubled to $697 million by the end of March 1996 largely because of Veronika Hirsch's draw as a star manager.

CHAPTER SIXTEEN

TAXES

EXECUTIVE SUMMARY

This chapter reviews the basic tax issues that affect the performance of mutual funds. It is not a substitute for professional advice regarding specific circumstances.

1. Mutual funds earn two different kinds of income. Investment income comes from interest, dividends, or the rental of real estate. Capital gains come from increases in the fund's asset values. Each type of income is taxed differently.

2. Mutual fund investments create tax liability in three ways:
   - The investments in the portfolio earns interest or dividend income, which is passed to unitholders.
   - The purchase and sale of investments for the fund portfolio by the portfolio manager create capital gains (and losses), which are passed to unitholders.
   - The unitholder sells the mutual fund investment for more (or less) than its purchase price, creating a capital gain (or loss).

3. A variety of factors affect the taxation of a mutual fund investment, including–
   - the type of investments held in the fund's portfolio
   - the fund's structure
   - the frequency with which the fund manager trades the investments in the portfolio
   - the switching of units from one mutual fund to another

INTRODUCTION

Taxes are one of life's inevitabilities. The purpose of this chapter is to outline the ways in which the tax system affects the operation of mutual funds so that investors can make wise choices.

In this discussion of tax issues, two points should be kept in mind. First, while taxes are important, tax considerations should not dominate an investor's decision making. The suitability of any investment should ultimately be governed by the investor's needs. Second, while we attempt to be as thorough as possible, the material in this chapter is not a substitute for advice on specific circumstances. Consulting with qualified tax professionals is strongly recommended.

Basic Concepts

Although the tax system can be confusing, many of the concepts on which it is based are straightforward. The following list summarizes some of the more basic principles:

- All income is subject to tax. It can be taxed now or later, but it will be taxed.

- Income is taxed according to the way in which it is produced. Some forms of income are more heavily taxed than others.

- In general terms, the more you make, the higher your ***marginal tax rate***. This means that as you earn more, Revenue Canada's "slice" will be larger, both as a percentage, and in absolute terms.

- Deferring tax permits investment capital to grow more quickly as a result of compounding.

- Corporations are subject to somewhat different rules than individuals.

Types of Income

The income received from a mutual fund is either ***investment income*** or capital gains.

Investment income takes three forms.

- Interest income is received on debt investments such as bank deposits, bonds, GICs, and mortgages. It is fully taxed.

- Dividend income is received as a share in the profits of a company in which the taxpayer has invested. Dividend income from Canadian corporations is accorded preferential tax treatment relative to earned income and interest income by virtue of the ***dividend tax credit.*** The net effect of the tax credit is to reduce the federal tax rate on dividends from Canadian corporations from 26 percent to approximately 16 percent. Since provincial taxes are usually calculated as a percentage of federal tax, the overall tax rate declines as well. As a result, a dividend of 10 percent provides the same ***effective return*** as an interest rate of 13.5 percent.

- Rental income is received from the rental of real estate. In principle, it is no different from interest income. However, it is eligible for ***capital cost allowance***, which is essentially a reduction in tax liability to compensate for the costs of maintaining the property. The practical result is that rental income is accorded preferential treatment.

Capital gains (or losses) come from increases (or decreases) in the value of assets, including units or shares of mutual funds. The current tax system taxes only three-quarters of any capital gain, so the effective tax rate is only 75 percent of the tax rate on earned income.

Table 16-1 indicates some approximate tax rates for different income brackets.

Table 16-1. Tax Rates by Source of Income

Taxable Income	To $30,000 (%)	$30,000 – $60,000 (%)	Over $60,000 (%)
Interest	27	42	52
Dividends	7	25	35
Capital Gains	20	31	39

Sources of Tax Liability

There are three sources of tax liability for an investment in mutual funds:
- income earned by the fund
- capital gains that are realized by the fund manager
- sales or ***dispositions*** of fund units by the unitholder

We'll look briefly at each of these.

Income Earned by the Fund

Many investments pay a regular income. Stocks can pay dividends; bonds make regular interest payments. Income from the investments in a mutual fund portfolio is passed on to unitholders, who become liable for any tax. The payments of income to unitholders are called ***income distributions***. The frequency of these distributions varies widely. Many money market funds make weekly distributions, while some growth funds make distributions less than once per year.

Capital Gains

When a mutual fund sells an investment in the portfolio for more than it paid to purchase that investment, it realizes a capital gain. Conversely, when a fund sells an investment below purchase price, it realizes a capital loss. The total of all the capital gains and losses in the portfolio are paid to investors at least yearly as a ***capital distribution***, which is taxable in the hands of the investor.

Investments in the fund portfolio that appreciate in value create unrealized capital gains, which are not subject to tax. The longer the investments in the portfolio are held while they appreciate, the longer the tax on the capital gain is deferred. Some funds actively attempt to defer tax in this way. For example, the intention of the *Templeton Growth Fund*, as described in its 1994 annual report, is "to minimize the payment of [distributions] so that the taxes on the increased value of shares are deferred. Only [distributions] which are required to reduce the Fund's tax burden are paid to shareholders."

A few points about distributions are noteworthy:

- A fund must make both an income distribution and a capital distribution at least annually, or the fund becomes liable for the tax, although this tax is refundable when the distributions are made to investors.

- The investor is liable for tax on the distributions whether they are received as cash or reinvested in additional units of the fund.

- The "attribution rules" of the Income Tax Act provide that distributions of interest and dividend income from a mutual fund (or other) investment made in the name of a minor are treated as income of the contributor rather than as income of the child. Capital gains, however, are taxable in the hands of the minor.

Dispositions

When mutual fund units are sold, the difference between the sale price and the cost of purchasing the units is subject to tax. The cost of purchasing the units is called the adjusted cost base and is not necessarily the same as the purchase price.

In calculating the investment's adjusted cost base, several factors have to be considered:

- Sales charges increase the adjusted cost base of the units.

If, for example, a sales charge of 4.5 percent is paid on a $5,000 purchase of mutual fund units with a net asset value of $10.00, the adjusted cost base of the units will be $10.47. Figure 16-1 sets out sample calculations:

Figure 16-1. Effect of Sales Commissions on Adjusted Cost Base

Initial investment	$ 5,000.00
Commission (4.5%)	$ 225.00
Amount of purchase	$ 4,775.00
Number of units @ $10	477.50
Adjusted cost base	$ 5,000.00 ÷ 477.5 =
	$ 10.47 per unit

- The adjusted cost base of units purchased at different times and prices is the average cost of the units.

The availability of both automatic reinvestment programs and pre-authorized payment plans makes this a very common concern. If, for example, 500 units of a mutual fund are bought for a total cost per unit (including sales charges) of $10.00, and a further 50 units are bought at a total cost per unit (including sales charges) of $11.00, the adjusted cost base of the units is $10.09. Figure 16-2 shows the calculation.

Figure 16-2. Average Unit Price as Adjusted Cost Base

500 units x $10 per unit		$ 5,000.00	
50 units x $11 per unit		$ 550.00	
		$ 5,500.00	
$5,500.00 ÷ 550 units	=	$ 10.09	per unit

- Distributions that include a return of capital (such as those made by funds with fixed distributions) reduce the investor's adjusted cost base by the amount of any return of capital.

For example, the adjusted cost base of units in the *Industrial Dividend Growth Fund* purchased on January 1, 1996, was $10.07. Over the year, the fund paid $0.60 per unit in distributions, of which $0.307 was a return of capital. As a result, the adjusted cost base of the units on January 1, 1997, was only $9.763.

In addition, investors should recognize that systematic withdrawal plans are dispositions. Depending on the timing of dividend reinvestments (or purchases) and withdrawals, each withdrawal will trigger a separate tax liability.

Factors Affecting Tax Liability

Fund Type

The return on equity investments is generated by dividend income and capital gains. The return on bonds and mortgages comes primarily from interest income and to a lesser degree from capital gains. The return on money market investments comes entirely from interest income. Since different categories of funds hold different types of investments, the category an investor chooses will have significant tax consequences. Table 16-2, for example, illustrates the different tax liabilities of a $1,000 investment in a bond fund and an income fund.

Table 16-2. Relative Tax Liability of Bond and Income Funds

	Bond Fund		Dividend Fund	
Total return	15% /	$150.00	15% /	$150.00
Distributions:				
Income		$ 70.00		$ 70.00
Capital gains		$ 30.00		$ 30.00
Unrealized gains		$ 50.00		$ 50.00
Tax on income	52% /	$ 36.40	35% /	$ 24.50
Tax on capital gains		$ 11.25		$ 11.25
Total tax		$ 47.65		$ 35.75
After-tax return		6.82%		7.62%

Although the realized capital gains of the two funds are equally taxed, the total tax payable on the return of the income fund is lower. The bond fund earns interest income, which is fully taxed at the investor's marginal rate. The income fund earns dividend income, on which the effective tax rate is about one-third lower. As a result, the after-tax or effective return of the income fund is significantly greater, although the pre-tax returns of the two funds are identical.

Fund Structure

Although the differences between mutual funds organized as unit trusts and those structured as investment corporations are usually unimportant, there are a few cases in which the legal structure is relevant. Real estate funds (and REITs), for example, are always structured as trusts. The reason for this is the preferential taxation accorded real estate investments through the capital cost allowance. If a real estate fund were structured as a corporation, the tax relief from any capital cost allowance would be available only to the corporation, but because real estate funds are organized as unit trusts, the benefit of this tax relief may be passed on to investors. Similar tax advantages for income from mining and oil and gas properties have lead to a proliferation of royalty trusts, which have some similarities with mutual funds.

It is important to recognize that many of the special tax advantages enjoyed by particular kinds of investments may be subject to recapture on the disposition of the investment. The capital cost allowance on real property, for example, depreciates the book value of the property at a specified rate. If the property is subsequently sold for more than the depreciated value, the tax system "recaptures" some of the tax relief previously allowed. Similarly, the tax relief that makes the returns of royalty trust units so attractive may be subject to recapture on the sale of the units, thereby significantly reducing the investment's net returns.

Portfolio Turnover

Portfolio turnover is the degree to which the investments in a portfolio are traded. A fund with low portfolio turnover may trade less than 10 percent of the portfolio's total value each year; while a fund with very high portfolio turnover may trade so frequently that more than 200 percent of the portfolio value is traded in a year.

Portfolio turnover is significant for two reasons. First, each time an investment in the portfolio is sold, a capital gain (or loss) is created. These gains and losses are ultimately passed on to the fund's investors. A fund with low portfolio turnover holds assets while they appreciate. The value of the fund rises with the increase in the value of the investments, but because the gain is unrealized until the investment is sold, no immediate tax liability arises. In contrast, a fund with high portfolio turnover will sell these investments more quickly and use the proceeds to purchase other investments. This "exchange" of investments creates a tax liability if it cannot be offset by capital losses.

High portfolio turnover is not necessarily bad. The investment strategy of the portfolio manager may rely on frequent trading of securities. The real issue is whether the returns of the fund are high enough to compensate for the tax liability that a trading strategy creates. What is clear is that two funds with identical pretax performance can have different after-tax returns because of the tax consequences of portfolio turnover. Table 16-3 illustrates the difference.

Frank Mersch, who manages the *Altamira Equity Fund*, is known as an active trader, with portfolio turnover well over 100 percent. In contrast, Alex Christ, who manages the Mackenzie Financial's *Industrial Growth Fund*, is considered to have more of a "buy-and-hold" approach. His portfolio turnover is reported to be a much more modest 30 to 35 percent.

The effect of taxation on the return of the *Altamira Equity Fund* is quite striking. Active trading resulted in $6.17 in capital gains, which attracted immediate tax of $2.31. In effect, only three-quarters of the gross return from the fund continues to compound. In contrast, the more restrained portfolio turnover of the Mackenzie fund produced no realized capital gain and thus enabled investors to defer tax, permitting the full amount of the return to continue to compound.

Figure 16-3. Tax Effects of Portfolio Turnover

	Altamira Equity	*Mackenzie Industrial*
Net asset value as of January 1, 1993	$ 23.41	$ 11.11
Net asset value as of December 31, 1993		
Before distributions	$ 34.31	$ 16.32
After distributions	$ 28.14	$ 16.32
Gross return ($)	$ 10.90	$ 5.21
Gross return (%)	46.55%	46.89%
Dividends	NIL	NIL
Taxable capital distributions	$ 6.17	NIL
Amount of tax (75% of gains at 50%)	$ 2.31	NIL
Return ($) net of taxes (gross return - amount of tax)	$ 8.59	$ 5.21
Return (%) net of taxes	36.69%	46.89%

Source: fund financial statements, 1993

Fund Switches

Most mutual funds are now part of fund groups or families. One of the chief advantages of such families is the possibility of ***switching*** from one fund to another within the group to meet changing investment objectives or to maximize return in cyclical markets without incurring additional sales charges. However, while sales charges may be waived, the redemption of units in the original fund will generally be regarded as a disposition for tax purposes, and will create a tax liability. This issue is particularly critical for ***asset allocation*** services.

The CI Group and more recently the AGF and GT Global groups have attempted to solve this difficulty by creating "umbrella" funds with multiple "classes" of shares, each of which represents an interest in a specific mutual fund. Shares of one class can be exchanged for shares of other classes under the umbrella without triggering the tax consequences of a disposition, in much the same way that portfolio managers can buy and sell shares of various companies in the portfolio of a mutual fund. Once an investor redeems out of the "umbrella" fund, a capital gain (or loss) will be triggered.

The entry of AGF and GT Global into the "multiclass" fund market has triggered considerable debate about the true tax liability entailed by these investments, and it is important to recognize that umbrella funds do not insulate investors from all tax liability. The potential tax liability from annual distributions remains: investors cannot escape the tax consequences of the fund's investment approach. As always, however, the tax implications of a switch should not deter an investor when switching funds is warranted.

A Note on Segregated Funds

Segregated funds are a type of investment fund offered by insurance companies that differs in some important respects from conventional mutual funds. One of these differences is the tax treatment accorded segregated funds on the death of the subscribing investor.

Most investments, including conventional mutual funds, are deemed to be sold on the death of the investor, triggering any potential tax liability. This tax liability can significantly reduce the value of any estate, notwithstanding the fact that only 75 percent of any capital gain is subject to tax. In contrast, in cases where the segregated fund investor designates a preferred beneficiary, the entire value of a segregated fund investment passes to designated beneficiaries, while the estate remains responsible for any tax liability.

A Note on Labour-Sponsored Funds

One of the chief benefits of labour-sponsored venture capital funds is the generous tax treatment they receive. (This tax treatment is covered in detail in Appendix E.) However, it is important to remember that choosing investments primarily on the basis of their anticipated tax benefits is imprudent.

Miscellaneous Issues

Foreign Taxes

Property held in foreign jurisdictions is generally subject to the law of those jurisdictions, and that includes tax law. There are a number of countries with which Canada has tax treaties, and there are therefore many instances in which tax liability in Canada can be reduced by the amount of any tax payable in foreign jurisdictions.

A review of interjurisdictional tax issues is far beyond the scope of this book. However, many Canadian investors may have to contend with U.S. tax laws, and these laws accordingly merit attention insofar as they apply to mutual fund investments.

Much tax payable by Canadians on income from U.S. sources is subject to tax treaties, and taxpayers are therefore eligible for credit against tax payable in Canada. However, because there is no Canadian equivalent to the federal estate tax levied in the United States, Canadians owning U.S.-based property have historically been largely ineligible for tax credits against U.S. estate taxes.

With the ratification of the Third Protocol to the Canada-U.S. Tax Convention in 1995, Canadians are now eligible, on a proportionate basis, for the same tax credit available to U.S. residents. The amount of the relief is determined by the proportion of the global estate composed of U.S.-based assets and is subject to reduction for any credits allowed on taxable gifts.

U.S. securities that are held by a mutual fund based in Canada are not regarded as U.S. assets in the hands of the taxpayer. Mutual funds are therefore an excellent way to participate in the U.S. market without incurring potential U.S. tax liability.

CHAPTER SEVENTEEN

TAX-SHELTERED PLANS

EXECUTIVE SUMMARY

This chapter reviews the basic issues that affect the use of mutual funds in tax-sheltered plans such as RRSPs and RRIFs.

1. The income and capital gains from investments held in tax-sheltered plans compounds tax-free.

2. The type of income earned by a fund inside a tax-sheltered plan is immaterial. Income withdrawn from a tax-sheltered plan is taxed at the investor's highest marginal rate, regardless of the way in which the income was earned.

3. It is important to maximize the foreign content of tax-sheltered plans.

4. Mutual funds are a convenient and flexible way to invest in tax-sheltered plans.

INTRODUCTION

Mutual funds are extremely popular investments in tax-advantaged plans like RRSPs, RRIFs, and registered education saving plans (RESPs). In this chapter we look at the basic framework of tax-sheltered plans and the way in which mutual funds can be used in them.

General Principles

Tax-Free Compounding

The main advantage underlying such plans is that the income of investments in the plan compounds without tax liability. When the return from an investment is reinvested with the amount of the original investment, the investment is said to *compound*. Ordinarily, tax is payable on investment income; this tax reduces the amount that can be reinvested. Sheltering an investment from tax allows the investment to grow much more quickly. Table 17-1 illustrates the effect tax sheltering can have on an investment of $5,000, assuming a return of 8 percent, and a combined federal and provincial tax rate of 50 percent.

Table 17-1. Effect of Tax Sheltering on $5,000 Investment

Year	Outside Tax-Sheltered Plan ($)	Inside Tax-Sheltered Plan ($)
1	5,200	5,400
5	6,083	7,347
10	7,401	10,795
15	9,005	15,861
20	10,956	23,305
25	13,329	34,242
30	16,217	50,313
35	19,730	73,927

An investment of $5,000 will grow in 35 years to $19,730 outside a tax-sheltered plan and to $73,927 inside a tax-sheltered plan. The difference in growth is remarkable. And the higher the return and the longer the period of compounding, the greater this difference will be.

The corollary of such tax-free growth is that the tax consequences for investments held outside such plans do not apply to investments in tax-advantaged plans. As a result, the type of income from these plans does not matter. There is, for example, no particular advantage to earning dividend income inside a tax-sheltered plan.

Deferred Tax

The second advantage of tax-sheltered plans is that investors can sometimes realize the benefit of their plans when their income is lower than it was when the investment was made, and accordingly, when the marginal tax rate on the realized value of the investment is smaller. By deferring the tax, investors may be able to reduce the amount of tax payable.

Types of Tax-Advantaged Plans

There are a variety of tax-sheltered plans. The most common are–

- registered retirement savings plans (RRSPs)
- ***locked-in retirement accounts (LIRAs)***
- registered retirement income funds (RRIFs)
- ***life income funds (LIFs)***
- registered education savings plans (RESPs)

We'll look at each of these in a little more detail.

Registered Retirement Saving Plans

These plans are funded by annual contributions from the investor. The maximum amount of the annual contribution is limited, but the amount of any contribution is deducted from the investor's ***taxable income***. Withdrawals from an RRSP are permitted but are fully taxed at the investor's highest marginal rate, regardless of the way in which the funds were earned. Beginning in 1997, an RRSP must be terminated no later than the end of the year of the investor's 69th birthday. Investors who turned 69 in 1996 must terminate their plans no later than the end of 1997.

Locked-in Retirement Accounts

These are analogous to RRSPs, but contributions are "locked in" because they are funded from an investor's irrevocable entitlement under a registered pension plan. Just as early withdrawals from a pension plan are not usually permitted, withdrawals from a LIRA are not permitted.

Registered Retirement Income Funds

When an RRSP or another tax-advantaged plan is terminated, the total value of the plan is subject to tax unless the assets are transferred to another tax-sheltered plan such as a RRIF. RRIFs operate like RRSPs in reverse. Each year, investors must withdraw a minimum percentage of the plan's assets, but there is no maximum limit on the amount that may be taken out. Withdrawals from a RRIF are fully taxed as ordinary income—the source of the income (interest, dividend, or capital gain) is immaterial. However, by facilitating the gradual depletion of assets, RRIFs reduce the tax consequences for the investor since only amounts withdrawn are subject to tax. The assets remaining in the RRIF continue to grow tax-free.

Life Income Funds

These funds are created from the assets of a terminated LIRA. As in RRIFs, a minimum percentage of the assets must be withdrawn from a LIF each year; however, there is also an upper limit on the yearly amount that may be withdrawn.

Registered Education Saving Plans

While there are fewer restrictions on the kinds of investments that can be held in an RESP than on those in RRSPs and RRIFs, there are also fewer benefits, since contributions to an RESP do not reduce taxable income. However, contributions of up to $4,000 per year, per beneficiary, to a lifetime maximum of $42,000 per contributor for a maximum of 21 years, are permitted to compound tax-free. Since the only benefit is tax-free growth, investments with the strongest prospects for growth make the most sense.

An RESP must be terminated no later than 25 years after it is established. If the funds are not used for educational purposes, the income generated within the plan may be returned to the subscriber, provided the plan has been in existence for at least 10 years and the contributor is a Canadian resident. In addition, any beneficiary must have reached the age of 21 and not be pursuing post-secondary education, nor have died. The RESP income will be subject to the subscriber's regular tax rate. Provided the subscriber has sufficient contribution room, up to $40,000 of RESP income may be transferred to the subscriber's RRSP or to a spousal RRSP. Where the RESP income exceeds the subscriber's available RRSP contribution room, or the $40,000 limit, the difference can be received directly as income, subject to a 20 percent charge in addition to regular taxes.

Allowable Investments

Investments that can be held in tax-advantaged plans are called ***qualified investments***. The general principle is that "tangible" assets and illiquid investments are not qualified for inclusion. Some common exclusions are–

- real estate
- works of art and collectibles
- precious metals and gemstones
- commodity futures contracts
- shares of many private corporations

A minimum of 80 percent of the ***book value*** of the investments in an RRSP, LIRA, RRIF or LIF must be Canadian property. Book value is the price at which an investment was acquired, as opposed to its market value. Canadian property consists of assets in Canada or securities of companies with a substantial presence in Canada. To qualify as Canadian property, at least 80 percent of a mutual fund's assets must be invested in Canadian securities or assets.

Maximizing the foreign content of any investment portfolio is a good idea, for two reasons. Foreign content provides additional diversification, which is always prudent. In addition, foreign investments offer the opportunity for superior returns. For the ten years ending December 31, 1996, the TSE 300 had a compound annual return of 10.1 percent. In contrast, the S&P 500, which is U.S.-based, had a compound annual return of 14.6 percent; the EAFE Index, which is biased towards Europe, had a compound return of 12.4 percent; and the MSCI, a world index, had a compound annual return of 11.1 percent. Appendix K provides an explanation of how to calculate allowable foreign content.

Mutual Funds in Tax-Sheltered Plans

Many mutual funds qualify for inclusion in tax-sheltered plans. They are well suited to such plans for a couple of reasons.

Mutual Funds Provide Flexibility

Since the purpose of RRIFs and LIFs is to provide retirement income, strong returns on their investments are necessary to ensure that the plans will not be exhausted prematurely. At the same time, however, since the rate at which RRIFs and LIFs are depleted is fixed, investors need to limit the risk that investments will need to be sold at a depressed price. Mutual funds provide a convenient and cost efficient way of switching to investments with lower volatility to insulate the plan against the danger of a forced sale.

Certain mutual funds also enable investors to hold unqualified investments in tax-sheltered plans. Choosing a qualified mutual fund whose portfolio includes unqualified assets allows individuals to invest indirectly in these unqualified investments. Mutual funds that specialize in precious metals and commodities are good examples.

Mutual Funds Are Convenient

A fund's eligibility for tax-sheltered plans must be indicated in the prospectus, and the major fund groups offer separate accounts for tax-sheltered investments. In particular, mutual funds can simplify the process of maximizing a plan's foreign content. There are, however, a number of issues of which investors should be aware:

- Each plan is treated as a separate entity for the purposes of applying the foreign content limits. As a result, investors who purchase tax-sheltered plans from a variety of sources are unlikely to maximize the allowable foreign content (20 percent) of their total investment. A common pattern for RRSP investors, for example, is to open a new RRSP plan each year to purchase a single investment at the institution offering the most competitive short-term rate. Over time, the investor accumulates a number of RRSP plans but since each plan holds only a single investment, none of the investments can be foreign property without exceeding the 20 percent limit in that plan. A plan containing multiple investments is needed, and the only realistic mechanism for maximizing foreign content is a ***self-***

directed plan, in which the choice of investments held in the plan is made by the plan-holder.

- Even with a self-directed plan, buying and selling investments may affect the proportion of the plan invested in foreign property. If, for example, an investor decides to switch a fund that makes up some of the foreign content in an RRSP, the purchase of a new foreign fund will establish a new book value for foreign content. If the value of the old fund has increased since its purchase, switching to a new fund may result in the 20 percent limit being exceeded and may trigger penalty taxes. The sale of Canadian content investments at a book loss can have a similar effect. If the book value of the Canadian content is reduced, the book value of the foreign content may be increased beyond the 20 percent limit, resulting in penalties.

- Reinvested income from assets held in RRSPs is added to the book value of the investment. As a result, automatic reinvestment plans can inadvertently increase the book value of the foreign content beyond the 20 percent limit.

- An increasing number of mutual fund companies are offering funds that attempt to reap the benefits of foreign exposure without losing their status as registered investments. For example, the Global Strategy group offers a "Diversified" series of funds in which a small portion of the portfolio is invested in derivatives linked to foreign investments. The bulk of the portfolio is invested in short-term Canadian securities such as T-bills to "cover" the risk of the derivatives. Since derivatives are leveraged, the effect they have on the returns of the fund is magnified, and the portfolio manager can therefore attempt to replicate the returns of a portfolio that is fully invested in foreign markets. In our view, the use of derivatives to achieve RRSP eligibility for foreign investments often reflects investment decisions based primarily on tax considerations.

A Note on Multiclass Funds in Tax-Sheltered Plans

We stated in Chapter 16 that multiclass or "umbrella" funds are designed to eliminate the tax consequences of switching from one fund to another. As a result, these funds offer no particular benefit inside tax-sheltered plans. In fact, however, these funds' organizational structure often makes them inappropriate as tax-sheltered investments. Although a different portfolio of investments corresponds to each class of shares, the portfolios of all the classes of shares are considered together for the purposes of calculating the fund's foreign content. While the portfolio of the "Canadian" class may be at least 80 percent Canadian property, the portfolios of the other share classes may not have any Canadian property, and the portfolio of the fund as a whole will generally be less than 80 percent Canadian property. The fund will therefore constitute foreign property even when an investor owns shares only in the "Canadian" class.

CHAPTER EIGHTEEN

FEES, LOADS, AND OTHER COSTS

EXECUTIVE SUMMARY

This chapter canvasses the various costs associated with mutual funds.

1. Contrary to popular belief, costs are the least important consideration in choosing a suitable mutual fund. Only investors who are concerned with identifying the cheapest fund rather than the best fund should be preoccupied with cost.

2. The return of the fund is reported in sales literature and the newspapers after expenses are deducted.

3. All funds charge a management fee. In some funds this fee covers all the expenses of the fund; in other funds, custodial and audit fees and similar costs are charged in addition to the management fee. The total of fees and expenses is calculated and reported as a percentage of fund assets on an annual basis and is called the management expense ratio.

4. The size of the expense ratio should reflect the value the manager adds in administering the fund. For money market and income funds, controlling expenses is important, and a relatively high expense ratio will probably reduce the long-term performance of the fund. For actively managed growth funds, higher expenses can often be absorbed in higher gross returns. The most important issue is whether expenses are reasonable.

5. Sales charges are the commissions paid to brokers and other dealers who sell the funds to investors. Commissions are calculated in a wide variety of ways.

6. Attempting to choose a fund on the basis of relative cost does not work.

7. It is a myth that no-load means no cost.

8. The important factors in choosing between sales charges are–
   - the needs of the investor
   - the specific advantages of a particular load

INTRODUCTION

A significant proportion of any fund prospectus is devoted to outlining the various costs of the fund, and this emphasis often leads to the conclusion that these costs must be extremely important. In our view, fees and costs are among the least important considerations in the process of evaluating and choosing a mutual fund. All other things being equal, costs may be relevant to the selection of the most suitable funds. Rarely, though, are all other things equal.

Mutual fund costs can be broken down into three basic categories:

- management expenses
- administrative charges
- sales charges

We'll deal with each of these in turn.

Management expenses

As the name implies, these are the costs related to managing the fund. They include–

- management fees
- transaction fees and commissions
- legal and audit expenses
- custodian and transfer agent fees
- accounting and bookkeeping costs
- office expenses
- marketing and promotional expenses
- GST (where applicable)

Management Fees

The ***management fee*** is the single most important management expense. It is the compensation the manager receives for administering the fund and is calculated as a percentage of the assets of the fund. The fee ranges from less than 0.5 percent for money market funds to as much as 3.0 percent for some equity funds.

The management fee covers a number of costs. Portfolio managers either internal or external, are paid out of the management fee. ***Trailer fees,*** which are continuing commissions paid to agents or brokers by many funds, are covered by the management fee. In some funds, a portion of the management fee is paid to limited partnerships which are responsible for paying sales commissions on some types of fund purchases. (We'll look at these last two in further detail in the section on sales charges.)

There are several points that should be made about management fees:

- The management fees of funds within a particular category should be comparable.

- The management fee belongs to the manager, and reducing the costs borne by the manager only increases the profitability of the manager: the returns of the fund will not be improved. For example, although many investors objected to Mackenzie Financial's sponsorship of a race car, believing that the expenditure reduced their returns from the fund, the costs of the car came out of the management fee, and cancelling the sponsorship would have increased the amount available to the shareholders of Mackenzie Financial Corp. rather than increasing the returns of the various funds the company manages. (The sponsorship was in fact terminated, not because of any negative effect on fund returns, but because the race car seemed an inappropriately extravagant corporate symbol during the recession of the early 1990s.)

  In an effort to control expenses, the portfolio manager sometimes agrees to accept less than the maximum percentage stipulated in the prospectus. Investors should be wary of this situation because the comparative return of the fund may be affected when the full fee is levied.

Other Management Expenses

Brokerage fees are the largest single expense next to management fees. For funds that are traded actively, brokerage fees can be significant. Brokerage costs for the *Altamira Equity Fund*, for example, were just over 1.1 percent of assets. For other funds, brokerage costs are quite modest. For the *Trimark Canadian Fund*, brokerage costs represented a mere 0.065 percent of fund assets in 1994. Other expenses, such as the fees of custodians, auditors, and lawyers, are relatively minor.

Management Expense Ratio

The management expense ratio relates total fund expenses to the total net assets of the fund. A fund with $500 million in assets and expenses of $15 million has a ratio of 3.0 percent. The management expense ratio for the last five years must be disclosed to investors in the prospectus and in the annual financial statements of the fund.

The management expense ratio is often used as a measure of a fund manager's efficiency. While this ratio can be helpful in some cases, its significance is too often exaggerated. The following points should be kept in mind:

- Investment returns are reported after management expenses have been deducted.

- Not all fund expenses are included in the expense ratio. Brokerage fees, for example, are generally not accounted for as an expense in the financial statements of a fund, but are instead incorporated into the "cost of investments sold." While this practice is consistent with the way in which investment income is reported for tax purposes, it does understate the total expenses of the fund. The greater the fund's brokerage expense, the greater the inaccuracy of the management expense ratio. Generally speaking, portfolio turnover has a direct effect on brokerage expense. For the *Trimark Canadian Fund*, which has very low portfolio turnover, the inclusion of brokerage costs would increase the management expense ratio from 1.56 to 1.625 percent. However, for the *Altamira Equity Fund*, which has very high portfolio turnover, the inclusion of brokerage costs would increase the expense ratio from 2.32 to 3.47 percent.

- By agreeing to accept less than the maximum fee permitted by the prospectus, the manager can manipulate the expense ratio.

- Management expenses should be related to the value added by the manager in administering the fund. Higher expenses can be justified when they result in higher net returns. In general, higher management expenses are acceptable in growth funds because the investment strategies of growth funds produce higher net returns. In income funds, high management expenses are harder to justify because there is far less variety in bonds than in stocks. It is even more improbable that the manager of a money market fund can add value by improving gross returns through the use of high-cost investment strategies. In passively managed funds, the manager does not add value, and higher expenses will almost always result in lower returns.

Administrative Charges

These charges are essentially user fees.

Set-up Fees

Some funds, particularly the no-load funds, levy a one-time charge ($25 to $50) to establish an account.

Switching Fees

Many fund groups permit one or two free switches from one fund to another within the family, and thereafter levy an administrative fee ($10 to $15). Some funds impose a further negotiable sales charge as a small percentage (up to 2 percent) of the net asset value of the exchanged units. While switching fees are a major irritant for many investors, the cost of a fund switch usually compares very favourably to the cost of a stock trade of similar size. A more significant fact is that a switch to a fund with a different commission structure may result in the payment of two sales commissions.

Systematic Withdrawal Plan Fees

Some funds impose a fee (about $50) to establish such plans. Other funds levy an administrative charge on a per-withdrawal basis. Some funds impose no charge but require investors to maintain a substantial minimum number of units in the plan.

Distribution Fees

This fee is levied by some funds in conjunction with the deferred sales charge. It is usually a small percentage (around 0.5 percent) of the net asset value, and is deducted from dividend reinvestments as they are received by the unitholder. This fee is particularly unpopular, and many funds that levied it in the past are phasing it out as part of fee restructuring.

Short-Term Trading Fees:
These fees (usually a percentage of net asset value) are levied on redemptions made soon after the fund was purchased to recoup processing costs associated with such transactions and commissions paid to brokers and dealers in the period prior to redemption.

Fees on Tax-Advantaged Plans
There are a number of separate charges included in this category. Many funds impose administration (or trustee) fees for RRSPs, RRIFs, and other tax-advantaged plans. (These fees can range from $15 to $75 per year.) Some funds charge a very small percentage of the net asset value of the plan, subject to maximums. Many funds do not charge administration fees if the fund is held in a self-directed RRSP account at a brokerage firm, but the brokerage firm will charge a fee.

In addition, most funds charge a termination fee when a tax-deferred plan is terminated or partially redeemed, or when a change in the beneficiary of the plan is made. Most funds exempt terminations when the proceeds are being transferred to a spouse in accordance with the Income Tax Act.

Sales Charges

Sales commissions are the payments to stockbrokers and other intermediaries who assist in the distribution of mutual funds to investors.

Types of Sales Charges

Sales charges can be charged in a number of different ways:

Front-End Load
Front-end loads, or front loads, are levied when the fund is purchased. In most cases, the amount of the commission is negotiable and is subject to a maximum that often declines with the size of the purchase. The front-end sales charges for the Mackenzie Financial Industrial group of funds (with the exception of the *Industrial Cash Management Fund* and the *Industrial Income fund*) for example, are shown in Table 18-1:

Table 18-1. Front-End Sales Charges for *Mackenzie Financial Industrial Group of Funds*

Amount Invested ($)		Maximum Charge (%)
up to	100,000	5
over	100,000	4
over	250,000	3
over	500,000	2
over	1,000,000	1

Source: fund prospectus, 11/96

Back-End Load

Back-end loads are also known as ***rear loads***, ***deferred sales charges***, or ***redemption charges***. Regardless of the designation, these charges are levied when the investment is redeemed or terminated. Some funds calculate the sales charge as a percentage of the amount originally invested, while others base it on the market value of the investment at the time of redemption or termination.

The most significant feature of back-end loads is that the percentage charged declines with the length of time the investment is held. Although the sales charge can be higher than a front-end load in the early years of an investment, long-term investors will pay no sales charges. Table 18-2 shows the redemption fee schedule for the *Trimark Select Canadian Growth Fund*. Deferred sales charges, however, are generally not negotiable.

Table 18-2. Redemption Fee Schedule for the *Trimark Select Canadian Growth Fund*

Date of Redemption	Deferred Sales Charge as a Percentage of the Price Paid
During the 1st year	4.50
During the 2nd year	4.00
During the 3rd year	3.50
During the 4th year	3.00
During the 5th year	2.50
During the 6th year	2.00
After the end of the 6th year	NIL

Source: fund prospectus

Another important feature of many funds purchased on a back-end load basis is that up to 10 percent of the investment may be redeemed each year without attracting a sales charge. Although the precise provisions of the feature vary from fund to fund, the basic privilege is fairly consistent. As an example, consider an investment of $50,000 at the beginning of 1994, which grows to $55,000 by year-end. In the absence of the redemption privilege, a redemption of 10 percent (or $5,500) of the investment in 1995 would attract a sales charge of about 5 percent ($275) leaving net proceeds of $5,225. With the redemption privilege, no sales charge would be levied on the $5,500 redemption. Assuming returns of 10 percent in 1995, the remaining investment (of $49,500) would be worth $54,450 at year-end, and the investor would be entitled to withdraw an additional $5,445 in 1996 without incurring a sales charge.

No-Load

There are an increasing number of no-load funds available. These funds charge no commission. Most banks, trust companies, and other financial institutions offer no-load funds, but many offer load funds as well. In addition, a number of independent funds are sold directly to the public. Altamira and Phillips, Hager & North are among the best-known no-load groups.

It is important to understand that *no-load* does not mean "no cost." The fees and expenses that we discussed earlier are charged by all funds, whether load or no-load. In addition, the no-load funds often have substantially greater marketing and promotional expenses than the load funds, which rely on their networks of dealers and sales staff to promote and distribute the funds.

Low Load

Low-load funds are relatively new. The sales commission for these funds is typically a very low (1 percent) front-end charge; the broker or dealer receives additional compensation in the form of trailer fees, which are paid by the manager of the fund out of the management fee.

- **Trailer Fees**

Trailer fees, sometimes referred to as service fees, are commissions paid to the dealer on a continuing basis. They can run from 0.25 percent to as much as 1 percent of assets, depending on the type of fund and the amount of assets under administration brought to the fund by the dealer. Trailer fees are paid from the management fee, and therefore do not directly affect the reported return of the fund.

Even some no-load funds pay trailers. Altamira, for example, pays brokers 0.25 percent annually on assets between $500,000 and $5 million in growth funds, and 0.70 percent annually on assets over $5 million.

Understanding Sales Charges

In the world of mutual funds, nothing arouses passions as much as the issue of sales charges. Largely because they are poorly understood, sales charges are very contentious.

To appreciate the true significance of sales charges, a variety of factors should be considered.

- The idea that sales charges on mutual funds are excessive is inaccurate. Mutual funds are not an individual security, but an investment "package" that includes portfolio diversification, professional management, and convenience.

  Consider the following example: to achieve even minimal diversification without investing in a mutual fund, a portfolio of at least six stocks is required (although a mix of six stocks does not begin to match the diversification of a mutual fund). To avoid excess costs associated with minimum commissions, a minimum of $6,000 per stock is required. The total minimum investment is therefore $36,000. For investments of this size, the commission will be approximately 2 percent per transaction. Furthermore, the portfolio of a mutual fund is regularly modified to maximize return. If the stock portfolio is modified or "turned over" completely just once, there are three transactions: initial purchase, sale, and subsequent purchase. The total commission on the stock portfolio will therefore be 6 percent. Compare this to the deferred sales charge on the Trimark funds, which is 4.5 percent at most and which declines to nothing if the fund is held for a reasonable period of time.

- The mistaken perception that commissions are excessive is reinforced by the existence of no-load and low-load funds. The question "why pay a sales charge when you can buy a similar fund with no sales charge?" is very common. The answer is that commissions are really payments for the experience and expertise a broker offers. Marketers of no-load funds assure investors that they will have access to professional advice, but it is unrealistic to expect the in-house sales representatives of no-load funds to provide a dispassionate view of the their funds' deficiencies.

In contrast, good brokers are true financial advisers, and the method of payment need not detract from the fact that they can provide investors with unbiased perspectives about investment performance and reassurance during periods of market turbulence and uncertainty. The claim that most brokers make recommendations based on the size of the commissions distorts the broker-client relationship. Long-term relationships are built on trust and confidence, and clients who do feel ill served can and do take their business elsewhere. Unfortunately, this preoccupation with broker compensation focuses attention on identifying the *cheapest* alternative, when the important issue is (or should be) finding the *best* alternative.

- Comparisons of sales charges based on attempts to calculate the relative costs of different kinds of commissions are fundamentally misguided. The principle is that by combining the total cost of management fees and sales charges over the time frame of the investment, the cheapest alternative can be identified. However, this kind of analysis simply cannot work. One reason is that cost-based evaluations are dependent on static assumptions about investment horizons. Even if it were possible to identify the cheapest load option for an investment of (say) ten years, there is no guarantee that the investor's needs will not change. A change in circumstances might easily transform an anticipated ten-year investment horizon into a six- or seven-year investment horizon, and such a change would entirely undermine the assumptions on which any cost analysis was based.

  The other reason cost-based evaluations can't work is that commission costs are truly a minor factor in investment performance. There are too many other variables affecting return to establish definitively that one type of sales commission or another is preferable. Those who accept the validity of a cost-based analysis argue, for example, that front-load funds outperformed deferred-load funds in the early 1990s because the management fees of the deferred-load funds were higher. In fact, the real explanation for the difference in performance lies in the portfolio characteristics of the funds rather than in their relative sales charges and management fees. Since deferred-load funds were far more popular during the early 1990s, more cash was invested in these funds. And since high cash balances reduce fund performance in a rising market, the deferred-load funds generally underperformed the front-load funds, which were more fully invested.

Choosing a Sales Charge

In our view, there are only two important issues regarding sales charges:

- **Does the sales charge meet the needs of the investor**

For investors who are clear about their financial goals and who are prepared to expend the time and effort necessary to properly research and monitor their investment, no-load funds may be acceptable. For investors seeking to maximize their investment performance, the contribution of brokers is undeniable. A recent study by Dalbar Inc. found that investors who used brokers earned higher returns than investors who attempted to "go it alone" even after adjusting for sales charges. Figure 18-1 illustrates this difference. From 1984 to 1995, the portfolios of investors who employed financial advisers grew by an average of 114.1 percent, while the portfolios of "go-it-alone" investors grew by 97.9 percent.

Figure 18-1. The Value of Advice

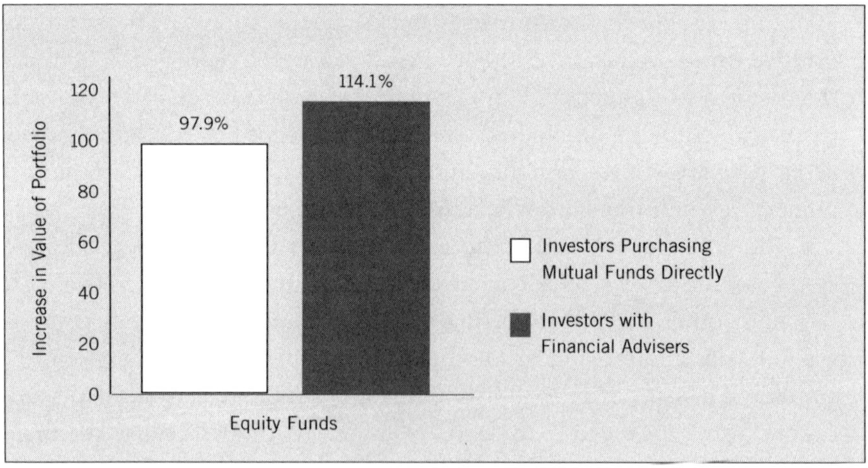

Source: Dalbar Inc., 1995

- **Is there a specific advantage to a particular sales charge?**

There are so many different commission structures that it is virtually impossible to meaningfully compare their relative costs. Costs aside, there may be a benefit to a particular type of sales charge, but many benefits are spurious. For example, one argument sometimes advanced for front-end loads is that they allow investors greater flexibility in deciding whether to change funds. Since the sales charge is paid up front, the investor's decision cannot be affected by the fact that a sale will attract a sales charge. In fact, this is nonsense. If an investor is willing to pay a sales charge to invest in a fund, it makes no difference whether that sales charge is paid when the investment is purchased or redeemed. More often than not, deferring the payment of the sales charge will result in paying less, since deferred charges decline over time. And while it is true that the deferred charges are typically higher in the early years, a decision to change investments in the first two or three years often reflects an inappropriate concern with short-term considerations. Over the long term, the incremental effect of a particular sales charge on the performance of an investment will be much, much smaller than the effect of superior portfolio management and sound portfolio characteristics.

PART FOUR
CHOOSING FUNDS

In Part Four, we draw together the previous three parts and outline an approach for evaluating and choosing funds. Choosing mutual funds is a three-stage process:

- establish your personal investment policy
- identify the types of funds that are appropriate for your needs
- identify the best funds within the appropriate groups

Chapter 19 focuses on explaining how the various classes of funds fit into an individual's investment policy.

Chapter 20 is a checklist of factors to consider once the kinds of funds that suit your needs have been identified. While there is an underlying order to the framework, the relative importance of individual considerations will depend upon the particular case. The checklist need not be followed rigidly. The flow charts in Chapter 21 and the case studies in Chapter 22 provide further guides to evaluating funds.

Chapter 23 is an overview of various sources of information available to investors.

CHAPTER NINETEEN

DEVELOPING AN INVESTMENT POLICY

EXECUTIVE SUMMARY

This chapter describes the basics for developing a personal investment policy and identifying the classes of funds that are most suitable for that policy.

1. The following are important considerations in developing an investment policy:
   - needs, goals, and objectives
   - time horizon
   - comfort level

2. Long-term objectives are always met best with equities (growth funds). Investors who are uncomfortable with volatility should choose less volatile funds. While the returns of less volatile funds are usually lower, less volatile funds may nevertheless be the most suitable choice.

3. Short- and medium-term objectives are best met with less volatile investments because the risk of loss over the short term is a very real possibility. The choice depends on the flexibility of the time frame and the investor's comfort level.

4. Owning too many funds is counterproductive. Most investors are reasonably served with one well-diversified domestic growth fund and one

global growth fund for long-term objectives. One income fund is usually suitable for shorter-term objectives.

5. Investing is not a static process. As the time horizon shrinks and long-term objectives become medium- and then short-term objectives, investors need to modify their portfolios. The conversion from growth investments to more stable investments should be done with foresight to decrease the chances that the conversion will take place when the values of the growth investments are depressed.

INTRODUCTION

An investment policy is an investor's financial "game plan." It incorporates a variety of considerations into an overall judgement about the most appropriate personal portfolio. A young investor with a stable income and no dependants, seeking maximum growth and feeling comfortable with the volatility of the stock market, will have a very different approach to investing than a widowed pensioner who requires a steady income and who is nervous about daily fluctuations in prices. The mixes of assets in the portfolios of these two investors will be very different, but the process of establishing the portfolio will be the same in both cases, and will be quite unlike that proposed by advocates of asset allocation and modern portfolio theory.

The most important feature of a meaningful investment policy is that it is personalized. No two investors share identical circumstances. While an "off-the-shelf" strategy is always the easiest approach, it is almost never the most suitable. The development of a policy that is tailored to an individual's requirements requires effort and the exercise of judgement, as well as technique.

The Criteria for an Investment Policy

There are a few basic considerations in any investment policy:

- needs, goals, and objectives
- time horizon
- comfort level

Needs, Goals, and Objectives

The process starts with the identification of needs because it is impossible to choose suitable funds unless the purposes for which they are intended are specified. The distinctions between needs, goals and objectives, although subtle, are nonetheless important. In our view, needs constitute the investor's requirements, while goals include more discretionary elements. For many investors, needs and goals may be the same. Objectives are the concrete targets that must be met to satisfy the needs.

The first step is to articulate investment needs and goals. Making a list helps to separate what is essential from what is not, and to clarify the objectives necessary to meet the needs and goals. For example, "providing for retirement" is vague: when you expect to retire, the kind of retirement lifestyle you envisage, and the cost of retirement living must all be spelled out.

The second step is to articulate objectives which will enable you to meet your needs and objectives. In essence, you have to attach a price tag to your needs by ascertaining how much money is required to satisfy the need. This may lead to a reconsideration of some of the objectives.

The third step is to ensure that your objectives are compatible. Pursuing some objectives may limit the ability to pursue others, and may also entail a reconsideration of some objectives, or the needs which underlie them.

Time Horizon

An investor's time horizon is the period over which he or she expects to invest. Different needs have different time horizons. These include–

- long-term goals (e.g., retirement)
- medium-term goals (e.g., university education)
- short-term goals (e.g., a trip)
- emergency funds

Long-term objectives can always be met most effectively with growth funds. The historical returns from equities are twice those of bonds and three times those of cash-equivalent securities. For long-term objectives the price at which investments are purchased does not matter—the important consideration is to "be invested."

Short- and medium-term goals require different approaches. Given the fact that equities are volatile in the short term, it is imprudent to commit resources for short- and medium-term objectives exclusively to equities. The degree to which one invests in equities in pursuit of medium-term goals will depend both on the specific time frame and on the attitudes of the investor. Generally speaking, the shorter the time frame, the lower the percentage of the portfolio that should be devoted to stocks. Investors who do not want to risk the possibility that the volatility of stocks will reduce the size of their investment in the short term or who have an inflexible time frame should choose investments other than mutual funds, such as short-term bonds or cash-equivalent investments such as T-bills.

Consider a couple who have $50,000, which they intend to use to purchase a house in two years. They want to invest the capital until it is needed. If they invest in growth funds, they might reasonably expect a "profit" of $10,000, since the historical return from equities is about 10 percent. Taxes, however will reduce these returns to about $6,000. Alternatively, the couple could buy bonds that mature in two years. The historical return from bonds is about 5 percent, and the current yield for two-year federal government bonds is about 4.3 percent. Taxes will reduce this to about 2.1 percent or $1,050 per year. So the difference in return between the two scenarios is nearly $4,000.

The difference in short-term risk, however, is far more significant. In two years, there is a real possibility that the value of the stock investment could drop by as much as 10 percent. In contrast, the bond investment will mature at par, ensuring the return of the original $50,000. The important question for the couple is therefore "is the additional $4,000 in returns worth the risk that the original investment may be worth less than $50,000 in two years?"

The Importance of Context

Although we firmly reject the strategy of market timing, it is nevertheless prudent to look at market conditions in making such judgements. If, for example, the market has been on a rise for a number of years, an income-based investment strategy (involving, for instance, a short-term bond or income fund) is probably most suitable for a time frame of less than five years. If, on the other hand, the stock market has just declined by 20 percent, an equity-based strategy (that involves, for example, a balanced fund) is probably acceptable for time frames of more than three years. It is critical to remember, however, that evaluations of market conditions are only approximations at best. Assessments of needs and comfort level can be far more certain than judgements about the trend of the markets.

Comfort Level

Regardless of investors' objective capacity for risk, personal portfolios are only appropriate if they are consistent with investors' comfort levels. Experienced or knowledgeable investors may be able to manage their anxiety in the short-term, but in the long-term investors ignore their comfort levels at their peril. When prices decline significantly, risk averse investors are very likely to panic and to sell their investments, thereby transforming a potential loss into a real loss. If investors can't stomach the fact that the short-term price volatility of stocks and stock funds can be pronounced, a strategy of investing in stocks is unlikely to be successful.

For risk-averse investors, an income fund may be best. Slightly less nervous investors may be most comfortable with a balanced fund—not because it provides both income and growth but because the short-term volatility of these funds is typically lower than that of growth funds. This lower volatility may alleviate the worry. The questionnaire in Appendix M may assist in identifying your personal comfort level.

For shorter time horizons, an investor's objective capacity for risk is far more important; the factors that have to be considered are canvassed in Appendix I.

Managing the Portfolio

Reconciling Objectives

Since the most suitable investments for long-term objectives will often differ from those most appropriate for short- and medium-term objectives, the issue of reconciling objectives is important. For example, as more people choose (or are forced into) early retirement, achieving the objective of providing current income while growing capital to provide a retirement nest egg is an increasingly common scenario. It is also one of the most critical combinations because the demand for current income conflicts directly with the growth of an investment through reinvestment of returns.

There are a number of ways in which competing objectives can be managed.

- The best approach to combining the competing objectives of long-term growth and current income is to invest entirely in a growth fund, and use the systematic withdrawal plans offered by most mutual funds to obtain a current income. However, there are a couple of drawbacks with such an arrangement. The volatility of the portfolio may limit the short-term ability of the investment to meet its dual objectives. There will be times when the return on the investment amply covers both the need for current income and the requirement for growth. There may, however, also be times when the annual return from the investment is inadequate to meet even the requirement for current income, let alone the requirement for growth. In the early stages, this situation may deplete the capital of the investment to the point where it cannot grow large enough or fast enough to meet future needs. As a result, caution must be exercised in the use of such plans, particularly during the early years of an investment program, when the size of the accumulated investment is modest.

In addition, the size of the investment relative to the amount of current income required may be a problem. An investment with a value of $750,000 can almost certainly tolerate systematic withdrawals of $37,000 per year, but would probably be threatened by withdrawals of $100,000 per year.

Finally, this approach will be unattractive to highly risk averse investors, since an aggressive investment strategy usually involves considerable volatility.

- Another approach to reconciling the objectives of growth and income is to use balanced funds. The attraction of these funds is that they tend to be less volatile, and therefore expose investors needing current income to less risk of encroaching on the accumulated investment. The clear disadvantage is that the returns from such investments are generally lower in the long run, and while current income may be adequate, the growth of the investment for the future may not be.

- A third approach is to segregate assets for long- and medium-term objectives: use growth funds for retirement plans and an income fund to provide current income. This approach permits the long-term investment to grow without risk of encroachment, but it is often unsuitable for conservative or risk-averse investors because the short-term volatility of the growth fund portfolio is not tempered by less volatile securities. This situation can cause substantial anxiety and result in an impulsive sale at an inopportune time.

- An increasing number of mutual fund families and other financial services companies now offer comprehensive asset management systems or asset allocation services. These programs divide an investor's assets into a number of individual funds. The funds and the proportion of assets in each fund are chosen with the needs of the specific investor in mind, although the assets in any particular investment will be pooled and managed together with the assets of other investors. These so-called mutual fund wrap accounts are promoted as an opportunity for smaller investors to reap the benefits of strategic asset allocation.

In our view, the benefits of these systems are seriously overrated. Most of these systems are impersonal: very few can be tailored to meet an individual's needs. In addition, even the most sophisticated of these programs is based on the conventional approach to risk management, rather than on a true long-term investment policy.

How Many Funds Should You Have?

The short answer is "as many as necessary to meet your objectives." The long answer is that most people have too many funds. In part, this is because many investors want "a small position" in the latest hot fund as a sort of insurance—just in case the fund *does* defy both logic and experience. In part, though, it is because investors are encouraged to buy increasing numbers of funds especially in conjunction with asset allocation programs.

There is, of course, a danger in missing out on the right fund, and we'll deal with how to avoid that problem in the next chapter. However, the danger in owning too many funds is that the purpose of active investing is defeated. A 1995 U.S. study by Prudential Diversified Investment Strategies concluded, for example, that combinations of even two domestic growth funds would often merely imitate the performance of an index fund. It makes no sense to pay for active management if the result is the performance of a passive fund.

Similarly, a combination of regional funds may superficially approximate a truly global fund, but in assembling such a combination, the investor assumes responsibility for determining which regions offer the best opportunities. This approach defeats the purpose of paying for professional management, which is to benefit from specialized expertise in the choice of good investments.

Some analysts argue that holding multiple funds is necessary to reduce the risk of cyclical underperformance caused by a fund manager's investment style, but in our view this risk is virtually eliminated by time. Over five years, and certainly over ten or more years, performance differences driven by style will largely cancel out.

In our view, one well-diversified domestic growth fund and one global growth fund are entirely adequate for long-term objectives. If growth funds cause too much anxiety, balanced funds can be substituted. For medium-term objectives, one income fund is almost always adequate. If the time horizon is specific, bonds with a corresponding maturity are probably most suitable. For short-term objectives, mutual funds are often unsuitable.

Modifying Allocations

Sooner or later, long-term objectives become medium-term objectives, and medium-term objectives become short-term objectives. Since the investments that are appropriate to long-term and to short- or medium-term objectives are different, consideration has to be given to modifying the portfolio by changing the investments.

The problem is that short-term price volatility can temporarily depress the price of investments. This effect is most serious in equity investments. Although there is virtually no risk of loss in a properly diversified long-term equity investment, short-term price volatility can reduce the size of an investor's gains if prices are depressed at the time the investment is sold.

The solution is to begin considering how to realize maximum benefit from the investment three to five years prior to when the proceeds are required. Readjusting the portfolio gradually, during periods when the equity markets are performing strongly, by reallocating assets from growth investments (equities) to less volatile investments such as balanced funds or income funds, ensures that the gains of a long-term approach can be preserved. Even though the return of the replacement investments will be lower than that from growth funds, there is less risk that price fluctuations will result in depressed gains when the investment is finally redeemed. The pace and extent of the realignment to suit changing circumstances will depend on the investor's new time frame and comfort level and on market conditions.

The same approach is appropriate as medium-term objectives become short-term objectives. Depending on the investor's comfort level, investments should be shifted from income and balanced funds to cash-equivalent securities such as money market funds anywhere from one to three years before liquidation. Stocks are simply not the vehicle for ensuring that an investment can be redeemed on short notice. There is nothing as stressful as worrying about whether an investment will be sufficient for college tuition or the down payment on a house. Converting to less volatile securities can ensure that the proceeds of an investment are available when required.

A Final Note

The process of developing a useful and workable investment policy is neither rigid nor static. Approaches that reduce the process of identifying needs and defining objectives to the mechanical application of formulas may seem adequate in the short term, but are unlikely to prove effective over the long term. Perspective, thoughtfulness, and flexibility are at least as important to the process as information and technical skill.

A Note on Formula Investing

Formula investing is the financial equivalent of paint-by-numbers. Its appeal is that it is effortless: the various formulas reduce the details of investing to a few simple rules. However, these rules are dangerous because they create a false sense of security.

The Ten Percent Rule

The most mindless of these formulas is undoubtedly the "10 percent rule." According to this rule, everyone—without exception or regard for circumstances—should invest 10 percent of income in growth mutual funds or other long-term investments. While setting aside 10 percent may be appropriate for many investors at some stage in their investment careers, a doctrinaire approach to investing is always hazardous. There are those for whom saving as much as 10 percent is unnecessary. There are many, many more for whom saving 10 percent will be wholly inadequate.

Life Cycle Investing

Advocates of ***life cycle investing*** are also misguided. The basic premise of this approach is that every individual's investment can be divided into four stages, each with a different "risk tolerance":

- **accumulation**
  In this phase, the investor has a very long time horizon and anticipates increasing income, and risk tolerance can be quite high.

- **consolidation**
  During this phase, gains amassed in the first phase are "locked in." Risk tolerance is accordingly somewhat lower.

- **transition**
  The focus in this phase shifts from growth to income and the preservation of purchasing power. Risk tolerance is lower than in the consolidation phase.
- **distribution**
  Expenses exceed current income during this phase, and there is a greater need for liquidity to finance current expenses out of accumulated capital. Risk tolerance reaches its lowest point.

The life cycle approach to investing is exemplified by the following formula:

100 – age = percentage of portfolio in equities

where equities are "risky" investments. Thus, when the investor is young, the percentage of the portfolio that may suitably be held in equity investments is high. As one grows older, the percentage appropriately invested in equities decreases.

It is not hard to spot the flaws in this system.

- It ignores the fact that some investors are by nature more aggressive, and less risk averse, than others.
- While younger investors typically have long-term horizons, they also have short-term goals requiring less volatile investments that can be realized more readily. Conversely, a long-term perspective is still essential for older investors since they may require an income for 20 to 30 years following retirement. Sir John Templeton, who is well into his eighties, believes that equities should constitute a minimum of 90 percent of one's portfolio at any stage.

It is obvious that there will be many occasions when this formula will be inappropriate and one or another of these phases will be missed. The most likely scenario is that of an individual who realizes relatively late (at age 45 or 50) that it is important to provide for retirement. The formula suggests that only about half of this investor's portfolio should be growth stocks. But this investor has a lot of catching up to do if he or she expects to retire comfortably. A significant investment in equities is essential. And, since a 20-year investment (to age 70) is still entirely feasible, such an aggressive approach is completely appropriate despite what the life cycle formula states about the suitability of "risky" investments.

CHAPTER TWENTY

EVALUATING FUNDS

EXECUTIVE SUMMARY

This chapter provides a checklist for evaluating funds.

1. Evaluating funds has two objectives:
   - to enable investors to choose the funds that are most likely to meet their expectations
   - to identify those funds with the greatest likelihood of future success, by differentiating performance based on investment skill from performance based on luck

2. Meaningful evaluation starts with examination of the fund's objectives in relation to the needs and objectives of the investor.

3. Performance data is only one consideration in evaluating funds. A proper analysis requires examination of the qualitative considerations on which the performance record is based.

4. In the evaluation of performance records, it is the manager's record, rather than the fund's, that is important.

5. In the analysis of management, the following considerations are important:
   - investment approach
   - decision-making approach
   - customer services record

   Our view is that an investment approach based on a long-term perspective and on fundamental security analysis offers the greatest likelihood of long-term success.

6. Costs are almost always the least important consideration in evaluating funds.

INTRODUCTION

As we saw in the previous chapter, the first step in choosing mutual funds is to determine your needs. The identification of needs makes it much easier to establish concrete and explicit objectives, and to develop an investment policy that combines them effectively.

An investment policy is, however, only the first step in the development of a comprehensive investment program. In this chapter, we outline a logical process for choosing the mutual funds that are best suited to one's investment policy. We identify the factors that are basic to evaluating all mutual funds, and indicate how various criteria may be important in meeting objectives. It is intended that the process be useful both in choosing funds and in reviewing existing investments to ensure they continue to meet the investor's needs.

Since individuals have different objectives, the criteria for choosing funds will differ, and the relative importance of the various factors will necessarily vary. As we've indicated, the process of evaluation is not rigid. There are very few ironclad rules, and the process of weighing the importance of the various factors takes judgement and perspective.

There are five factors common to the assessment of all mutual funds:

- investment mandate
- performance
- investment approach
- customer service
- costs

The format we have chosen is to set out the important issues as questions, followed by commentaries that examine how and why the answers are useful in choosing funds. Where appropriate, we've included cross-references for further elaboration. Particularly important considerations are highlighted in bold.

Investment Mandate

A fund's investment mandate encompasses both its fundamental investment objectives and its investment policies. In the evaluation of the investment mandate, four considerations are important.

1. How clear is the fund's mandate?

The name of the fund is a notoriously poor way to determine the fund's mandate, and the objectives and policies specified in the prospectus are very often too vague to be helpful. The reputation of the fund or the fund's sponsor may be useful in assessing the accuracy of the description in the prospectus, but there is generally no substitute for evaluating the fund's investment portfolio over a number of years to determine definitively the fund's investment mandate.

2. How broad is the fund's mandate?

The broader the fund's mandate, the greater the discretion on the part of the manager to shape the fund's character. There are two points of view to consider:

- Investors may want to allow the manager the greatest possible latitude to maximize returns without constraint.
- Investors may want a fund to adhere closely to a specific mandate on which they can rely in constructing a personal investment portfolio.

Investors should recognize that the broader the mandate, the greater the potential for changes in the fund's risk profile.

3. How consistent is the fund's mandate?

The fund's mandate should be consistent over at least five, and preferably ten, years. **A track record based on a prior mandate is meaningless in evaluating performance.**

4. How risky is the fund's mandate?

Investors should consider the risk profile of the fund's mandate as well as the fund's performance profile. For example–

- Funds that invest in emerging markets typically entail greater risks than funds that invest in developed markets.
- In the evaluation of bond funds, the maturity and duration of the portfolio have a strong influence on the fund's risk profile. Investors should consider the manager's latitude in regulating the portfolio's maturity and duration.

- Funds that invest in derivatives may entail greater risks than funds that do not. Investors should carefully consider the extent to which derivatives are used, as well as the purpose and type of such investments.

Performance

Typically, fund assessment has been dominated by appraisals of performance data. There are a couple of reasons for this. Predicting returns involves speculation; past performance is real, concrete, and indisputable. This appeal is reinforced by those who market funds. It is much easier to sell the benefits of big numbers than the nuances of an investment approach. Finally, most investors think the question "how much will I make?" is the only important issue. Our view is that other factors are equally important, although they cannot be reduced to simple numbers. Nevertheless, performance data provides a starting point for identifying those funds with the greatest probability of superior future performance.

Answers to the following questions are helpful in evaluating performance.

5. What is the fund's long-term compound return?

Compound annual return describes an investor's experience in owning an investment over the reported period of time (Chapter 4), and is an essential element in the evaluation of performance. Although it is important to understand the shortcomings of compound annual return, they should not detract from the data's fundamental importance.

Long-term records are a far more reliable guide to future performance than short-term results, regardless of how spectacular the short-term numbers seem. A track record of five years is an absolute minimum. Our view is that a ten-year record is necessary to properly evaluate performance, but there are only a limited number of funds with a ten-year record, and many investors may find that standard too restrictive.

Investors should focus on funds with compound annual returns in the top two quartiles. A quartile is one-quarter, or 25 percent, of the funds in a particular group or class. The top quartile is the quarter of the group with the highest returns (Chapter 4).

A fund may have an excellent ten-year record even though its more recent performance has slipped somewhat. It is possible, for example, for a fund to post top-quartile performance over ten years, and second-quartile performance over the most recent five years. Conversely, it is possible for a fund to post second-quartile performance over ten years and top-quartile performance over the most recent five-year period.

Some sources regard recent results as more significant than more dated performance. In our view, this reflects an inappropriate short-term bias. The manager's style is a cyclical component of performance and an emphasis on more recent performance attracts investors to funds that employ the current "hot" style.

In the examination of compound returns, the following considerations are important:

- **Fund classifications must be reasonable.** It is important to look beyond the classification to ensure that funds within a particular class are truly comparable.

- **Compound returns provide no context.** Reducing performance to a single number makes it impossible to evaluate that performance in different market conditions. It is, for example, impossible to judge from compound annual return how well or poorly a fund performs in bear markets.

- **Compound returns minimize the significance of variations in performance.** Reducing performance to a single number obscures fluctuations in return. This makes it difficult to determine whether the performance of the fund is skewed by unusual performance in one or two years. In addition, a single indicator of overall performance does not permit an assessment of the consistency of the fund's returns.

6. How consistent is the fund's performance?

Year-over-year returns permit investors to evaluate the consistency of a fund's performance. The more consistent the performance, the greater the likelihood that the fund's compound annual return accurately indicates performance in the future. One way to evaluate the consistency of returns is to calculate a fund's modified compound return by eliminating the best and worst years from the performance record. The more closely this modified compound return corresponds to the actual compound return, the more consistent is the fund's performance (Appendix G).

Year-over-year returns also permit an investor to evaluate how the fund performs in a variety of market conditions. The performance of the fund in bear markets is of particular interest because it allows investors to judge worst case scenarios.

7. How often does the fund lose money?

The risk of loss is time-frame dependent and should be evaluated over a period of time that corresponds to the investor's anticipated holding period (Chapters 5 and 6). If, for example, the investor has a time horizon of ten years, the test should evaluate the number of ten-year holding periods in which the fund has declined in value.

8. How volatile is the fund?

Volatility is a poor indicator of total financial risk. The way in which volatility is measured does not reflect the fact that the risk of loss varies with the time frame of an investment. The time period over which the investment's volatility is measured should correspond to the anticipated holding period for the investment. In other words, if the investor anticipates holding the fund for ten years, the appropriate indicator is the volatility of the fund's ten-year compound returns. It is unhelpful to assess the volatility of a long-term investment on the basis of monthly price fluctuations (Appendix H).

Volatility is nevertheless useful in evaluating–

- the potential risk of loss in the event of a forced sale
- the degree of anxiety associated with an investment

Generally speaking, the higher the fund's volatility, the greater the anxiety it will cause.

Investment Approach

The investment approach describes the strategies and techniques used by the portfolio manager to achieve the fund's objectives. There are a number of different investment approaches, and some approaches are more appropriate than others.

In evaluating a portfolio manager's investment approach, a number of considerations are important.

9. What is the fund's investment approach?

The "declared" approach should be the actual approach. Descriptive terms such as *value*, *fundamental*, *growth*, *conservative* and *long-term* have very positive connotations and are widely used to describe a manager's investment strategy, even when they are inaccurate. Investors should be cautious in relying on a manager's "self-portrait." In addition, investors should ensure that the manager does not covertly rely on "techniques" such as market timing and closet indexing.

There are circumstances in which the passive management of an index fund is desirable or advantageous, provided the index is suitable.

The manager's investment approach should be disciplined. A manager that constantly changes his or her investment approach really has no approach. There are, of course, circumstances in which a change in the investment approach may be appropriate, but such changes should be gradual and infrequent. The manager should not modify the investment approach merely to bolster short-term returns.

Different investment approaches have different time horizons. Our view is that approaches based on short-term perspectives are less reliable and that funds with long term investment approaches are preferable. We are also of the view that, over the long term, the most successful approaches are based on the premise that equity investing is about buying *businesses* rather than about buying stocks.

The investor should be comfortable with the investment approach. Confidence in the merit of the approach will provide reassurance during times when the performance of the fund lags.

All investment approaches have cycles and perform better at some times than at others. Investors should avoid choosing funds that are attractive only because recent performance has been strong. By the same token, funds should not necessarily be rejected because of recent weak performance.

Caution must also be exercised when making the decision to change an existing investment. Investors rarely change investments when performance is strong. Typically, changes are made when performance has been lacklustre. It is therefore important to be sure before selling that the lag in performance is not merely temporary.

10. What is the portfolio manager's track record?

The track record of the fund is really the track record of the fund manager. The length of a fund's performance record is irrelevant if the manager responsible for the record no longer handles the fund. Conversely, a fund with a short performance record may be acceptable if the manager of the fund has experience handling other funds with similar investment mandates.

In evaluating track records, investors should note the following considerations:

- It is misleading to conclude that a manager who has exhibited success in managing a pension fund or closed-end fund will have similar success with open-end mutual funds. While success in managing other types of funds is superficially compelling, the particular characteristics of mutual funds mean that a manager's track record with other forms of investments will be of only limited use.
- Investors should also be extremely wary of track records derived from back-testing because they are based on the unlikely assumption that the future will be similar to the past.
- A change in the investment approach of the portfolio manager will invalidate a performance record based on a prior approach.
- Changes in management often result in changes in a fund's investment approach.
- Generally speaking, funds that are "for sale" by sponsors should be reviewed closely because the likelihood of management changes is substantial, regardless of the prior manager's record. The sale of the Bolton Tremblay funds to the BPI group in 1994 is typical: both in-house and contract managers of all but one of the BT funds were replaced.

11. How does the portfolio manager make decisions?

The way in which decision making is organized is extremely important. In our view, portfolio management based on a team approach is most conducive to stability and discipline in the investment approach. In this kind of arrangement, members of the management team work collaboratively, with shared views of the general investment policy, while focus and flexibility are secured by the ultimate decision-making authority of a lead manager.

The fact that a fund claims to be managed collectively should not be taken by itself as evidence of continuity in management. A collective management structure may be merely a way to disguise frequent changes in personnel.

The relationship between the portfolio managers and the fund sponsor is also important. Our view is that internal portfolio management is preferable because it contributes to the consistency of the investment strategy. In contrast, external or contract managers are more vulnerable to the temptation to seek high short-term results to avoid being fired for lacklustre performance. There will be occasions, however, when other considerations—such as performance or the desire for exposure to particular foreign markets—will outweigh the benefits of in-house management.

The length of a manager's relationship with a fund is important. If the fund managers have changed frequently in the past, it is probably a good bet that they will do so again.

Managers should be chosen on the basis of their investment acumen, and not on the basis of their marketing appeal. This is not to say that high-profile managers with market appeal cannot have financial ability. However, the priorities of funds with managers chosen primarily on the basis of marketing rather than financial considerations can conflict. No sponsor will acknowledge that its funds are driven by marketing considerations, but there is little doubt that marketing is far more important in some organizations than in others.

One of the most important considerations in assessing the management of mutual funds is the way in which management succession is provided for, since it is highly unlikely that the current manager of a fund will remain in place 15 to 20 years into the future.

12. What are the characteristics of the investment portfolio?

An examination of portfolio characteristics is helpful in a number of ways. Among other things, it can help in clarifying–

- the true objectives of the fund
- the risk profile of the fund
- the tax implications of the investment

It is a myth that small funds outperform large funds. By itself, the size of a fund is irrelevant. The following considerations are important:

- Some investment approaches work better in small funds than in large funds. In particular, strategies based on frequent trading and investment in speculative and illiquid securities are more suited to smaller funds. Although smaller funds have greater investment opportunities, this advantage does not appear to result in superior performance in either growth funds or income funds.
- Larger funds, and those that are part of a larger fund family, may have "deeper benches" from which to recruit new talent (Chapter 14). This may contribute to the stability of management, and therefore to the long-term consistency of a fund's performance.

The fund's general asset mix will provide an indication of both the objectives of the fund and the relative riskiness of the fund. The following considerations are relevant in examining the asset mix:

- Growth funds always invest primarily in equities. The aggressiveness of the fund is determined by the concentration and quality of the investments.
- Income funds choose a variety of investments: bonds, preferred shares, and dividend-paying common shares, mortgages, and MBSs. Watch out for income funds that are heavily weighted in equities: they are typically substantially more volatile and therefore inappropriate for investors uncomfortable with significant price fluctuations. For similar reasons, watch out for funds with longer average maturities and durations.
- Balanced funds combine the objectives of growth and income. The portfolios of funds that emphasize growth (such as the *Trimark Select Balanced Fund*) are composed primarily of equities; the portfolios of income-oriented funds have a greater proportion of income-earning investments.

The asset mix of a fund should be evaluated for a minimum of five years. The asset mix is never constant, and just as performance should be evaluated over a full market cycle, the character of the portfolio is best examined over a longer time frame.

The greater the degree of portfolio concentration, the riskier the fund. Since one of the major benefits of mutual funds is the reduction of risk through diversification, investors should be concerned about the extent to which a portfolio is concentrated in or overweighted with particular segments of the market. In evaluating portfolio concentration, investors should consider the following points:

- **While sector and other specialty funds are appropriate as niche investments, they should never be the core holding in an investment program.** Sector funds are deliberately overweighted (Chapter 12). It is also possible to overweight a fund with particular regions or particular qualities of investments. There is a place for these funds in some portfolios, but the accompanying level of risk makes them inappropriate for many investors.

- Even in "mainstream" or "broad-based" funds, some investment approaches, such as sector rotation, overweight the portfolio. In some cases, overweighting merely reflects the manager's view that a particular sector or region represents good value. However, a portfolio that is dramatically overweighted may indicate a strategy of market timing (Chapters 6 and 13). The extent to which a growth fund varies its cash position can also be indicative of an attempt to time the market.

Investors should investigate very carefully the degree to which derivatives are part of a fund's investment strategy or style. The risk level of derivatives varies. While the risk in some forms of derivatives is limited to the (generally) modest cost of an option, the risk in other forms of derivatives can be unlimited. The fact that most mutual funds that invest in derivatives claim to use them solely for limiting risk through hedges should not necessarily be interpreted as a guarantee of low risk because the boundary between a hedge and more aggressive uses is so vague (Chapter 3).

The manager of a fund with a portfolio that closely resembles the broader market may be employing a "strategy" of closet indexing. The management of these funds adds no value and should be avoided.

For funds held outside tax-sheltered plans, the asset mix has tax consequences. A fund portfolio composed of interest-bearing investments will attract greater tax liability than a portfolio composed of investments that generate dividend income or capital gains.

The quality of the fund's portfolio is important in assessing its risk profile. The following considerations are also important in assessing the credit quality of a fund:

- **credit rating**

  Volatility does not reflect the credit risk of income funds. It is therefore important to get a sense of the credit rating of the investments in a portfolio, to ensure that the fund is not boosting return by unduly reducing the average credit quality of the portfolio (Chapter 5).

- **reliance on appraised values**

  Determinations of an investment's value based on appraisals are less reliable than those indicated by the securities markets. This can be a particular concern in funds which use derivatives extensively (Chapter 3), labour-sponsored funds (Chapter 2), and real estate funds (Chapter 12)

- **investment in illiquid securities**

  Investors should determine the degree to which the performance record of a fund is based on investments in illiquid securities. Although such investments may constitute no more than 10 percent of a fund portfolio, the definition of *illiquid investment* is extremely vague. There are many, many investments that are illiquid, although they are not defined as such by Canadian securities regulators (Chapter 2).

- **use of derivatives**

  The risks of investing in derivatives are not apparent from performance data (Chapter 5). The market behaviour of derivatives can be quite different from that of other securities. Our view is that the potential for harm presented by derivatives generally outweighs their potential benefits.

13. What is the fund's portfolio turnover?

Portfolio turnover indicates the rapidity with which the fund's investments change. The greater the portfolio turnover, the greater the tax liability of the fund. For funds held outside tax-sheltered plans, a fund with high portfolio turnover will have relatively lower after-tax return than a fund with low portfolio turnover (Chapter 14).

Portfolio turnover can also have an effect on fund expenses. High turnover means high transaction costs.

Customer Service

In the evaluation of a fund's customer services, answers to the following questions are important:

14. How does the fund handle administrative issues?

Questions and difficulties should be resolved promptly. Errors inevitably occur from time to time. Funds maintain client services departments to handle precisely these sorts of issues, and independent financial services professionals should know which organizations have good reputations. Often, these professionals can help resolve problems, especially when they have an established relationship with the fund.

Do not be mesmerized by superfluous gimmicks. Features such as 24-hour "hotlines" and dial-in conference calls with the portfolio manager may seem attractive, but their contribution to enhanced investment value is doubtful.

15. How is the fund rated in independent surveys?

Data on the relative performance of no-load funds is generally not available. Both Marketing Solutions and Dalbar Inc. conduct research on the attitudes of the brokerage and financial planning industries toward various fund groups. In assessing the results of such studies, investors should look for funds and fund groups that meet a certain minimum level of customer service rather than focusing exclusively on funds or groups with the highest rankings. Customer service is important, but it should not dominate the evaluation of investment potential.

Costs

In our view, costs are generally the least important consideration in the evaluation of funds.

In evaluating costs, investors should ask the following questions.

16. Are the management fees and expenses consistent with industry norms?

For growth funds, the idea that "if expenses were lower, returns would be greater" is a myth. **It is immaterial whether fees are high or low, as long as the net returns are suitable.**

For income funds, costs are usually more important because there is generally less potential for the portfolio manager to outperform similar funds.

Only in money market funds and in index funds is the control of costs critical.

Changes in the level of fees are relevant to the performance record of a fund. If fees have gone up, investors should adjust the long-term performance record down at a comparable rate.

17. Is there a significant advantage to a particular sales charge or load?

It is a mistake to think of sales charges as merely the cost of processing the transaction. Much more important are the information, advice, expertise, and perspective that good financial services professionals offer in assisting investors to choose the most suitable funds.

No-load funds are not cost-free. If you insist on focusing on incremental differences in cost, make sure you are thorough in your investigation.

It is unreasonable to expect the in-house representatives of the no-load funds to paint a dispassionate view of the merits and drawbacks of their own funds.

A FINAL NOTE

The process of combining these considerations into a unified judgement about the suitability of a fund cannot be mechanical or rigid. As we indicated at the outset, the performance data must be tempered by thought, care, and knowledge of the objectives of the investor. While the process is not quick, perseverance will result in the selection of mutual fund investments that truly suit the needs of the individual investor.

CHAPTER TWENTY-ONE

A MUTUAL FUND SELECTION CHART

INTRODUCTION

In this chapter, we outline the steps in evaluating and choosing funds in flow-chart format. The charts are useful both in choosing new investments and in reviewing existing investments to ensure that they continue to meet your needs.

There are two flow charts: one for investments held outside tax-sheltered plans and one for tax-sheltered plans such as RRSPs. The purpose of the charts is to gradually narrow the number of funds being considered. While we regard these steps to be essential for choosing suitable funds, investors may nevertheless want to make changes or add their own considerations to the evaluation process.

Chart 1: Investments in Tax-sheltered Plans

Step 1

Determine your investment horizon and comfort level.

Table 21-1 provides a convenient way to identify the fund category most appropriate to your circumstances. See Part 2 and Chapter 19 for a fuller discussion.

Table 21-1. Funds Categorized by Time Horizon and Comfort Level

	Highly Conservative	Moderately Conservative	Aggressive
Less than 3-5 years	Money market fund	Short-term bond (income) fund	Balanced fund
More than 3-5 years	Short-term bond (income) fund	Balanced fund or Long-term bond fund or Dividend fund	Growth fund

Step 2

Do you want a foreign asset fund?

If yes: Go to Step 3.
If no: Go to Step 6.

Step 3

Have you already maximized your allowable foreign content?

If yes: Go to Step 4.
If no: Go to Step 5.

Step 4

Do you want to exceed allowable foreign content through the use of derivative-based funds?

If yes: Identify qualifying funds.
A foreign fund that is eligible for 100 percent of the RRSP's assets almost certainly uses derivatives to achieve its objectives. See Chapter 3 and Appendix F for a fuller discussion of derivatives.
Go to Step 5.

If no: Using derivative-based funds is the only way in which you may exceed foreign content limits. If you do not want to invest in a derivative-based fund, you must invest in a domestic fund.
Go to Step 6.

Step 5

What kind of foreign or international fund do you want?

- global
- regional
- country
- emerging markets

See Part 2 for a discussion of the different fund categories.
Look at the investment mandate and portfolio composition of the fund to evaluate the fund's objectives.

Is the degree of diversification adequate for your comfort level?

If yes: Go to Step 8.
If no: Re-evaluate your choice.

Step 6

What kind of domestic fund do you want?

- large-cap or small-cap
- concentrated or broad-based

See Part 2 for a discussion of the different fund categories.
Look at the investment mandate and portfolio composition of the fund to evaluate the fund's objectives.

Is the degree of diversification adequate for your comfort level?

If yes: Go to Step 7.
If no: Re-evaluate your choice.

Step 7

Choose funds with a five- to ten-year track record.

See Chapter 4 for an explanation of the importance of track records of at least five years. Our view is that the ten-year compound annual return is the appropriate standard, but there are a very limited number of funds with ten-year records, and many people may find this standard too restrictive. A list of funds with a five-year track record as of December 31, 1996 is included in Part 5. Inevitably, however, this list will become outdated. Chapter 23 suggests a number of sources for finding current information in the future. The track record of the fund should encompass a full market cycle, including performance in a bear market. The five-year track records for funds listed in Part 5 do not encompass performance in a bear market.

Step 8

Of the funds chosen, identify those with a five-year compound annual return in the top two quartiles.

This data is available from any of the mutual fund database services. See Chapter 23 for a review of the services available. Our view is that top-quartile ranking over a ten-year period is necessary, but there are a very limited number of funds with ten-year records, and many people may find this standard too restrictive. See Chapter 4 for a discussion of quartiles and the limitations of five-year records.

Step 9

Of the funds remaining, identify those with good management.

This information is available from a variety of sources, including mutual fund database services and the fund companies themselves. See Chapter 14 for a discussion of the important considerations. A manager's track record with other comparable funds is relevant to the quality of management.

Step 10

Of the funds remaining, identify those with consistent records.

The consistency of the record can be determined only from a comparison of annual returns. Look, for example, at the range of annual returns, the number of years the fund loses money, and the extent of those losses. See Chapter 23 for sources for this data.

Step 11

What are the costs of the fund?

It is important to keep the issue of costs in perspective. In the long term, differences of 0.5 percent shouldn't be an important consideration. See Chapter 18 for a more detailed discussion of the issue of costs.

Step 12

Re-evaluate your choice.

- Does it meet your needs?
- Is it compatible with your comfort level?
- How does its long-term performance compare with that of other funds?

Chart 2: Investments outside Tax-Sheltered Plans

Step 1

Determine your investment horizon and comfort level.

Table 21-2 below provides a convenient way to identify the fund category most appropriate to your circumstances. See Part 2 and Chapter 19 for a fuller discussion.

Table 21-2. Funds Categorized by Time Horizon and Comfort Level

	Highly Conservative	Moderately Conservative	Aggressive
Less than 3-5 years	Money market fund	Short-term bond (income) fund	Balanced fund
More than 3-5 years	Short-term bond (income) fund	Balanced fund or Long-term bond fund or Dividend fund	Growth fund

Step 2

What kind of fund do you want?

- large-cap or small-cap
- concentrated or broad-based
- global
- regional
- country
- emerging markets

See Part 2 for a discussion of the different fund categories.
Look at the investment mandate and portfolio composition of the fund to evaluate the fund's objectives.

Is the degree of diversification adequate for your comfort level?

If yes: Go to Step 3.
If no: Re-evaluate your choice.

Step 3

Choose funds with a five- to ten-year track record.

See Chapter 4 for an explanation of the importance of track records of at least five years. Our view is that the ten-year compound annual return is the appropriate standard, but there are a very limited number of funds with ten-year records, and many people may find this standard too restrictive. A list of funds with a five-year track record as of December 31, 1996 is included in Part 5. Inevitably, however, this list will become outdated. Chapter 23 suggests a number of sources for finding current information in the future.

The track record of the fund should encompass a full market cycle, including performance in a bear market. The five-year track records for funds listed in Part 5 do not encompass performance in a bear market.

Step 4

Of the funds chosen, identify those with a five-year compound annual return in the top two quartiles.

This data is available by subscribing to any of the analytical services. Our view is that top-quartile ranking over a ten-year period is necessary, but there are a very limited number of funds with ten-year records, and many people may find this standard too restrictive. See Chapter 4 for a discussion of quartiles and of the limitations of five-year records.

Step 5

Of the funds remaining, identify those with good management.

This information should be available from fund companies. See Chapter 14 for a discussion of the important considerations. A manager's track record with a comparable fund is relevant to the quality of management.

Step 6

Of the funds remaining, identify those with consistent records.

The consistency of the record can be determined only from a comparison of annual returns. Look, for example, at the range of annual returns, the number of years the fund loses money, and the extent of those losses. See Chapter 23 for sources for this data.

Step 7

What are the costs of the fund?

It is important to keep the issue of costs in perspective. In the long term, differences of 0.5 percent shouldn't be an important consideration. See Chapter 18 for a more detailed discussion of the issue of costs.

Step 8

Re-evaluate your choice.

- Does it meet your needs?
- Is it compatible with your comfort level?
- How does its long-term performance compare with that of other funds?

CHAPTER TWENTY-TWO

CASE STUDIES

INTRODUCTION

In this chapter we present four case studies, which are designed to show–

- how the flow chart is applied in practice
- which specific mutual funds we think are appropriate
- when investments other than mutual funds are appropriate

The studies are based on real cases. The names have been changed, and the facts somewhat simplified to emphasize particular issues, but there is nothing artificial about the circumstances.

Mr. and Mrs. Black

Jim and Mary Black are married and live in Ontario. Both are in their early forties, and both are employed.

Beginning in 1990, both Jim and Mary decided to begin investing in RRSPs.

Jim had had previous experience with mutual funds and can tolerate moderate volatility. Mary's previous investing experience had been limited to GICs, and a review of her comfort level (using a questionnaire similar to the one in Appendix M) revealed a significant aversion to the price fluctuations of stocks.

While both felt that early retirement would be nice, they realistically expected (and continue to expect) to work until age 65. Their respective investment horizons were therefore between 20 and 25 years.

Jim's investment horizon, his previous experience, and his tolerance of volatility suggested that growth funds would be the most suitable investment for him.

Since the potential returns from foreign investments typically exceed those from domestic funds, Jim was anxious to maximize the foreign content of his RRSP. However, because he was starting with a single foreign fund, he wanted to keep it as broadly based as possible. As a result, he restricted his search to global funds rather than regional funds.

At the beginning of 1990, there were ten true global or international equity funds with ten-year track records:

- *Bolton Tremblay International Fund*
- *CGF International Growth Fund*
- *Cambridge Diversified Fund*
- *Cundill Value Fund*
- *Fonds Desjardins International*
- *Guardian Global Equity Fund*
- *Montreal Trust Excelsior International Fund*
- *Templeton Growth Fund*
- *United Venture Fund*
- *Viking International Fund*

The *Fonds Desjardins International* is not available in Ontario. Of the remaining nine, the six funds with the highest ten-year compound annual return are listed in Table 22-1.

Table 22-1. Funds with Highest Ten-Year Compound Annual Return at the Beginning of 1990

	Compound Annual Return		
	5-Year 1980–1984 (%)	5-Year 1980–1984 (%)	10-Year 1980–1989 (%)
BT International	20.5	15.1	19.3
Cundill Value	21.5	14.1	18.0
Templeton Growth	15.8	16.4	16.6
Viking International	18.3	13.2	15.9
MT Excelsior International	13.3	16.0	15.8
Guardian Global	16.8	14.2	15.6

Of these funds, the performance of the *Templeton Growth Fund* is significantly more consistent than any of the others, as the data in Table 22-1 shows.

The management of the Templeton fund has been extremely stable; until 1988, Templeton himself administered the portfolio, and he continued to play an important supervisory role after Mark Holowesko assumed day-to-day responsibility. The discipline and rigour of the Templeton approach is well documented.

On the basis of this analysis then, Jim chose the *Templeton Growth Fund* for the foreign content portion of his RRSP.

For the Canadian component of his plan, Jim employed the same sort of analysis. One of the strongest funds over the previous five- and ten-year periods was Mackenzie Financial's *Industrial Growth Fund*. However, the *Trimark Canadian Fund*, managed by Robert Krembil, had marginally outperformed the Mackenzie fund over the preceding five years. Although the Trimark fund did not have a ten-year track record, Krembil's ten-year record was impeccable. Prior to starting the Trimark funds, he and his team had managed the *Bolton Tremblay Canada Cumulative Fund* and the *Bolton Tremblay Taurus Fund*, both of which had outstanding long-term performance records. Jim also felt more comfortable with the bottom-up stock-picking approach employed by Krembil than with the top-down approach employed by Alex Christ at the *Mackenzie Financial Industrial Growth Fund.*

Mary also wanted an investment with strong growth potential. However, she realized—given her previous investing experience and her psychological profile—that she might be uncomfortable with volatility, and accordingly focused her attention on balanced funds. In 1990, there were 11 balanced funds with a ten-year track record available in Ontario. One of these was an affinity fund with restricted circulation. Four were segregated funds, which Mary chose to avoid because they were subject to less rigorous supervision of their investment objectives. One was sold only by sales agents of the fund sponsor, and two were no load funds that were generally not sold through the broker network. Given the conflict between her desire for growth, and her aversion to volatility, Mary recognized the importance of ongoing advice and guidance, and felt that it was important to purchase a fund through a registered broker. Of the three remaining funds, none was attractive, either because the size of the fund's bond portfolio limited returns too much, or because the investment strategy was based on attempts to "time" investment decisions, or because the current manager was not responsible for the fund's track record.

Because her husband had invested in a Trimark fund, Mary examined Trimark's balanced fund, the *Trimark Growth and Income Fund.* It was strongly oriented to stocks: a bond component of only about 30 percent provided moderated fluctuations in price without severely impairing returns. Its investment approach was bottom-up stock picking. Although it lacked a five-year track record, Mary took considerable comfort from the superior track record of the manager's other funds. It is important to note, however, that it was only because her expectations were best met with a fund oriented towards equities that the prior record of Trimark's management was relevant. Had she wanted a fund with a greater emphasis on bonds, the Trimark fund would not have been the most appropriate choice.

Since 1990, Mary's investment policy has changed somewhat. Having developed some familiarity and confidence with the way in which a mutual fund investment grows, she has used RRSP contributions for 1992 and 1993 to acquire growth funds for both the domestic and foreign content portions of the plan.

It is interesting to note that Mary's move from GICs to mutual funds took place well before the emergence of "GIC refugees" seeking better returns than those available from fixed-income investments in 1992 and 1993. It is particularly interesting to note that Mary's experience with mutual funds encouraged her to take a slightly more aggressive investment stance. Most telling is the fact that she did not seek to scale back her exposure to growth funds in the wake of the cyclical downturn that occurred in early 1994.

Mr. Brown

Mr. Brown is 70 years old. He has considerable experience in investing in the stock market, and has fairly well diversified holdings, with a current value of about $1 million. In 1991, he became interested in the potential of the Far East markets and wanted to make an investment in the region. He liked the format of mutual funds because they provided "instant diversification," permitting him to invest easily in a cross-section of the market.

In 1991 there were four funds with a five-year track record investing in the Far East, three of which were devoted exclusively or predominantly to Japan. Brown was not interested in the funds specializing in Japanese investments, and rejected the *CI Pacific Fund* because it employs a top-down investment style, which Brown felt depended too much on the manager's guesses about economic developments.

Of the four funds with track records of one or two years, none was associated with a manager with a well-entrenched investment discipline. However, both AGF and Fidelity introduced Asian funds in 1991. Although neither had a track record, Fidelity's bottom-up stock-picking investment discipline was well known. Because Fidelity offered similar funds in the United States, the United Kingdom, and various countries in Southeast Asia, the company could provide a substantial pool of management and research expertise on which the new manager of the *Fidelity Far East Fund* could draw. Shortly after the *Fidelity Far East Fund* was established in September 1991, Brown invested $10,000. Since Brown's portfolio is relatively large, the specialized investment that a regional fund represents was appropriate.

Ms Green

Ms Green is 64 years old. She is widowed, with no dependent children. She has taken an offer of early retirement and has been given a lump-sum severance equal to the commuted present value of her pension—about $245,000—with which she has established a LIF, which is similar to a RRIF. She also has an RRSP with a value of about $130,000. From this capital, she requires an income of about $20,000 which will rise as inflation erodes its earning power. Her previous investing experience has been limited to GICs, and she is unaccustomed to the volatility of the stock market.

Given her age and lack of sophistication, Green's requirements are most appropriately met with a portfolio that is comprised only partly of mutual funds. Within the LIF, she has invested approximately $45,000 in five-year non-prepayable MBSs, and a further $20,000 in three-year prepayable MBSs. Finally, she has purchased about $45,000 in one-year T-bills. This capital, together with the income it generates, will provide a guaranteed income of $20,000 for the next eight years. To provide the groundwork for the future, Green has invested the remaining $130,000 in eight-year strip bonds yielding 9.5 percent and in a growth mutual fund.

The strip bonds were chosen for reasons related to Green's risk aversion. Most importantly, their future rate of return is known with certainty. In addition, this return is very attractive in the present economic context and will more than meet Green's anticipated requirements.

In choosing the mutual fund, Green and her financial adviser considered a number of factors. Given Green's circumstances, superior returns are essential to secure income for the future. Her nest egg is quite small and therefore particularly vulnerable to the potential ravages of inflation. However, since Green has no experience with mutual funds, it is important to ensure that she is comfortable with the investment, since premature or inopportune withdrawal could seriously jeopardize the security of future income.

Since foreign investments have historically provided returns that are superior to those on Canadian investments, an international or global fund is preferable. To ensure that the foreign content of the LIF does not exceed 20 percent of book value, the mutual fund investment has been limited to $45,000.

Of the various global funds available, Green has chosen the *Templeton*

Growth Fund because of both the consistency of its long-term performance and the stability of its management. For Green, the fund's track record of more than 15 percent over 40 years provides enormous reassurance.

Green's other major investment asset is her RRSP. It is composed of GICs, each of which constitutes a separate RRSP account. The GICs have a variety of maturity dates and no foreign content.

As part of Green's overall financial plan, the RRSP needs to be rationalized. Since the proceeds of the RRSP will not be required for at least ten years, a more aggressive investment stance is tolerable in the RRSP than in the LIF. Based on the fact that the LIF could easily fund her expenses for that period of time, Green thought that she would be comfortable with about 50 percent of the RRSP portfolio invested in stocks and the remainder invested in strip bonds. It is important to stress that there is no magic in these percentages: they are dictated entirely by the comfort level of the investor.

The portfolio of GICs has been reviewed. The proceeds of those that can be terminated early with no penalty have been used to buy strip bonds and mutual funds. As the remaining GICs mature, their proceeds will be used to acquire additional bonds and fund units.

The full 20 percent foreign content of the RRSP is invested in the *Templeton Growth Fund*, rather than the potentially more volatile *Templeton Global Smaller Companies Fund*, and the remainder of the domestic component of the RRSP is invested in the *Trimark Select Canadian Growth Fund*.

Mr. White

Mr. White is 42 years old and married, with two children, aged 8 and 4. Although he fully expects that they will go to university, he wants to ensure that he has the resources to provide them with the opportunity to pursue their goals, whatever they may be, without seriously straining his resources. He recognizes that the cyclical nature of his commission-driven income may constrain his ability to assist them at the relevant time.

A possible solution to White's situation would have been to purchase an RESP. The chief benefit of such a plan is that income from contributions to the plan (up to $1,500 per year) is tax sheltered. The principal drawback of RESPs is that the purposes to which such an investment can be put are limited.

Because his time horizon was relatively long, White chose instead to establish an informal trust by purchasing mutual funds in the names of his children. This alternative provides more flexibility than an RESP in the uses for the proceeds, but it lacks the tax-free growth offered by a formal plan. It is possible, however, to manage the tax considerations of such an informal plan. Only realized capital gains are taxable, and by choosing a fund with low portfolio turnover, White could minimize the extent to which gains are realized. In addition, by choosing a fund which earns the bulk of its returns from capital gains as opposed to interest or dividend income, White could minimize his tax liability. Interest and dividends are taxable in the hands of the trust's contributor while capital gains are taxable in the hands of the beneficiary. Since the child's tax rate is typically much lower than that of the parent, the tax liability will be smaller.

The investment is not restricted in any way because it is not part of a formal plan. Since returns from funds that invested abroad have historically been superior to returns from funds that invest mainly in Canada, White decided to invest in foreign funds. He has decided that global funds, rather than more narrowly focused regional or country funds, are most suitable, and has diversified his investment by purchasing two funds that complement each other.

Of the funds available with a ten-year track record, White particularly likes the *Templeton Growth Fund*. It has a very stable management team and a strong investment discipline. Of particular interest is the fund's distribution policy which is specifically intended to defer taxes by minimizing the payment of dividends.

White also likes the *Templeton Global Smaller Companies Fund*. Although it does not have a ten-year track record, it is attractive for a couple of reasons. It shares the management discipline of the *Templeton Growth Fund*. In addition, smaller companies present better investment bargains than large-cap stocks, which the *Templeton Growth Fund* emphasizes. Finally, by choosing two funds with the same manager, White ensures that the combination will not "water down" the investment strategy.

The most important risk associated with growth funds is the possibility that the fund will have to be sold during a cyclical market low, thereby reducing the potential return from the investment. In White's case, a number of factors combine to limit this risk. First, because the proceeds from the fund are expected to be used for university education, not all the proceeds will be required at once. Second, it is always possible to shift the funds into a less volatile fund closer to the date when the proceeds of the fund will be required. Finally, if other resources permit, it may be possible for White to meet some of the costs of university using current income and "repay" himself when the mutual fund is sold at a more advantageous time.

CHAPTER TWENTY-THREE

SOURCES OF INFORMATION

INTRODUCTION

A proper evaluation of mutual funds requires information. The better informed an investor is, the more likely it is that the chosen investments will be appropriate to his or her circumstances.

There are two types of information that is relevant to investors. First, general information about economic and financial circumstances is important because it places the performance of mutual funds in context. For example, information about anticipated trends in interest rates may help investors decide whether short-term bond funds or money market funds are appropriate for fund investments of up to about five years. Second, specific information about mutual funds is necessary both to assess how well a particular fund meets one's objectives and to make choices between funds with similar objectives.

Not all information is equally useful. Some information is objective: daily newspaper reports of fund net asset values are an example. However, a great deal of information is much less objective: it is part of a report with a point of view. While information is not useless simply because it has a particular slant, it is important to bear the slant or perspective in mind when assembling and reviewing data.

Information is available from a multitude of sources. Among the most prominent are–

- mutual fund companies
- newspapers

- financial services professionals
- newsletters
- independent databases
- electronic media

We'll look at each of these in some detail.

In addition, articles covering every conceivable aspect of mutual funds appear constantly in the popular press. While the quality varies considerably these articles sometimes provide useful insights and pieces of information that can contribute to the investor's overall knowledge.

Mutual Fund Companies

As we stated in Chapter 2, mutual funds are required to provide investors with the following documents.

Prospectus

Typically, the information regarding the investment objectives and relative "riskiness" of the fund is too general to be of real assistance. While the information regarding fees, dividends and distributions, and redemptions is usually detailed, our view is that it is relatively unimportant.

Annual Reports

The annual report and semi-annual reports (including the financial statements) provide useful information about the fund on an ongoing basis, although such data is usually somewhat dated by the time it is distributed. A review of a number of reports may, however, give some indication of the portfolio turnover of the fund and the general extent to which the portfolio is concentrated in particular sectors.

The annual report also often provides some information about the manager. There is frequently an indication of the manager's basic investment approach and outlook, and changes in the personnel responsible for portfolio management are sometimes disclosed.

Account Statements

Account statements provide investors with important information on how their personal investments are performing. Many fund companies are striving to improve the quality of the statements, and many now indicate the investor's overall rate of return.

Annual Information Form

Investors are entitled to this document but must generally request it. This document is essentially a supplement to the prospectus, but it contains virtually no greater detail on the important issues of investment objectives and risk factors.

Marketing and Promotional Material

Fund companies inundate clients and prospective clients with promotional and marketing information. While this material is clearly intended to portray the funds in the best possible light, it nevertheless includes useful data. Typically, such publications outline historical performance and identify the asset mix of the fund. For growth funds, this material may include a breakdown of investments by sector or geographical region; for income funds, it may specify term to maturity and credit qualities.

This marketing material can also often provide some information about the investment strategy of the fund, but it is important not to put too much stock in the management's own description of the investment approach or strategy unless these descriptive claims are supported by other evidence. Words such as *growth, value, long-term,* and *fundamental* are very subjective and can easily convey an impression that is not justified by the facts. Look for clues that reveal discrepancies between the claim and the reality. For example, a fund whose portfolio changes substantially from one year to the next while professing a bottom-up approach to security selection is either confused or unsure about its real investment strategy.

Newspapers

Daily Quotations

All the major daily newspapers publish daily reports on mutual fund performance. In most cases, the data is received from Fundata Canada Inc. and is therefore identical from paper to paper. The excerpt from the *Globe and Mail* in Table 23-1 is representative.

The first column is the fund name. In the daily fund quotations, names of funds are listed alphabetically by fund group. Money market funds are listed separately because the data reported for these funds is different. We'll look at them later.

The second column contains various letters that are codes for various features. The meaning of the codes is explained in the legend at the beginning of the section. The codes differ from paper to paper, so it's important to read the legend.

Most of the codes are self-evident, but a few require explanation.

- *Z* indicates that the fund is an "affinity" fund, the sales of which are restricted to certain groups. Sales of *MD Growth Fund*, for example, are restricted to members of the Canadian Medical Association and their families.

- *x* denotes *ex dividend*, which signifies that the net asset value is quoted after the most recent distribution has been deducted.

- *n* indicates that the fund sponsor is not a member of the Investment Funds Institute of Canada. This agency is part watchdog, part lobby group, and part educator.

The third column indicates the net asset value (per share) of the fund. As we mentioned in Chapter 2, this is the total value of all the securities in the mutual fund portfolio, less any liabilities, divided by the total number of outstanding shares or units in the fund. As the price of the securities in the fund portfolio changes, this value changes as well.

Table 23-1. Daily Mutual Fund Quotations

Recent prices of investment funds supplied by Fundata Canada Inc. at 6:00 p.m. June 30. Prices reported by funds are the net asset value per share or unit last calculated and are for information purposes only. Confirmation of price should be obtained from the fund. Chg—penny change from last valuation; D—distributed by fund sponsor; G—redemption charge; I—distributed by independent dealers; L—sales charge; N—no sales charge; O—optional front—end or redemption charge;B—choice of front or back redemption charge; R—eligible for RRSPs; Z—not available for sale; m—minimum purchase of $150,000; u—U.S. currency; x—ex—dividend; (n)—not a member of IFIC; (Date following fund denotes last valuation).

Fund	Load	RSP	Dist	Val	Chg
ABAX(n)					
uBradys Oblig 06/26	L		I	10.82	—
ABC FUNDS					
mAmer-Value 05/30	N		D	5.66	—
mFully-Mgd 05/30	N	R	D	8.27	—
mFund-Value 05/30	N	R	D	12.41	—
ACADIA INVESTMENT FUNDS					
Balanced 06/27	N	R		12.79	+.02
Bond 06/27	N	R		11.44	-.00
Mortgage 06/27	N	R		10.02	unch
AGF GROUP OF FUNDS					
20/20 Aggr Gbl	O		I	5.87	-.02
20/20 Aggr Gth	O		I	15.12	+.10
20/20 Cdn Res	O	R	I	21.69	+.10
20/20 Emerg Mkt	O		I	5.16	-.03
20/20 India	O		I	2.26	+.04
20/20 Latin Am	O		I	8.18	-.03
20/20 Mgd Fut	O	R	I	6.37	+.03
20/20 RSP Ag Eq	O	R	Z	6.41	+.01
20/20 RSP Ag Sm	O	R	I	5.51	unch
AGF Amer Grth	O		I	18.87	-.10
AGF Amer TAA	O		I	17.37	-.02
AGF Asian Grth	O		I	16.28	unch
AGF Cda Class	O		I	5.95	+.05
xAGF Cdn Bond	O	R	I	5.44	-.03
AGF Cdn Equity	O	R	I	14.53	+.11
AGF Cdn Growth	O	R	I	20.95	+.09
AGF Cdn TAA	O	R	I	5.24	unch
Amer Equ Valu	O		I	9.16	-.04
Amer Small Co	O		I	32.68	+.50
Asia Pacific	O		I	11.31	+.04
Cdn Balanced	O	R	I	5.35	-.02
xCdn Bond	O	R	I	4.95	-.04
Cdn Equ Value	O	R	I	9.51	+.03
Cdn Mid-Cap	O	R	I	10.00	—
Cdn Resource	O	R	I	19.07	+.01
Cdn Small Co	O	R	Z	12.51	+.13
xDiv Income	O	R	I	12.20	+.03
Emer Markets	O		I	14.96	-.01
Glo Bal RSP	O	R	I	15.79	unch
Glo Equity	O		I	23.15	-.05
xGlo RSP Bond	O	R	I	10.69	-.06
Glo Small Co	O		I	20.50	+.11
xHigh Income	O	R	I	10.71	unch
Inc & Growth	O	R	I	10.00	—
Intl Equ Val	O	R	I	10.00	—
BPI MUTUAL FUNDS U$					
uAmer Equ Val U$	O		I	6.65	-.01
uAmer Sml Co U$	O		I	23.71	+.40
uAsia Pacific U$	O		I	8.21	+.05
uEmer Markets U$	O		I	10.85	+.01
uGlo Equity U$	O		I	16.80	unch
uGlo Small Co U$	O		I	14.87	+.10
uIntl Equ Val U$	O	R	I	7.26	—
CALDWELL SECURITIES					
Amer Equity	O	R		5.00	—
Associate	O	R		7.42	-.09
Cdn Equity	O	R		5.00	—
Cdn Income	O	R		5.00	—
International	O			6.02	-.06
CAMAF(n)					
Camaf 06/20	N	R	D	14.49	—
CANADA TRUST					
AmeriGrowth	N	R	D	12.82	-.10
AsiaGrowth	N	R	D	10.15	+.06
xBalanced	N	R	D	18.22	-.01
xBond	N	R	D	11.97	-.07
xDiv Income	N	R	D	14.88	+.01
EmergMkts	N		D	13.28	-.03
EuroGrowth	N	R	D	11.57	-.12
GlobalGrowth	N	R	D	11.32	-.06
xIntl Bond	N	R	D	10.37	-.02
Intl Equ	N		D	26.08	-.07
xMortgage	N	R	D	60.44	-.05
North Amer	N		D	44.73	+.01
xRetirement Bal	N	R	D	10.00	-.02
xSht Term Bnd	N	R	D	10.18	-.04
Special Equity	N	R	D	24.20	+.19
Stock	N	R	D	20.95	+.04
US Equity	N		D	20.11	-.04
CAPSTONE GROUP(n)					
Internat'l	N		I	7.42	-.04
Investment 06/27	N	R	I	8.15	—

Source: *Fundata Canada Inc.* and the *Globe and Mail*

The fourth column indicates any change in the net asset value from the previous quotation. Most funds quote net asset value daily, but not all do. Real estate funds, in particular, are required to quote net asset values only quarterly. The newspaper quotations typically indicate the date of the price quotation, if that day is not for the most recent trading day.

Daily fluctuations in the net asset value are unimportant. What is important, although it does not appear in the daily newspaper quotations, is the gradual rise or fall in the net asset value. However, since the rise and fall of this value does not reflect the value of distributions and dividends, analysis of simple changes in net asset value is unreliable as a method of calculating returns.

Money market fund quotations are somewhat different, as the sample in Table 23-2 illustrates.

Table 23-2. Daily Money Market Fund Quotations

MONEY MARKET FUNDS

Cur—current yield (actual return over past 7 days, annualized); Eff—effective yield. Effective yield includes compounding. Yields will vary; Chg—change from previous yield.

Fund	Dist	Cur	Eff	Chg
ACADIA INVESTMENT FUNDS				
MMF 09/19		1.76	1.78	+.08
AGF FUNDS INC.				
xMMF	I	1.70	1.71	unch
xuUS MMF	I	4.50	4.60	unch
AIC GROUP				
MMF	I	2.46	2.48	+.01
AIM MUTUAL FUNDS C$				
Cash Prf	I	2.77	2.81	+.20
ALLSTAR FUND GROUP LTD.				
Money Market	D	2.44	2.47	unch
ALTAMIRA				
T-Bill	I	3.06	3.11	+.01
ATLAS ASSET MGT: ATLAS				
uAm MMF	I	4.52	4.62	-.00
MMF	I	2.27	2.30	+.01
T-Bill	I	2.04	2.06	-.03
BANK OF MONTREAL				
FC MMF	D	2.36	2.39	-.10
FC T-Bill	D	2.27	2.30	-.05
BEUTEL GOODMAN(n)				
MMF	I	3.10	3.15	-.01
BISSETT				
MMF		3.28	3.33	-.10
BNP (CANADA) FUNDS				
MMF 09/19	D	2.06	2.08	-.32
BPI MUTUAL FUNDS				
T-Bill	I	2.93	2.97	+.02
uUS MMF		4.69	4.80	-.02
CANADA TRUST				
MMF	D	2.42	2.45	+.01
Pr MMF	D	2.80	2.84	+.03
CAPSTONE GROUP(n)				
Cash	I	2.66	2.70	-.00
CI MUTUAL FUNDS C$				
MMF	I	2.67	2.71	unch
CI MUTUAL FUNDS U$				
uU$ MMF	I	4.83	4.95	+.01
CIBC FUNDS				
Cdn TBill	D	2.39	2.42	+.01
MMF	D	2.62	2.65	+.02
mPrem TBill	D	2.80	2.84	+.02
uUS MMF	D	4.44	4.54	unch
CLARINGTON GROUP OF FUNDS				
MMF	I	2.11	2.13	+.03
CONCORDE				
MMF 09/19	I	2.77	2.81	+.02
CORNERSTONE				
Govt M	D	2.25	2.27	+.01
DESJARDINS FUNDS				
MMF 09/19	D	3.01	3.05	+.01
DYNAMIC MUTUAL FUNDS				
xDyn MMF	I	2.00	2.02	-.02
ELLIOTT & PAGE				
EP Mon	I	2.72	2.76	unch
T-Bill	I	1.47	1.48	unch
EMERALD PRIVATE CAPITAL				
MMF	D	2.57	2.60	-.01
ETHICAL FUNDS				
MMF	I	2.45	2.48	+.06
FICADRE FUNDS				
MMF 09/19	D	3.15	3.20	-.01
FIDELITY INVESTMENTS C$				
CdnST	I	2.20	2.22	unch
FIDELITY INVESTMENTS U$				
uUS MMF	I	4.32	4.41	unch
GBC FUNDS(n)				
MMF 09/16	I	2.39	2.42	—
GLOBAL STRATEGY				
MMF	I	2.80	2.84	+.01
GT GLOBAL C$				
MMF	I	2.75	2.79	-.01
GUARDIAN GRP CLASSIC				
Cdn MMF	I	2.58	2.61	unch
uUS MMF	I	4.89	5.01	-.02

Source: *Fundata Canada Inc.* and the *Globe and Mail*

In these tables, the first column is the fund name, and the second contains various codes, which are the same as those in the previous tables. The third column is the current yield, and the fourth is the effective yield, which as we saw in Chapter 12, is based on the assumption of reinvestment at the current yield. The fifth column indicates any change in net asset value.

Periodic Reports

Many newspapers also publish quarterly or monthly summaries of mutual fund activity and performance. The examples below are typical. Table 23-3A shows the legend, and Table 23-3B an excerpt from the "Canadian Equity" category.

Table 23-3. (A) Monthly Performance Data—Legend

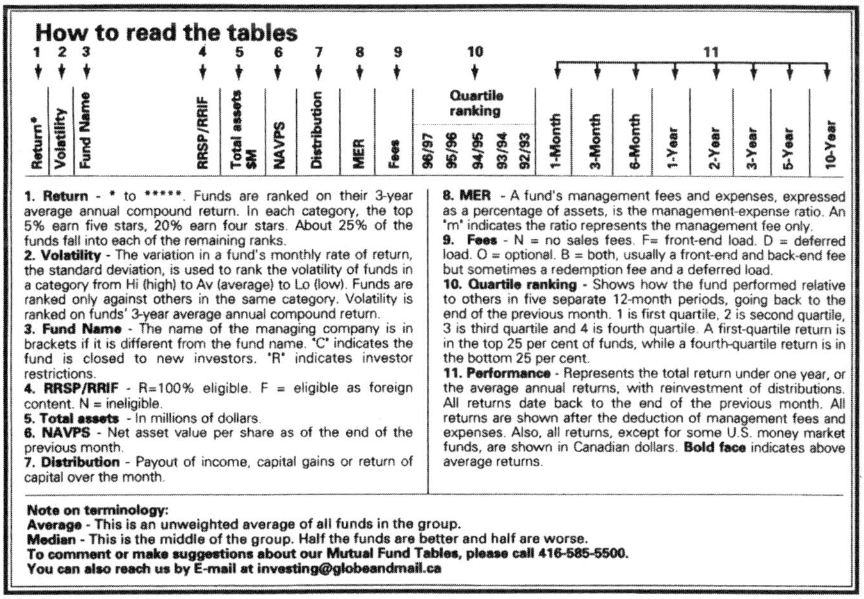
How to read the tables

1	2	3	4	5	6	7	8	9	10					11							
									Quartile ranking												
Return*	Volatility	Fund Name	RRSP/RRIF	Total assets $M	NAVPS	Distribution	MER	Fees	96/97	95/96	94/95	93/94	92/93	1-Month	3-Month	6-Month	1-Year	2-Year	3-Year	5-Year	10-Year

1. Return - * to *****. Funds are ranked on their 3-year average annual compound return. In each category, the top 5% earn five stars, 20% earn four stars. About 25% of the funds fall into each of the remaining ranks.
2. Volatility - The variation in a fund's monthly rate of return, the standard deviation, is used to rank the volatility of funds in a category from Hi (high) to Av (average) to Lo (low). Funds are ranked only against others in the same category. Volatility is ranked on funds' 3-year average annual compound return.
3. Fund Name - The name of the managing company is in brackets if it is different from the fund name. 'C' indicates the fund is closed to new investors. 'R' indicates investor restrictions.
4. RRSP/RRIF - R=100% eligible. F = eligible as foreign content. N = ineligible.
5. Total assets - In millions of dollars.
6. NAVPS - Net asset value per share as of the end of the previous month.
7. Distribution - Payout of income, capital gains or return of capital over the month.
8. MER - A fund's management fees and expenses, expressed as a percentage of assets, is the management-expense ratio. An 'm' indicates the ratio represents the management fee only.
9. Fees - N = no sales fees. F= front-end load. D = deferred load. O = optional. B = both, usually a front-end and back-end fee but sometimes a redemption fee and a deferred load.
10. Quartile ranking - Shows how the fund performed relative to others in five separate 12-month periods, going back to the end of the previous month. 1 is first quartile, 2 is second quartile, 3 is third quartile and 4 is fourth quartile. A first-quartile return is in the top 25 per cent of funds, while a fourth-quartile return is in the bottom 25 per cent.
11. Performance - Represents the total return under one year, or the average annual returns, with reinvestment of distributions. All returns date back to the end of the previous month. All returns are shown after the deduction of management fees and expenses. Also, all returns, except for some U.S. money market funds, are shown in Canadian dollars. **Bold face** indicates above average returns.

Note on terminology:
Average - This is an unweighted average of all funds in the group.
Median - This is the middle of the group. Half the funds are better and half are worse.
To comment or make suggestions about our Mutual Fund Tables, please call 416-585-5500.
You can also reach us by E-mail at investing@globeandmail.ca

Source: The *Globe and Mail*, 1997

Table 23-3. (B) Monthly Performance Data

Return	Volatility	Fund Name	RRSP/RRIF	Total Assets ($M)	NAVPS	Distributions	MER	Fees	Quartile Ranking 96/97	95/96	94/95	93/94	92/93	Percentage Return 1-Month	3-Month	6-Month	1-Year	2-Year	3-Year	5-Year	10-Year
★	LO	All-Canadian CapitalFund	R	13.3	10.82		2.00	F	4	4	1	2	2	-1.7	-4.1	-3.2	-5.6	4.3	5.4	9.6	4.9
★	LO	All-Canadian Compound(C)	R	11.9	14.06		0.00	N	4	4	1	2	2	-1.7	-4.0	-3.2	-5.4	3.8	5.1	9.4	4.8
★	LO	All-Canadian ConsumerFund	R	0.9	3.69		1.96	F	4	4	1	3	·	0.3	**3.9**	6.9	7.9	5.3	5.4	·	·
★★	AV	Allstar AIG Canadian Equity Fund	R	4.3	11.20		3.00	F	2	4	4	4	4	**3.1**	**0.5**	**9.1**	**20.9**	18.3	10.9	9.6	·
★★★★	HI	Altafund Investment Corp.	R	302.2	23.91		2.30	N	2	1	4	1	1	**1.6**	-1.5	4.3	**17.3**	**26.8**	**14.7**	**20.1**	·
★	AV+	Altamira Capital Growth Fund	R	133.4	15.46		2.00	N	4	4	2	2	2	**2.5**	-2.6	5.0	4.1	9.0	7.4	10.9	**7.9**
★★	AV	Altamira Equity Fund	R	2453.7	30.10		2.28	N	4	1	2	1	1	0.2	-1.9	3.6	5.5	14.5	10.7	**17.2**	·
★★	AV	Altamira North American Recovery	R	87.2	14.67		2.30	N	1	4	4	·	·	**3.1**	**3.9**	**16.5**	**26.6**	**20.9**	12.0	·	·
★★★	LO	Associate Investors Ltd.	R	9.5	9.81		2.09	N	1	4	3	2	4	**2.8**	**1.7**	**8.2**	**28.9**	**20.7**	**13.7**	12.5	**7.8**
★★★★	LO	Atlas Canadian Large Cap Growth	R	138.8	17.47		2.47	N	1	2	2	4	4	**2.4**	**1.2**	**12.0**	**23.9**	**22.4**	**15.5**	11.8	6.4
NA	·	Atlas Canadian Large Cap Value Fund	R	23.2	12.85		2.69	N	3	4	·	·	·	**2.6**	**-1.2**	7.1	12.4	12.7	·	·	·
NA	·	Azura Growth RSP Pooled(R)	R	23.9	12.07		2.23	O	4	·	·	·	·	-0.2	-3.7	5.8	10.3	·	·	·	·
★★★	LO	ABC Fundamental Value Fund(R)	R	205.6	11.71		2.00	N	2	2	4	1	1	**2.7**	**3.4**	**11.0**	**21.1**	**22.3**	**13.3**	**28.8**	·
★★	AV+	ADMAX Canadian Performance Fund	R	35.5	7.89		2.61	O	4	2	3	3	3	**3.1**	-3.0	4.4	10.7	15.9	9.8	10.6	·
★	LO	ADMAX Canadian Select Growth Fund	R	7.1	5.77		2.63	O	4	4	2	4	4	**1.9**	-3.3	2.5	7.6	7.9	6.3	5.7	·
NA	·	AGF Canada Class(R)	F	3.6	5.62		2.00m	O	·	·	·	·	·	1.3	-7.0	·	·	·	·	·	·
★	AV+	AGF Canadian Equity Fund	R	695.4	13.65		2.81	O	4	1	4	2	3	0.9	-7.6	0.0	0.3	13.5	6.9	10.0	3.9
★★	AV-	AGF Canadian Growth Fund	R	300.6	19.49		2.43	O	3	4	2	2	4	**3.3**	-1.6	**8.6**	14.1	13.2	9.8	10.7	·
★	AV+	AGF Growth Equity Fund	R	774.3	25.95		2.44	O	4	1	4	1	1	-0.6	-5.2	5.2	9.8	**20.4**	8.8	**18.2**	**8.0**
★★★★★	HI	AIC Advantage Fund(C)	R	1360.8	50.45		2.45	O	1	1	3	1	2	**2.0**	**1.7**	**20.3**	**48.9**	**53.5**	**32.6**	**29.2**	**16.3**
NA	·	AIC Advantage Fund II	R	1272.2	6.26		2.71	O	·	·	·	·	·	**2.8**	**2.0**	**20.6**	·	·	·	·	·
NA	·	AIC Diversified Canada Fund	R	516.8	21.95		2.55	O	1	1	·	·	·	**2.7**	**1.0**	**17.1**	**47.1**	**43.7**	·	·	·
★★★★	AV-	AMI Private Capital Equity	R	1.5	14.14		1.75	N	1	2	3	2	3	**2.7**	**1.4**	**12.2**	**25.6**	**23.4**	**15.2**	**14.6**	·
NA	·	APEX Canadian Stock Fund(R)	R	6.3	5.08		2.55	O	·	·	·	·	·	**2.8**	**0.6**	·	·	·	·	·	·
★	AV+	APEX Equity Growth Fund(R)	R	62.1	5.79		3.00	O	4	1	4	·	·	**1.7**	-7.6	1.0	3.7	14.3	7.9	·	·
★★	LO	Batirente - Section Actions(R)	R	2.4	19.67		1.61	N	1	3	3	·	·	**2.3**	**-0.3**	**9.1**	**21.8**	**19.3**	**12.3**	·	·
★★★	AV	Beutel Goodman Canadian Equity	R	43.0	15.65		2.20	N	2	4	1	2	4	**3.1**	**0.0**	**9.8**	**17.9**	16.1	**12.7**	12.4	·
★★★★	AV-	Bissett Canadian Equity Fund(R)	R	71.5	33.85		1.33	F	1	1	2	2	1	**2.2**	**0.6**	**13.6**	**27.8**	**26.9**	**18.0**	**18.4**	**10.8**
★★★	AV	BNP (Canada) Equity Fund	R	6.3	34.26		2.26	N	2	3	2	4	2	-0.6	-2.1	**9.6**	**18.6**	**19.1**	**13.4**	12.4	·
★★	AV+	BPI Canadian Equity Value Fund	R	360.8	8.96		2.69	O	4	1	4	4	1	-0.1	**-1.4**	6.8	10.6	**22.8**	10.8	12.8	·
NA	·	BPI Canadian Opportunities RSP Fund(C)	R	129.4	35.04		2.50	O	2	·	·	·	·	-4.8	-9.7	0.6	**19.2**	·	·	·	·
★	AV	C.I. Canadian Growth Fund	R	1120.0	6.72		2.38	O	4	3	2	1	·	**1.5**	-5.1	2.3	4.0	11.6	8.3	·	·
★	AV+	C.I. Canadian Sector Shares	F	54.5	6.30		2.43	O	4	3	2	1	1	**1.6**	-5.1	1.8	3.4	10.8	7.8	12.9	·
★★★	AV-	Canada Life Canadian Equity S-9	R	586.8	155.72		2.25	R	2	3	2	3	4	**3.6**	**-0.6**	**8.7**	**19.2**	**18.8**	**12.7**	12.4	**7.8**
★	LO	Canada Trust Everest Stock Fund	R	785.9	19.06		1.86	N	2	4	3	2	1	**3.3**	**0.3**	**10.3**	**18.4**	16.1	9.8	13.0	·
★	LO	Canadian Protected Fund(R)	R	2.0	10.53		2.40	R	4	4	2	4	2	-0.2	**-0.1**	-2.4	-1.8	3.2	2.9	6.2	6.5

Source: The *Globe and Mail*, 1997

Column 1 is a ranking system that highlights the relative performance of the funds over the preceding three years. It is not based on quartiles.

Column 2 (Volatility) indicates the price volatility of the fund. The *Globe and Mail* uses the "HI/AV/LO" scale shown here, while the *Toronto Star* uses a scale from 1 (low volatility) to 10 (high volatility). Although these scales can be useful for crude comparisons of funds' relative volatility, they are unhelpful for more precise analysis.

The *Financial Post*'s tables use three-year standard deviation as the measure of price volatility. It is very important to understand what this statistic means: it is an indicator of variations in monthly return measured against the three-year average. It is not an indicator of the variation in three-year returns. While it is certainly more exact than the *Globe*'s scale, it does not help in evaluating the long-term risk of an investment.

In addition to the tables of fund performance, the papers publish the performance of various benchmarks, an example of which is shown in Table 23-4.

Table 23-4. Benchmarks

Benchmarks

Index	Total return 1 mo.	3 mo.	6 mo.	1 yr.	Average annual compound return 2 yrs.	3 yrs.	5 yrs.	10 yrs.
Canada Savings Bonds Rate	0.2	0.7	1.4	3.8	4.8	5.4	5.6	7.6
CPI - All Items	0.1	0.5	1.2	1.8	1.6	1.9	1.6	2.9
Hang Seng Total Return Index	4.5	1.1	9.0	24.2	29.8	16.9	26.8	22.1
Mexico IPC (Bolsa) Price Index	1.1	5.0	23.5	13.4	21.1	-12.0	-2.0	-
Midland Walwyn Canadian Bond	1.0	0.5	1.1	11.9	11.1	9.6	-	-
Midland Walwyn Canadian Equity	1.5	-1.4	6.7	12.6	15.8	9.9	-	-
Midland Walwyn Global Bond	1.0	1.1	1.2	4.8	6.6	4.7	-	-
Midland Walwyn International Equity	1.5	3.3	11.1	9.9	14.0	9.0	-	-
Midland Walwyn U.S. Equity	3.8	-0.1	9.7	12.4	21.2	16.1	-	-
Morgan Stanley - Europe	0.7	8.0	16.7	24.6	20.5	16.2	17.7	11.6
Morgan Stanley - EAFE	1.7	6.4	6.0	2.0	6.8	6.0	14.4	5.8
Morgan Stanley - Japan	4.9	6.4	-9.6	-25.1	-11.7	-7.5	8.4	-1.1
Morgan Stanley - World Index	4.5	6.2	12.3	13.8	16.5	13.8	17.4	9.2
Morgan Stanley - Emerging	1.4	5.5	15.7	7.1	10.7	4.7	14.0	-
Nesbitt Burns Cdn Small-Cap Index	-1.0	-4.3	3.3	9.0	18.9	9.9	15.5	6.4
Nikkei 225 Price Index	5.0	3.6	-12.6	-26.4	-12.0	-7.7	6.2	-0.5
Russell 100 Growth Index	3.6	-5.0	3.3	9.5	17.3	10.3	11.9	-
Russell 100 Value Index	2.3	1.9	12.4	29.2	24.4	19.0	17.4	-
Russell 300 Growth Index	2.8	-5.0	3.7	9.5	17.8	10.3	12.2	-
Russell 300 Value Index	1.8	1.4	11.6	27.4	23.4	17.9	17.3	-
S&P 500 Total Return Index	7.0	6.3	19.7	28.2	29.4	24.5	20.8	14.6
Salomon Brothers World Gov't Bond	5.2	1.2	-0.5	3.4	3.2	6.6	11.5	8.8
ScotiaMcLeod Universe Bond Total Return	1.2	0.9	1.7	13.7	12.8	11.5	11.3	11.1
TSE300 Total Return	2.2	-1.7	7.7	18.4	20.7	14.4	15.0	8.0
1-Year Average GIC Rate	0.2	0.6	1.3	3.1	4.1	5.0	5.0	7.5
5-Year Average GIC Rate	0.4	1.2	2.4	5.5	6.0	6.8	6.8	8.7
91 Day Treasury Bill	0.3	0.7	1.5	3.8	5.5	5.7	5.8	8.2

Note: All Benchmarks are expressed in Canadian Dollars
Source: Datastream, ScotiaMcLeod, Frank Russell Canada, Morgan Stanley Capital Int'l

Source: The *Globe and Mail*, 1997

Year-over-Year Data

Semi-annually, the *Globe and Mail* publishes tables of funds' year-over-year performance. This is a very useful complement to the more common compound annual rates of return because it allows an analysis of the consistency of fund returns. Used in conjunction with the compound annual return, it enables investors to evaluate the risk of loss.

A Note on Fund Classifications

While the daily reports organize individual funds by fund group, the periodic tables organize them according to fund category. To facilitate comparisons, the "highest," "lowest," and "average" returns are often identified. However, as we indicated in the introduction to Part 2, the classification of a fund can have consequences for its relative performance. A particular classification system can be useful or frustrating, depending on what sorts of comparisons an investor wants to make.

Financial Services Professionals

There is a broad array of investment professionals with a wide range of qualifications and perspectives.

- Certified Financial Analysts (CFAs) are designated by the Association of Investment Management and Research.

- Certified Investment Managers (CIM) are designated by the Canadian Securities Institute (CSI) after having successfully completed the Canadian Investments Management course.

- Registered Representatives, are licensed by the provincial securities commissions to sell securities. Among other professional standards, they are required to have passed the Canadian Securities Course (CSC). Loosely referred to as "brokers", they are known variously from firm to firm as "account executives (AEs)," "financial consultants (FCs)," "investment advisers (IAs)," or "investment executives."

- Certified Financial Planners (CFP) are designated by the Financial Planners Standards Council of Canada (FPSCC).

- Registered Financial Planners (RFP) are designated by the Canadian Association of Financial Planners (CAFP).

- Mutual fund dealers are companies and individuals licensed by provincial securities commissions to sell mutual funds only. Individual salespersons employed by registered mutual fund dealers must have successfully completed the Canadian Investment Funds Course, as an alternative to the CSC. The independence of these dealers varies. Some are completely independent, while others sell the funds of only selected fund sponsors. The quality of the advice provided varies widely.

- Banks and bank personnel are major players in the mutual fund industry. Most of the banks offer a full line of their own bank-sponsored funds. Some also offer a limited number of independent funds through their branch networks.

- A number of organizations have sales forces dedicated exclusively to the sale of their products. Investors Group is the best known of these organizations, but many insurance companies selling segregated funds have similar arrangements.

- Various other professionals, such as accountants, lawyers, and even life insurance sales staff, are permitted to give some investment advice, as an adjunct to their other responsibilities.

Choosing an Adviser

A good adviser should be able to provide several different kinds of service.

- **evaluation of alternatives**
  This is the most crucial service. A good adviser should be conversant with a range of choices. Ordinarily, superior evaluation requires comprehensive training: it is, for example, generally unrealistic to expect a lawyer to be able to provide the same level of investment expertise as a broker. There is nothing wrong with a particular point of view: the important issue is whether there is a sound basis for the position.

- **provision of information**
  Good judgements demand good data. Good advisers will know, for example, whether control of a particular mutual fund company is likely to change, and whether this will affect the management of the fund. They should also know the reputation and investment strategy of specific managers.

- **facilitation of transactions**
  The process of order taking is the least important of these services, and it is a mistake to see the fees that the adviser charges as compensation for simply placing an order.

Newsletters

There are several investment newsletters devoted to mutual funds in Canada. Peter Brimelow, the senior editor of Forbes magazine, describes investment newsletters as "the guerrilla troops of the financial world" because they constitute the very personal perspective of their authors, and are generally unburdened by any corporate orthodoxy. In reviewing newsletters, it is important to consider both the qualifications of their authors and the framework of criteria on which their analysis is based. Our view is that most newsletters advocate some form of asset allocations, and that many are more notable for their hype than their substance.

Two publications which do deserve the attention of mutual fund investors are the *Morningstar Mutual Funds* and the *Value Line Survey of Mutual Funds*. Although both are published by U.S.-based organizations, and are directed specifically at the U.S. market, they provide a comprehensive analytical framework for evaluating funds. Morningstar also publishes the *5-Star Investor*, which contains summary data on the top 500 funds covered by Morningstar together with articles and commentaries on various mutual fund issues. Value Line is newer to the mutual fund field, but the *Value Line Investment Survey*, which evaluates individual stocks, is widely acknowledged to have an exceptional record in identifying superior stock investments.

Independent Databases

There are now four major databases available for Canadian mutual funds:

- BellCharts
- Southam Sourcedisk/Sourcebook
- Portfolio Analytics PALTrac
- *Globe and Mail* HySales

The Southam database is available in both book and computer disk form; the remainder are available only on disk.

All these databases offer a comprehensive compilation of Canadian mutual fund data, including information on the sponsor, the portfolio adviser, minimum investments, asset allocations, and risk/reward analysis.

The benefit of the computer-based versions is that they permit manipulation of data: it is possible to isolate a group of funds according to specific criteria. For example, investors can identify Canadian equity funds with below-average standard deviations (volatility) and above-average ten-year compound return. It is also possible to "graph" data, although the usefulness of this feature for the average investor is debatable.

BellCharts and Sourcedisk are designed primarily for broad comparative analysis. Paltrac has considerably more detail about portfolio composition than either BellCharts or Sourcedisk, and is more suitable for in-depth analysis of specific funds. HySales is marketed at financial planners and offers advanced presentation utilities.

Electronic Media

The reach of the Internet continues to grow and mutual funds are now within that reach. Table 23-5 provides a list of some of the sponsors and related sites on the World Wide Web. In some cases, much of the material at these sites is marketing material, providing little more than up-to-date information on net asset values and the amount and value of the most recent distributions. Some sites, however, are much more informative and offer more sophisticated options, such as retirement and educational "calculators," which allow the user to determine the future value of investments by specifying projected rates of return and annual contributions.

A number of companies also offer "fax on demand" services, which provide information on various funds.

Table 23-5. Mutual Fund Web Sites

AGF	(www.agf.com)
AIC	(www.aicfunds.com)
Altamira	(www.altamira.com)
Atlas Funds	(www.atlasfunds.ca)
Bank of Montreal	(www.bmo.com/fcfunds)
BellCharts	(www.bellcharts.com)
CIBC Funds	(www.cibc.com/products/investment/mfunds)
C.I. Mutual Funds	(www.cifunds.com)
Canada Trust Funds	(www.canadatrust.com/mutual/ctmutualfunds)
Cundill Funds	(www.cundill.com)
Dynamic	(www.dynamic.ca)
Elliott & Page	(www.fundlib.com/ellpage.html)
Fidelity Investments	(www.fidelity.ca)
Financial Pipeline	(www.finpipe.com)
Fund Library	(www.fundlib.com)
GT Global	(www.gtglobal.ca)
Guardian Group	(www.guardianfunds.com
Investment Funds Institute of Canada	(www.mutfunds.com/ific)
Investors Group	(www.investorsgroup.com)
Mackenzie Financial	(www.mackenziefinancial.com)
Mawer Funds	(www.mawer.com)
Royal Bank	(www.royalbank.com/english/fund)
Cambridge Funds (Sagit Mgmt)	(www.direct.ca/funds/)
Scotia Excelsior	(www.scotiabank.ca/nonreg.html)
Saxon Funds	(www.inforamp.net/~saxon)
Scudder Funds	(www.scudder.ca)
Spectrum United Funds	(www.spectrumunited.ca)
Talvest	(www.talvest.com)
TD Bank	(www.tdbank.ca/tdbank/mutual/index.html)
Templeton	(www.templeton.ca)
Trimark	(www.trimark.com)
University Avenue	(www.fundlib.com/univers.html)

PART FIVE

APPENDICES

APPENDIX A

Closed-End Funds

Like open-end or mutual funds, closed-end funds invest in a portfolio of securities on behalf of the investors in the fund. However, despite this superficial similarity, closed-end funds differ from mutual funds in a number of ways.

- **Closed-end funds have a limited number of shares.**
  While there is no limit on the number of shares or units that a mutual fund can issue, the number of shares a closed-end fund can issue is restricted by the terms of the prospectus or the offering memorandum. In some circumstances, the number of shares may be increased, but only with the approval of a majority of the existing shareholders.

- **Shares of closed-end funds trade on an exchange.**
  The shares of an open-end mutual fund are purchased from, and sold to the fund company, which will sell or redeem shares or units any day on which net asset values are determined. In contrast, a closed-end fund takes no role in the purchase and sale of shares following the initial distribution. Instead, the shares are listed on an exchange, and are bought and sold for whatever price the market will bear.

- **Shares of closed-end funds do not necessarily trade at net asset values.**
  Typically, the shares of a closed-end fund trade at a discount to their net asset value, although they can sometimes trade above net asset values (at a premium). There are a couple of reasons for these discounted values. The first is that, although the shares are listed on an exchange, they are frequently very illiquid and can be sold only at discounted values. The second is that market sentiment has an effect on their price. Although there are only a fixed number of shares, the possibility that the fund will issue more shares, diluting the value of the current shares, always exists.

  Notwithstanding their discounted values, the shares of closed-end funds can be attractive for a couple of reasons. First, the yield on the shares may be very favourable. Second, closed-end funds are often terminated or wound up, at which point the shares of the fund are redeemed at their net asset value. The difference between the discounted purchase price of the shares and their net asset value at redemption constitutes a capital gain.

The relative size of the discount is often the most important price consideration. For example, a fund that has historically traded at a 20 percent discount may be a bargain when it trades at a 30 percent discount, but may be overvalued when it trades at a mere 10 percent discount.

- **There are fewer restrictions on the investment practices of closed-end funds.**
  Unlike mutual funds, closed-end funds may issue preferred shares and debt securities. There are also fewer restrictions on the use of derivatives and on practices such as short-selling.

- **Investment mandates of closed-end funds are more restricted.**
  Closed-end funds with mandates to invest broadly are the exception rather than the rule. The majority of closed-end funds have relatively narrowly focused mandates. Most of the closed-end funds that trade on the TSE, for example, invest in specific countries or industry sectors.

- **Management of closed-end funds is subject to different constraints.**
  Most closed-end funds are fully invested. Open-end funds hold a certain percentage of cash assets both because it is impossible to invest new cash assets immediately upon receipt and because a certain level of cash is required to meet the unpredictable demand for redemptions. In a closed-end fund, there are no cash flows aside from those generated by the fund's investments, and it is much easier to forecast these accurately.

Royalty trusts, income trusts and real estate investment trusts are similar to closed-end funds both because they have a fixed number of shares or units, and because they trade on exchanges.

APPENDIX B

The Prospectus

The rules governing prospectuses are found in the various provincial securities acts and in National Policy Statements #36 and #39, which establish the procedures applicable to mutual funds. The purpose of the prospectus is to provide "full, true and plain disclosure" of all material facts relating to the mutual fund, especially its investment objectives, management and risk factors.

Although the content of the prospectus is closely regulated, there are very few restrictions on its form. While the language of most prospectuses is rather legalistic, an increasing number of funds are attempting to reduce the jargon and communicate in plain language.

Some prospectuses are organized in a question-and-answer format, in an effort to be more readable for investors. Others are more conventionally structured around a table of contents. Sponsors offering multiple funds often issue a common prospectus for all the funds, with subsections to address matters specific to each fund.

Regardless of the format, the following information must be included:

i) **cover statement**
This statement appears on the cover of the prospectus and must indicate that the financial statements of the fund form part of the prospectus.

ii) **summary of fees, charges, and dealer compensation payable by the securityholder**
Reference to this summary must be made on the cover page or inside facing page, and the summary itself must be organized in tabular form.

iii) **introductory statement**
This appears on the first page of the prospectus and should include–
- a description of the regulatory framework in which the fund operates
- a statement that the information in the simplified prospectus is summary in nature

- a statement that securityholders have statutory rights, which are described in the prospectus
- a description of where investors may obtain documents forming part of the permanent information record

iv) **name, constitution, and description of the business of the sponsor**

v) **risk factors**

The prominence and content of this information varies. There must be some reference to the risks of the investment on the first page of the prospectus, and a cross-reference to fuller additional information in the body of the prospectus, where appropriate. Some funds situate information about risk factors after the information on objectives and policies, while others put it at the back of the prospectus.

Surprisingly, perhaps, there are few specific requirements for disclosing the risks of the investment. Depending on the nature of the investment, the prospectus should discuss risks regarding the following items:

- general market conditions
- fluctuations in net asset value
- credit worthiness of the investments that the fund makes
- changes in interest rates
- changes in currency exchange rates
- foreign investments
- illiquid investments
- derivative investments

The intention of the rules is to ensure that investors have a "clear understanding" of the risks, but sometimes the complexity of the descriptions can defeat this goal. In other cases, the descriptions are too vague or qualified to be helpful.

vi) **description of the investment**

This description should include all material characteristics of the investment, including–

- dividend rights
- distribution rights

- purchase and redemption rights, including the authority of the manager to suspend redemptions
- voting rights
- conversion or transfer rights between funds
- liquidation rights
- any liability of the securityholder to assessments
- any provisions governing the modification of securityholder rights

vii) **price of securities**

This section covers–

- method of distribution
- minimum initial and subsequent investments
- process by which the price of the securities is determined
- sales charges to which transactions are subject
- procedures for purchasing and redeeming securities
- provisions for reinvestment of distributions

viii) **responsibility for principal functions**

The principal functions include–

- management of the issuer
- investment management
- investment analysis and decisions
- distribution of units

In addition, the prospectus must explain–

- how administrative and managerial functions are performed
- how functions are coordinated
- how potential conflicts of interest are managed
- how management agreements are terminated

ix) **management fees and other expenses**

The prospectus must explain–

- what fees and expenses are charged to unitholders
- what fees and expenses are borne by the manager
- how fees and expenses are calculated

x) **investment objectives and practices**

These include–

- the investment aims of the fund
- any restrictions on the fund's investment practices
- the types of securities in which the fund proposes to invest
- the status of the fund for retirement savings plans and other savings plans

xi) **dividends and distributions**

These provisions cover–

- the timing of distributions of the fund's net income. Distributions must be made at least annually, but some funds will make distributions more frequently.
- the application of reinvestment programs

Dividends should be set out on a per-security basis in the form of notes to the financial statements, which must be incorporated by reference in the prospectus itself.

xii) **tax status of unitholders**

This should indicate in general terms the tax consequences of–

- distributions in the form of interest, dividends, and capital gains
- sale or redemption of the fund
- transfers between funds

xiii) **purchasers' statutory rights**

Securities legislation provides a number of protections for investors, that must be described in mandatory language. These rights include–

- the right to withdraw from an agreement to purchase mutual funds ("right of rescission") within 48 hours of receipt of the confirmation of the purchase (this period is sometimes longer in the case of purchases under a contractual plan)
- the right to sue for damages, if the prospectus contains a misrepresentation

There are time limits imposed on the exercising of these rights, and investors who feel wronged should obtain legal advice promptly.

APPENDIX C

Dollar Cost Averaging

The rationale behind dollar cost averaging is to overcome the difficulties investors confront in their attempts to "buy low" and "sell high." It is difficult to tell if the share or unit price is low enough to buy or high enough to sell. In addition, most investors are psychologically reluctant to buy when prices are depressed. A strategy of dollar cost averaging overcomes these difficulties by investing a set amount at regular intervals. When the price of the investment is high, the set amount will buy fewer shares or units. When the price of the investment is low, the (same) set amount will buy more shares or units. Over a longer time frame, with multiple periodic investments, calculating the average price of the shares will get complicated because the price of the shares is constantly changing.

The misguided conventional view is that dollar cost averaging reduces the average cost of an investment, thereby increasing returns. The reality is that share prices are usually rising, and that (except in very unusual circumstances) dollar cost averaging actually increases the average price per share compared to a lump-sum investment. In addition, advocates of dollar cost averaging ignore the fact that the benefits of compounding are maximized in a lump-sum investment. In dollar cost averaging, only the earliest contributions get the full benefits of compounding. Contributions made near the redemption date derive virtually no benefits from compounding.

Figure C-1 shows the relative performance of a lump-sum investment and a periodic investment plan based on dollar cost averaging. Over the 100 months from September 1, 1987 to December 31, 1995, a $10,000 lump-sum investment in the *Trimark Income Growth Fund* grew to $22,628, while regular investments of $100 per month grew to $15,888. It is worth noting that the investment period includes the "crash" of October 1987, which shaved about 25 percent off the value of the market, providing dollar cost averagers with a classic opportunity to prove their case.

Figure C-1. Dollar Cost Averaging and Lump-sum Investing

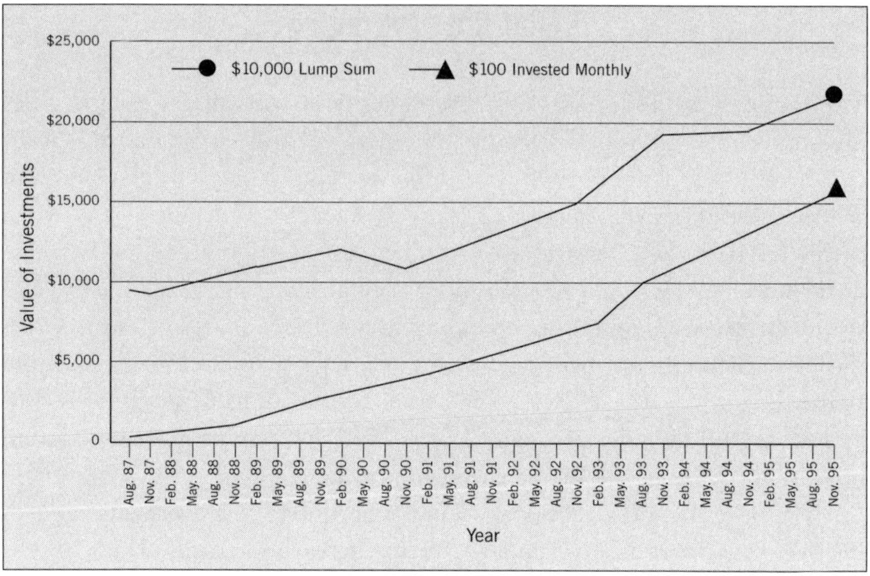

The fact that the upper line (illustrating the performance of the lump-sum investment) does not begin at $10,000 reflects the fact that a 4 percent sales charge has been deducted from the total amount invested.

APPENDIX D

Segregated Funds

Segregated funds are finanical products issued by insurance companies. They are exempted from supervision by securities regulators in a number of ways:

- Disclosure requirements are generally less onerous. At the time of purchase, investors must be given, and acknowledge receipt of, a summary information folder, but there is no requirement that it disclose the fund's objectives, risks, fees or expenses. A prospectus is not required.

- There are fewer limits on permissible investments. While conventional open-end funds may not invest more than 10 percent of assets in any single security or hold more than 10 percent of any single issue, segregated funds are subject to no such restrictions. In addition, investment in illiquid securities and derivatives is unrestricted in segregated funds.

- There is less regulation of the way in which investments are valued for the purpose of determining net asset values.

- Financial statements and reports to investors are not required.

- Changes in segregated funds are not subject to review. Segregated funds are not required to seek the approval of investors for a change in either the manager or the objectives of the fund.

- The calculation of performance is largely unregulated. There is no standard format in which segregated funds must report performance, and they are not required to disclose the basis on which performance is calculated.

- People who sell conventional mutual funds are licensed by provincial securities commissions, while those who sell segregated funds are regulated by provincial insurance legislation and various insurance councils or commissions.

APPENDIX E

Labour-Sponsored Investment Funds

Labour-sponsored investment funds are governed by the federal Income Tax Act and various provincial laws such as the Labour-Sponsored Venture Capital Corporations Act (Ontario).

Investment Restrictions

Labour-Sponsored Investment Funds are subject to both federal and provincial investment restrictions. Provincial investment restrictions apply only to investments by residents of the particular province. In general, the following rules apply:

1. Labour funds may invest only in eligible investments, which are typically defined as corporations or partnerships that–
   - do not have more than $50 million in assets or more than five hundred employees
   - pay 50 percent of their wages and salaries to employees ordinarily employed in a permanent establishment in the province in which the fund operates
   - have 50 percent of their employees employed in eligible businesses carried on in the province in which the fund operates

2. Labour funds may not purchase securities of publicly traded companies in the secondary market (that is, on a stock exchange) but may purchase such securities as part of an initial public offering or a private placement provided these securities are held by the fund for a minimum of six to eighteen months.

3. Labour funds must hold at least 20 percent of their assets in liquid securities. These are investments that can be readily bought and sold without their prices being significantly affected.

4. Labour funds must make investments within certain time frames.
   - The provincial rules typically give these funds up to two to three years to invest 70 percent of the fund assets.

- The federal rules originally required these funds to invest at least 80 percent of the fund assets for the first five years of operation, and at least 60 percent of fund assets acquired after the first five years.

  Failure to meet these requirements could result in penalty taxes and revocation of registration as a labour fund.

5. Under the provisions governing labour funds in Ontario, investments in single enterprises prior to 1997 cannot exceed the lesser of $10 million or 10 percent of the fund's equity capital, and cannot constitute a control position. For 1997 and subsequent years, the limit has been increased from $10 million to $15 million.

6. The Ontario rules also require labour funds to dispose of investments that no longer qualify as eligible businesses by virtue of the growth of such businesses. Failure to do so may attract penalty taxes.

In 1994, as a result of the slow rate at which some of these funds, were making the kinds of investments intended, the federal government changed the regulations, requiring a minimum of $100 million to be invested by February 1995 and a further $100 million to be invested by February 1996. Nevertheless, despite the rhetoric of investing in small companies requiring venture capital to expand, most of the money in labour funds is invested in government-guaranteed T-bills. As of early 1996, the funds had on average less than 30 percent of their assets invested in eligible investments.

Risk Factors

1. Many of the investment rules applicable to mutual funds do not apply to labour funds. In particular, rules directed at ensuring liquidity and diversification of investments do not apply.

2. While conventional mutual funds generally value their investments at the closing market price at which they can be bought and sold, labour funds must often rely on appraisals to determine values because there is no published market for the investments that these funds are required to make. Although all labour funds have comprehensive methodologies for determining the values of these investments, such values may not reflect the amounts for which the investments can actually be sold.

3. Although labour funds are liable for penalty taxes and revocation of registration in the event they do not meet investment requirements, there is no assurance that these funds will find or make sufficient eligible investments.

4. The costs of managing labour funds are typically greater than the costs of managing conventional mutual funds because–
   - there are additional costs in valuing the funds' assets
   - the eligible investments require a greater degree of analysis

5. The marketing and promotion of labour funds focuses on their tax benefits. The generous nature of these benefits unfortunately implies that investors can receive something for nothing. This is highly misleading. In fact, most labour-sponsored funds are truly high risk. There is a significant possibility of absolute loss in these funds because of the kinds of investments they make. Indeed, the relatively low after-tax price of such investments merely offsets the substantial illiquidity and default risks of these portfolios.

Tax Considerations

1. Prior to 1996, the federal government allowed a 20 percent tax credit (that is, a deduction from the amount of tax payable) on invested amounts up to $5,000. The maximum investment would therefore reduce the investor's tax by $1,000 ($5,000 x 20 percent). For 1996 and subsequent years, the maximum investment eligible for the federal tax credit has been reduced to $3,500, and the tax credit has been modified to match the credit in the taxpayer's province, subject to a minimum of 10 percent and a maximum of 15 percent.

2. A number of provinces also allowed tax credits. In Ontario, prior to 1996, the tax credit was 20 percent, up to a maximum of $5,000. The maximum investment in Ontario would therefore reduce the investor's tax by a total of $2,000 (the federal credit plus the provincial credit). For 1996 and subsequent years, the maximum investment eligible for the provincial credit is $3,500, and the tax credit has been reduced to 15 percent.

3. To benefit from these tax credits, the investment must be maintained for a minimum period of time. Prior to 1996, the minimum period was five years. Investors who redeemed early had to repay the credit. Investors who redeemed after the minimum period were entitled to additional tax credits for new investments. For 1996 and subsequent years, the holding period has been extended to eight years from five. In addition, investors who redeem after the minimum period are now subject to a waiting period of three years before new investments are eligible for additional tax credits.

4. It is important to distinguish the specific benefit of the tax credit on labour-sponsored funds from the general tax deductions allowed on any RRSP-eligible investment. The marketing material of most labour-sponsored funds suggests that such investments offer tax breaks of up to 90 percent. Figure E-1 illustrates this claim for Ontario labour funds.

Figure E-1. Advertised Tax Treatment of Labour-Sponsored Funds

Investment (maximum)	$3,500
Federal tax credit (15%) (for Ontario residents)	($ 525)
Ontario tax credit (15%)	($ 525)
RRSP tax benefit (assuming 50% marginal rate)	($1,750)
Total tax advantage	$2,800
Cost of investment	$ 700

The "total tax advantage" claimed for labour-sponsored funds is misleading: only a portion of the tax relief is attributable to the nature of the investment. Up to 50 percent of the potential tax relief arises from buying the fund inside an RRSP, and is available from any RRSP-eligible investment. Such promotion is analogous to advertising shares of Bell Canada at half price for RRSPs. The real tax advantage of labour funds is shown in Figure E-2.

Figure E-2. Actual Tax Treatment of Labour-Sponsored Funds

Investment (maximum)	$3,500
Federal tax credit (15%) (for Ontario residents)	($ 525)
Ontario tax credit (15%)	($ 525)
Total tax advantage	$1,050
Cost of investment	$2,450

APPENDIX F

Derivatives

Derivatives have been used for centuries. There is evidence that rudimentary commodity and agricultural derivatives were used as early as the 13th century, and the Chicago Board of Trade which provided a formal exchange for the commodity derivative market was created in 1848.

Financial derivatives are derivatives based on financial assets such as stocks and bonds. Financial derivatives have also been employed for some time, but grew markedly in importance following the establishment of a formal market at the Chicago Board of Options Exchange in 1973. During the past six or seven years, both the derivatives market and the number of derivatives exchanges has grown rapidly. In Canada, the "notional value" of derivatives (that is, the value of assets subject to derivatives contracts) in 1995 was $1,826.4 billion, and the market value of the derivatives contracts themselves was $46.1 billion.

Derivatives are becoming an increasingly important feature of many mutual funds. Surveys by the Equion Group in latter 1994, and the Fraser Institute in early 1995 both found that about 70 percent of mutual funds in Canada used some form of derivative. Historically, the use of derivatives has been focused on managing and reducing investment risks, but a growing proportion is driven by increasing competitive pressure, and the need to enhance returns.

Types of Derivatives

The range of derivatives is extremely diverse. Some of the more common types include:

Forwards

This is the simplest of derivatives, in which one party agrees to buy (and the other to sell) an asset in the future, at a price fixed today. The asset can be anything: commodities like grain, oil, or pork bellies; or financial assets such as Canadian dollars or shares of IBM. A future is merely a forward contract which trades on an exchange.

Options

In an option, the buyer acquires the right, but not the obligation, to deal with an asset for a period of time. A ***call*** is the right, but not the obligation, to purchase an asset at some specified time in the future. A ***put*** is the right, but not the obligation, to sell an asset at some specified time in the future.

Swaps

A ***swap*** is a financial derivative that involves the exchange of assets' cash flows. In an interest rate swap, for example, one party to the contract has an obligation to pay a fixed rate of interest, while the other party, the ***counterparty***, has an obligation to pay a floating rate. By swapping obligations, the party with the floating-rate obligation can eliminate exposure to the risk that interest rates will rise. This can be advantageous to a company that purchases raw materials with borrowed funds. At the same time, the counterparty to the transaction can increase its interest rate sensitivity. This can be beneficial to a financial institution that must pay a floating rate on deposits, but receives the bulk of its income from fixed-income loans (such as mortgages). By exchanging its fixed-income obligation for a floating-rate obligation, the company can more nearly match its revenues to its liabilities.

Collateralized Mortgage Obligations

As the name suggests, these derivatives are based on mortgages. The simplest of these are similar to MBSs. The difference is that an MBS constitutes a direct interest in all the mortgages in the underlying pool, while a collateralized mortgage obligation constitutes an interest in only part of the underlying mortgage assets. A principal only (**PO**) entitles an investor to an interest in only the principal of an MBS. POs behave like strip bonds, with the added uncertainty of prepayment. An interest only (**IO**) entitles the investor to an interest in only the income stream of the MBS. Unlike conventional bonds, the price of IOs varies directly with interest rates: as rates rise, so does the value of the IO.

Structured Investments

These are the most complex of derivatives. They are typically tailor-made for a particular party, and combine a number of simpler derivatives.

Exchange-listed derivatives, such as simple options and forwards, have standardized terms regarding expiry dates and methods of settlement. Their market behaviour is therefore relatively predictable. Less standardized derivatives such as swaps, and more complicated combinations of these basic derivatives are traded "over the counter" through an informal network of investment dealers. The most exotic and complex derivatives are often designed for a specific party and counterparty. Their complexity makes their market behaviour difficult to predict, particularly during volatile periods, and the fact that they are assembled for specific parties usually makes them extremely illiquid and therefore almost impossible to sell.

Uses of Derivatives

Hedging

There are a variety of uses for derivatives. Traditionally, financial derivatives have been employed largely as mechanisms for reducing risk. The most widespread use has been to hedge investments. A currency forward, for example, can insulate bond yields from currency devaluations. If Argentinian bonds offer an attractive coupon rate, but there is a chance the peso will be devalued relative to the Canadian dollar, it is possible to use a forward contract to sell pesos in the future at the current exchange rate, thereby protecting (at least some of) the profit from the bonds. Similarly, puts can protect a stock portfolio from declines in the price of its investments by "locking in" the price at which specific stocks can be sold.

Leveraging returns

More recently, less conservative uses for derivatives have emerged. These uses are all more or less dependent on the fact that derivatives are leveraged. Since a derivative is merely based on an underlying asset, owning a derivative investment is generally less costly than owning the asset itself. This fact implies that derivatives are inherently leveraged. An investment in a derivative is similar, in many cases, to putting a deposit on a purchase. Investing only a small proportion of the underlying asset's value allows control of the asset itself, as the following example shows. On May 3, 1996, shares of Alcan traded at $44.50. An investor who wanted to buy 100 shares in anticipation of an increase in the price would have to spend $4,450. In contrast, July 1996, calls at $45 (that is, the right to purchase shares of Alcan at $45 per share until the end of July) traded at $1.95. An investor would therefore have to pay only $195 to exercise control over 100 shares of Alcan, and could still have benefited from any increase in the share price of $45 before the end of July 1996.

The leverage of derivatives can be exploited in a variety of ways. It can be used to improve the cost efficiency of a portfolio by reducing execution costs. For example, while the commission costs on a portfolio of $100 million invested in S&P 500 stocks would be about $150,000, the commission on stock index futures to achieve the same market exposure would be only about $12,000. In addition, the use of derivatives significantly increases the speed of transactions. Purchasing index futures takes far less time than assembling a $100 million stock portfolio, even if the market distortion effects of such an investment are discounted. In fact, the injection of $100 million into the market would have a significantly greater effect on prices than the purchase of index futures.

The inherent leverage of derivatives can also be employed to simulate exposure to foreign markets while preserving the fund's eligibility for tax-advantaged plans such as RRSPs. One technique is to invest the allowable foreign content of the fund in derivatives based on foreign investments, and the remaining bulk of the fund's assets in short-term Canadian securities such as T-bills. Since derivatives are leveraged, the effect they have on the portfolio is magnified, and the portfolio manager can thereby attempt to replicate the returns of a portfolio which is fully invested in foreign securities. Another technique is to employ swaps. A fund that owns Ontario Hydro bonds, for example, can exchange the cash flow with an investor holding a portfolio of U.S. stocks. In return for the fixed income from the bonds, the U.S. stockholder agrees to pay the fund the rate of return on the S&P 500. The fund thereby achieves exposure to the U.S. market without violating foreign content rules, since it still owns the bonds. Not incidentally, the credit quality of the fund is preserved, since the bonds are guaranteed.

Problems with Derivatives

Despite the benefits they offer, derivatives can involve considerable risks.

Lack of Liquidity

Although there is nothing inherently wrong with illiquid securities, it is important to recognize the consequences of their limitations. The prospectus of the *AGF Germany Fund*, for example, describes the following problem:

> The Fund's successful use of [derivatives such as] options and futures...is subject to numerous risks. The ability of the Fund to close out an option or future position will depend upon the existence of a liquid secondary market in such option or futures con-

> tract, and there is no assurance that such [a] market will exist for any particular option or future contract at any particular time.

While most exchange-traded derivatives are reasonably liquid, those traded over the counter and particularly those engineered for specific parties are usually highly illiquid. One of the most important consequences of illiquidity is the difficulty of valuing securities, and this can pose significant problems when derivatives are included in the portfolios of mutual funds. For the most part, mutual funds are based on the premise that they can be bought and sold readily. This premise in turn presupposes that the net asset values of the funds can be easily established. If net asset values cannot be accurately determined, and the fund cannot be sold at its quoted price, much of the attraction of mutual funds is lost. As Don Phillips, the publisher of the *Morningstar Five Star Investor*, observes: "open end mutual funds offer many advantages, but efficient participation in illiquid securities is not one of them."

Difficulties in Valuation

For most exchange-traded derivatives, values can be ascertained relatively precisely. In part, this is a function of the liquidity created by exchange listing. In addition, the terms of an exchange-traded contract are standardized, facilitating comparisons to other derivatives. For "over the counter" derivatives, however, valuations can often be extremely difficult. The process of auction by which values are determined for liquid investments does not work well for illiquid investments, and many over the counter derivatives are valued by appraisal. In attempting to establish the value of an illiquid security, analysts rely on the value of similar instruments that do trade, and on the bid prices of dealers and computer models that incorporate variables such as interest rates and prepayment schedules into estimates of value. The difficulty is that despite the volume of data processed, the result is still only an educated guess. In addition, the only computer-based financial models suitable for evaluating the instruments are often proprietary products of the very institutions which market the derivative, making independent assessment almost impossible. The more complicated the instrument, the more difficult the valuation. James Midanek, a risk management consultant in California, says: "I don't care how big your computer is, you can't get your arms around them."

The consequence of misvaluing an asset is that projections about its market behaviour are much less reliable. If, for example, investors believe an asset priced at $10 has an actual value of $12, they will generally consider it a good investment. But if the asset's actual value *is* $10, it is much less attractive as an investment. This is, in fact, precisely what happened to the *Piper Jaffray Institutional Government Income Portfolio* in the United States. Piper Jaffray's computerized financial models valued its derivative investments far above the price set by the market, and the fund suffered substantial losses when the investments were realized.

Inherent Instability

The past three or four years have witnessed a number of financial disasters precipitated by derivative investments. To some degree these failures are rooted in the failure of management in the companies and funds that use derivatives to adequately monitor their use. Some of these fiascos, such as those involving Procter&Gamble in the United States, and Metallgeselschaft in Germany, are attributable to errors in judgement. In the P&G case, for example, pressure on the treasury department to contribute directly to corporate profitability encouraged speculative investments in a portfolio intended merely to hedge financial risk. What seems to have been overlooked is that a hedge requires balance: if a position produces significant gains, it is capable of producing significant losses. In the case of Metallgeselschaft, the difficulties seem to have arisen from an ill-considered attempt to shut down, or "unwind," a hedged position in midcycle, at the point when paper losses were greatest.

Other failures are attributable to so-called rogue traders using derivatives for speculative purposes. The losses suffered by Kidder Peabody and the collapse of Barings Bank were both the result of unauthorized and unsupervised activity.

Yet while careful supervision and monitoring of derivative use can alleviate some of these difficulties, other parts of the problem are far more intractable. Typically, the value of a derivative is conditional on the value of its underlying security. Most of the time, changes in the values of the underlying security are sufficiently gradual that a rough equilibrium is maintained between the value of the security and the value of the associated derivative. Difficulties arise when this equilibrium is disrupted, threatening expectations that are based on it. In such circumstances, the value of the derivative can have an independent impact on the value of the underlying security. In effect, the derivative "tail" can wag the security "dog," resulting in a kind of circular pricing that is highly unstable.

The catch is that the equilibrium has an unfortunate habit of breaking down when it is needed most—during periods of market turbulence and uncertainty. One of the precipitating causes of the 1987 "crash," for example, was the collapse of the traditional relationship between stocks and stock futures. Prior to the crash, a number of institutional investors had employed a technique called "portfolio insurance" to insulate their portfolios against loss. By selling futures on the stocks in the portfolio, losses on the stock portfolio could be offset by gains on the stock futures. To be successful, portfolio insurers must be able to execute transactions quickly, so that the price on the futures exceeds the market price for the stock. However, when the markets opened on Monday October 19, 1987, the overwhelming preponderance of sell orders almost paralyzed the administrative capacities of the clearing systems, making it virtually impossible to obtain timely information about securities prices. Once underway, the decline was fueled rather than retarded by portfolio insurers' attempts to limit losses by closing out positions.

In an effort to prevent the possibility of uncontrolled loss, most Canadian jurisdictions restrict the use of derivatives in mutual funds. These controls–

- prohibit the use of leverage by requiring funds to provide collateral to "cover" any leveraged positions
- restrict investments in derivatives for "nonhedging" purposes to a maximum of 10 percent of the portfolio in instruments with a term of no more than three years
- limit investment in illiquid investments to no more than 10 percent of the portfolio

In fact, these rules are very difficult to police. In the case of leverage, for example, the problems of valuation referred to above can often make it very difficult to determine the actual size of the position to be covered. In the case of hedging, the line or boundary between "hedging" purposes and "nonhedging" purposes is extremely hard to define or enforce. There are more—and less—imperfect hedges, and the point at which a hedge ceases to be a technique for limiting risk and becomes a technique for speculating is very grey, indeed. The same is true of illiquid investments. There are many,

many investments that are very illiquid, although the officially sanctioned definition of *illiquid* does not cover them all. These difficulties of enforcement become more pronounced as the derivatives become more complex, and are almost impossible to manage when "normal" financial relationships are disrupted.

Derivatives themselves vary in their level of risk. Funds that limit their use of derivatives to exchange-traded instruments for the purpose of hedging volatility are unlikely to suffer significant losses. As we indicated above, for example, the risks involved in using put options as a form of portfolio insurance in equity funds are few. Similarly, the use of interest rate futures by bond funds usually provides a reasonably efficient way to insure debt portfolios.

In contrast, funds that exploit derivatives for more aggressive purposes are on far less certain ground. For example, RRSP-eligible funds that use derivatives in an attempt to replicate exposure to foreign markets are implicitly engaging in a form of speculation. By using the leveraged quality of derivatives to produce dramatic returns from only 20 percent of the portfolio, the fund hopes to compensate for the mediocre returns of the remaining 80 percent, which is invested in domestic money market securities. The comparison of the foreign and RRSP-eligible versions of some Global Strategy funds is illustrative. To the end of August 1996, the two-year compound return for the *Global Strategy Asia Fund* was –2.6 percent, while the performance of the derivative-based *Global Strategy Diversified Asia Fund* over the same period was –5.2 percent.

The problem is that the real uses that a portfolio manager makes of derivatives are often extremely difficult to evaluate. A detailed analysis of portfolio transactions is the only reliable way of differentiating between a hedge and a speculation, but detailed information on portfolio transactions can be very hard to obtain.

In our view, the fundamental problem with derivatives is not so much that they are inherently bad, but that they involve a great deal more *potential* for harm than conventional investments. The recent widely publicized losses suffered by various sophisticated institutional investors show that in some cases derivatives can have negative consequences entirely out of proportion to the benefits they may offer.

APPENDIX G

Calculating Compound Annual Return

Compound annual return is an ***average***. Like other averages, it describes the point around which data points tend to cluster. The calculation of compound annual returns is straightforward. The equation is

$$(Y1 \times Y2 \times Y3 \times \text{..........}Yn)^{\sqrt{}(1 \div n)}$$

where n = the number of years
Y = annual return

The annual returns must be expressed as "wealth relatives." For example, an annual return of 10 percent is expressed as 1.10. An annual return of 21.4 percent is expressed as 1.214. An annual return of 112 percent is expressed as 2.12 percent. A negative annual return of –8.5 percent is expressed as 0.915.

Any calculator with scientific functions will perform the calculations: a computer is not necessary.

If, for example, a fund had annual returns for the past five years as follows,

1991:	**13.1 percent**
1992:	**15.6 percent**
1993:	**35.6 percent**
1994:	**–2.3 percent**
1995:	**22.7 percent**

then the calculation is as follows:

$$(1.131 \times 1.156 \times 1.356 \times 0.977 \times 1.227)^{\sqrt{}(1 \div 5)} = 1.1627$$

The five-year compound annual return is therefore 16.27 percent.

Modified Compound Return

In evaluating the distribution of data, statisticians are often confronted by data that does not fit the overall pattern of distribution. This anomalous data can distort statistical analysis. Establishing the central point around which data tends to cluster will be affected by data points that are unusually high or unusually low.

To ensure accuracy, statistical analysis often includes mechanisms for discounting the importance and effect of this anomalous data. Measures of dispersion, such as standard deviation, generally minimize the importance of peripheral data. In a normally distributed sample, 95 percent of the data typically fall within two standard deviations of the mean: the importance of the top 2.5 percent and the bottom 2.5 percent of the data is discounted. Similarly, the results of political polls and other survey research are often expressed with a confidence level of 95 percent, which means that the data in the poll is accurate 19 times out of 20.

To calculate modified compound annual return, the highest and lowest annual returns are removed, and *n* is reduced by 2. For the above example,

$$(1.131 \times 1.156 \times 1.227)^{\surd(1 \div 3)} = 1.1706$$

The modified compound annual return is 17.06 percent.

While the technique of excluding the best and worst years in calculating compound annual return is relatively crude, it is consistent with more sophisticated statistical techniques.

APPENDIX H

A Primer on Volatility

Measuring Volatility

Measurements of volatility are actually measurements of probability.

Beta reflects the extent to which the returns of an investment fluctuate in comparison to the fluctuations in the returns of the general market, which represents a kind of "peer group." Strictly speaking, beta is the correlation coefficient of the investment return to the market return. Mathematically, it is calculated as follows:

$$\beta = \text{cov}(\, R_i \times R_m) \,/\, \sigma^2{}_m$$

where

R_i	is the return of the investment
R_m	is the return of the market
$\sigma^2{}_m$	is the variance of the market

A beta of 1.0 indicates that the price fluctuations of the investment are equivalent to those of the broader market. An investment with a beta less than 1.0 fluctuates in price less than the broader market; a beta greater than 1.0 indicates that the price fluctuations of the investment are greater than those of the broader market.

Standard deviation reflects the extent to which the returns of an investment fluctuate in comparison to its own average return. Mathematically, it is the square root of the variance of an individual investment and is calculated as follows:

$$s = \sqrt{(\,\Sigma(x_i - x_m)^2 \div (n - 1))}$$

where

$(x_i - x_m)$	is the difference between each return and the mean of the returns
n	is the number of returns

A standard deviation of 3.0, for example, means that the price fluctuations of an investment will be within 3 percent of the average price two out of three times, or 67 percent of the time, and within 6 percent of its average price 95 percent of the time.

The Volatility of Portfolios

The beta of a portfolio is merely the weighted sum of the betas of the individual investments. The computation of the standard deviation of a portfolio is more complex because it requires not only the variance of the individual investments but also the covariance of each pair of investments.

Relative Advantages

The chief attraction of beta is that it provides a reliable statistical measure of investment variability relative to an independent benchmark. While standard deviation is useful in evaluating individual stocks or portfolios, comparisons to a group average are usually not possible because information about the covariance of the funds in the group required to compute the standard deviation of the group is generally unavailable.

On the other hand, since standard deviation does not depend on an external benchmark, it is less likely that extraneous factors will influence the measurement. Beta, in contrast, can be affected by a variety of factors unrelated to the merits of an investment. For example, thinly traded stocks often have high betas, simply because the price movements of the stock are susceptible to the activities of only a few investors. In addition, the beta of an investment is heavily dependent on the composition of the benchmark. Comparing the variability of foreign investments to benchmarks based on domestic markets (such as the TSE 300 or even the S&P 500) is meaningless, but there is often no entirely appropriate benchmark.

Standard deviation expresses variance in terms of percentages. It is therefore straightforward to understand. For example, the actual returns of an investment with an average return of 6.0 percent and a standard deviation of 3.0 percent will fluctuate between 3.0 and 9.0 percent in 67 percent of cases, and between zero and 12.0 percent in 95 percent of cases. Beta, by contrast, expresses variance relative to the (chosen) benchmark and thus depends on an appreciation of the benchmark's variance to be intelligible. For example, an investment with a beta of 1.1 is 10 percent more volatile than the benchmark, but unless the volatility of the benchmark is known, the implications of the measurement cannot be fully evaluated.

Limitations as a Measure of Financial Risk

As a measure of financial risk, volatility has a variety of limitations.

- The way in which volatility is measured exaggerates the importance of short-term fluctuations in return because it is typically calculated on the basis of individual *monthly* returns. Standard deviation is most frequently calculated on the average of monthly returns measured over one year (12 months), although calculations on the average monthly returns over three years (36 months) and five years (60 months) are common, and even calculations over ten years (120 months) are used. Beta is most commonly calculated on the average of monthly returns measured over three years (36 months).

For investments held for relatively short periods of time, calculating deviations from the average monthly price may make sense, since long-term trends are often not apparent over the short term. For long-term investments, though, calculating deviation on the basis of average monthly return exaggerates the significance of short-term influences. A more accurate picture of financial risk is obtained when the variability is evaluated on the basis of the expected holding period. If, for example, the anticipated holding period is five years, the important question is how much will actual five-year returns deviate from the average five-year return.

The following two charts depict variations in performance for the *Trimark Canadian Fund* from August 1986 to August 1996. Figure H-1 shows the fund's monthly performance, while Figure H-2 shows the fund's five-year compound return to the end of each month.

Figure H-1. Monthly Returns of *Trimark Canadian Fund*

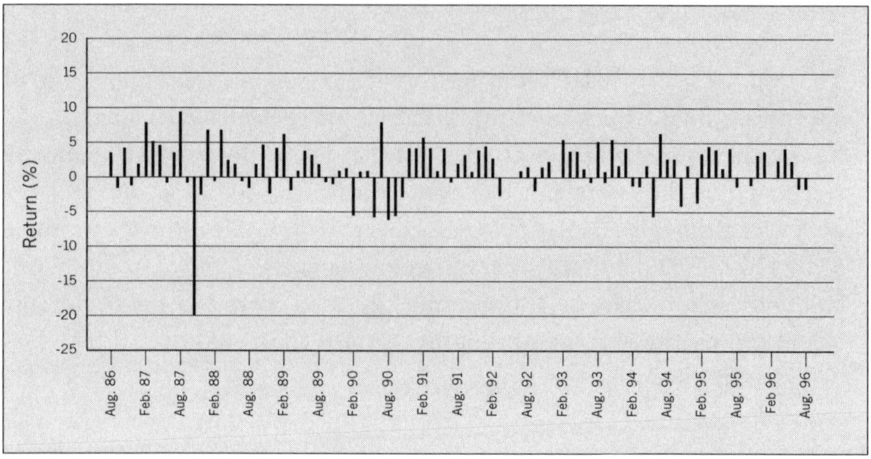

Figure H-2. Five-Year Compound Returns of *Trimark Canadian Fund*

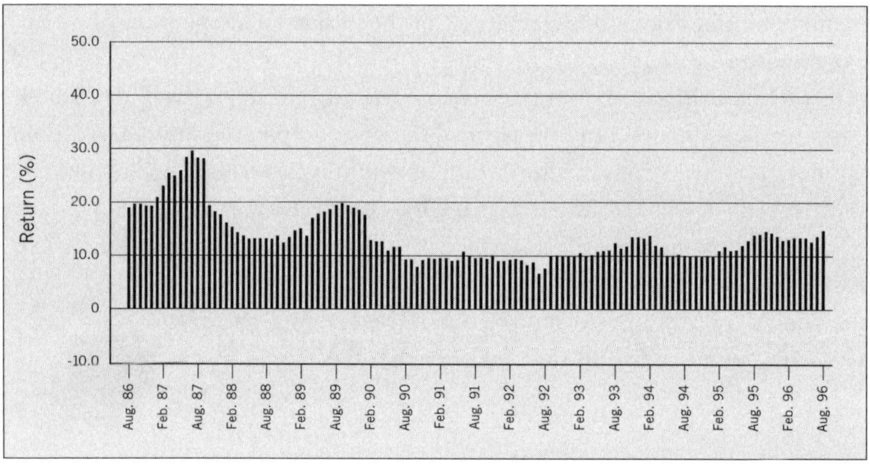

Two points are noteworthy about this data. The first is that the range of fluctuations in monthly returns is greater than the range of fluctuations in five-year compound returns. Monthly returns vary from +8.8 percent to –19.8 percent, a range of 28.6 percent, while the rolling five-year compound returns vary from +6.1 percent to +29.5 percent, a range of only 23.4 percent.

Even more telling is the difference in the risk of loss that the two charts imply. More than 35 percent of the monthly returns is negative—that is, the fund lost money. In contrast, none of the five-year compound returns are negative—the fund has never lost money over a five-year holding period.

- Volatility reflects only risks that cause fluctuations in market prices. Credit risk and default risk are often poorly reflected in the volatility of an investment. The credit rating of Olympia & York debt, for example, was investment grade right up to the point of default.

- Measures of volatility do not distinguish between variability above or below the average or anticipated level. In financial terms, volatility does not distinguish between returns that fluctuate up and those that fluctuate down. As a result, an investment that declines in value slowly and steadily will appear to be low risk, while an investment that increases in value abruptly and erratically will be characterized as high risk. In fact, it is really only downward fluctuations that constitute a risk: upward fluctuations reflect increasing investment returns.

- The calculation of the volatility of a portfolio is based on the assumption that the portfolio does not change. However, portfolios are constantly changed as individual investments are added and removed by the manager. The more the investments in the portfolio are changed, the less accurate the measure of volatility will be.

APPENDIX I

The Components of Risk Tolerance

In modern portfolio theory, risk tolerance is one of the considerations in identifying an investor's most suitable portfolios. Conventionally, risk tolerance consists of both objective and subjective factors.

OBJECTIVE COMPONENTS

- **investment horizon**

All other things being equal, the shorter the time period of an investment, the less risk the investor can tolerate. In the short term, the cyclical activity of the markets may depress the price of the investment. Longer time frames provide the opportunity to recover from any early losses.

- **net worth**

The ***net worth*** of an investor is the total value of his or her assets after deducting all liabilities. Individuals with greater net worth are usually able to tolerate greater risk: their existing wealth provides a cushion against potential losses. Individuals with low net worth are less likely to be able to absorb losses without a significant impact on their standard of living.

- **income level**

Individuals with lower incomes are generally less tolerant of risks, believing they lack the capacity to absorb any loss.

- **stability of income**

Individuals with secure income are typically willing to accept greater risks than those whose future income is uncertain. In effect, individuals with an irregular income often act as if their income were lower than it actually is. Source of income is also relevant. Those who are dependent on investment income are typically less risk tolerant than those with employment income because the consequences of a disruption in investment income are greater.

- **need for liquidity**

A liquid asset is one that can be sold quickly without a significant capital loss. There are a number of reasons why liquidity may be required:

- emergencies
- short-term objectives
- tax planning

Generally, individuals whose circumstances require greater liquidity have less tolerance for risk.

Subjective Components

- **level of sophistication**

The knowledge and understanding of investments varies widely. Individuals with a more limited grasp of financial matters will generally have less tolerance for risk than more sophisticated investors. The most naïve will avoid investments of any kind, believing that the stock market is essentially a gamble and that success is largely a matter of good luck. Others, for whom the concept of variable return is completely foreign, restrict themselves to "guaranteed" investments such as Canada Savings Bonds, GICs, or term deposits. Still others are quite sophisticated and are entirely comfortable with a broad range of securities.

- **psychological profile**

Some individuals are naturally less risk averse than others. Even individuals who have identical objective circumstances may make different choices about the kinds of investments they are most comfortable with.

Risk Tolerance and Comfort Level

In our view, including objective factors in the evaluation of risk tolerance makes the process of asset allocation somewhat circular. The time horizon, for example, is one of the factors to consider in evaluating risk tolerance, but the time horizon is also an independent consideration in identifying the most suitable portfolios.

We believe objective and subjective considerations should be distinguished in evaluating the suitability of an investment or portfolio. Objective considerations are largely addressed in assessments of the time horizon: it is the subjective considerations that determine an investor's comfortability with a given investment.

APPENDIX J

Modern Portfolio Theory and Asset Allocation

Modern portfolio theory is an investment approach based on the idea that financial risk is synonymous with volatility. The objective of this theory is to identify efficient portfolios, in which return is maximized for a given level of risk (or risk is minimized for a given level of return).

The basic principle underlying the theory is that the volatility of some investments in a portfolio can be offset or moderated by the volatility of other investments. This principle is called ***correlation***. When two investments are perfectly correlated, changes in the return of one investment are exactly matched by changes in the return of the other: the correlation is +1.0. When there is no association between the returns of the two investments, the correlation is zero. When changes in the return of one investment are matched by equal but opposite changes in the return of the other investment, the two investments are negatively correlated, and the correlation is --1.0. Combining investments with strong negative correlations reduces the overall volatility of the portfolio. Diversification is the method by which this goal is achieved. Table J-1 illustrates this effect.

Table J-1. Correlation of Investment Returns

	Year #1 (%)	Year #2 (%)	Year #3 (%)	Year #4 (%)	Average Return	Variance (Risk)
Investment A	–10	35	20	15	15	0.2625
Investment B	30	–15	0	5	5	0.2625
Total return (INVEST. A + INVEST. B)	10	10	10	10	–	Nil (riskless)

In reality, identifying investments with perfect negative correlations is impossible because the relationships between investments are never perfectly stable. As it turns out, however, the most stable negative correlations are found between the different returns of asset classes. It is therefore considerably easier to diversify portfolios by combining asset classes than by combining individual investments. The process of combining asset classes is called asset allocation.

Asset allocation is the basic process by which risk is managed in modern portfolio theory. In general terms, asset allocation refers to the process of adjusting the proportions of different asset classes in a portfolio. It is based on the fact that the return and the volatility of each asset class differ. Varying the proportion of different asset classes in a portfolio changes the overall or average volatility.

To make decisions about the most suitable mix of assets, it is necessary to know the anticipated return and the anticipated volatility of each asset and the correlation or covariance of each pair of assets. Tables J-2 and J-3 illustrate this process. Table J-2 shows the return, volatility, and correlation for the three basic asset classes. Table J-3 shows the return and the volatility of a portfolio composed entirely of bonds (Portfolio B), and of two portfolios composed of stocks, bonds, and cash (Portfolios A and C). Combining stocks and cash with bonds in different proportions decreases the volatility of the portfolio without decreasing return. Alternatively, the return of the portfolio can be increased without increasing volatility.

Table J-2. Return, Volatility, and Correlation for Three Asset Classes

Asset Class	Return (%)	Standard Deviation (%)	Correlation with Stocks	Correlation with Bonds	Correlation with T-Bills
Stocks	10.30	20.60	–	0.30	–0.80
Bonds	4.80	8.60	0.30	–	0.10
T-Bills	3.60	3.30	–0.8	0.10	–

Table J-3. Return and Volatility for Three Portfolios

Asset Class	Portfolio A (%)	Portfolio B (%)	Portfolio C (%)
Stocks	4.0	0.0	30.5
Bonds	80.0	100.0	69.0
T-Bills	16.0	0.0	0.5
Return	4.8	4.8	6.5
Volatility	7.1	8.6	8.6

To evaluate the efficiency of a particular allocation, modern portfolio theory relies on the concept of risk-adjusted returns. To explain how the process works, an analogy may be helpful. In baseball, batting ability is measured not by the number of hits, but by batting average. If one player has 100 hits, while another has 50, it can't be said that the first is "better" than the second because the number of opportunities each has had is unknown . If the first batter has had 400 "at bats" while the second has had only 150 "at bats," then it is the second player who is better. The first batter has a relatively ordinary .250 batting average (that is, hitting once in every four "at bats"), while the second batter has an impressive .333 batting average (hitting once in every three "at bats"). In short, meaningful comparisons can be made only on the basis of hits per "at bat."

Modern portfolio theory applies the same principle to comparisons of the returns of investments. If portfolio X has an annual return of 18 percent while portfolio Y returns only 12 percent, it cannot immediately be concluded that portfolio X is "better" than portfolio Y. Instead of batting averages, the relevant statistic is the return per unit of risk. If portfolio X has twice as much risk as portfolio Y, then our initial perception of portfolio X as the better investment is wrong: its superior return required a disproportionate level of risk.

The process of identifying the most efficient allocations is called mean-variance optimization. Although it is supposed to be extremely accurate, the data on which it is based is rather imprecise. The calculation of allocations requires information about three variables:

- expected returns
- expected correlations
- expected volatility

The most commonly used measure of return is compound annual return, but compound return is an average, and the actual return in any year can deviate widely from the expected return. Similarly, the correlation of each pair of assets is an average derived from historical observations. The measurement of volatility creates ambiguity because standard deviation is a measure of probability. As a result, specifying the return of a portfolio really means that the expected return will be somewhere around the projected return, most of the time.

Additional ambiguity is created by the short-term bias of the input variables. The anticipated return is *annual*, while the typical measurement of volatility indicates the extent of variations in *monthly* return over a three- or five-year average of *monthly* returns. As a consequence, the resulting allocations are likely to be "efficient" only over the short term.

There are two distinct approaches to asset allocation. Tactical asset allocation, or market timing, involves the active attempt to increase returns by modifying the portfolio's asset mix to capitalize on anticipated changes in the markets. A market timer who anticipates a downturn in the stock market, for example, will typically decrease the proportion of the portfolio invested in stocks, and increase the proportion invested in cash equivalents. Market timing has a seductive appeal because the clarity of hindsight allows analysts to see in retrospect precisely the best times to buy and sell. However, the approach suffers from two shortcomings.

First, there is an enormous difference between identifying the best way to maximize return *after the fact*, and identifying the best approach *before the fact*. It is extremely unlikely that anyone will be right, or wrong, all the time. In short, the fact that market timing can explain market performance does not make the approach possible, although this fairly basic point seems to be largely ignored by its proponents. In reality, there is a substantial possibility investors attempting to "time" the market will find themselves "whipsawed"—buying high only to have the price drop.

The other major limitation of market timing is that its practical effects are not nearly as great as one might anticipate. The following example, developed by Professor Geoffrey Hirt, of the Department of Finance, DePaul University, illustrates the limited benefits of the strategy. Two investors are each able to invest $1,000 per year in a fund that mirrors the stock market. One is lucky at predicting market developments and unerringly invests at the low point in the market each year. The other is utterly witless and always invests at the worst possible time each year. Over 30 years, the compound annual return for the fortuitous investor will be 11.08 percent, while the hapless one will realize a return of 9.40 percent. This really isn't that big a difference.

The academic evidence also increasingly indicates that market timing does not work. Dalbar Inc., of Boston, has recently shown that an approach of holding investments through short-term price fluctuations outperformed a strategy of market timing by three to one over the past ten years. Mark Hulbert, the author of the *Hulbert Financial Digest*, which reviews investment newsletters, has similarly demonstrated that the "buy-and-hold" strategy is far superior to market timing.

The second approach is strategic asset allocation, which is based on more gradual adjustments to an investor's portfolio. In this approach, timing is less important than risk tolerance. The lower the investor's tolerance for risk, the less volatile the appropriate portfolio. A young, single professional can tolerate the risk of a portfolio composed predominantly of equities, while a less volatile portfolio of bonds is more suitable for a widowed senior dependent on investment income.

The attraction of this version of asset allocation is that it appears to have academic support. A 1986 analysis of 91 pension funds by Gary Brinson, Randolph Hood, and Gilbert Beebower that appeared in *Financial Analysts Journal* is widely, if mistakenly, misunderstood to have concluded that more than 90 percent of a portfolio's performance is attributable to its asset allocation, while security selection and timing accounted for less than 10 percent of the variation. And if asset allocation is the most important factor affecting portfolio performance, then modifying the asset mix must be the most effective method of portfolio management. Although modern portfolio theory recognizes that it is possible to increase returns by varying the specific investments that make up each asset class, such improvements are generally portrayed as inferior on a risk-adjusted basis.

Unfortunately, the conclusions of this study have been widely misconstrued. A careful reading of the study reveals that this conclusion is enormously exaggerated. The study's actual conclusion is only that varying a portfolio's asset allocation from its long-term average allocation accounts for more than 90 percent of the resulting variation in return over time. Put another way, the effect on variations in portfolio return of decisions about changes in the basic mix of asset classes is greater than the effect of decisions about the choice of specific investments within each asset class. Increasing the proportion of bonds in the portfolio, for example, will have a greater effect on portfolio's variations in return than choices about specific bond issues. Since it is well known that the short-term volatility of bonds is lower than that of stocks, this conclusion is rather unexceptional.

In order to justify the broader conclusion conventionally attributed to the study, it would be necessary to assess the effects of both security selection and timing decisions by "controlling" for the effects of changes in basic asset mix. In a 1991 study in *Canadian Investment Review*, Colin Carlton and John Osborn attempted such a study by evaluating the relationship between a fund's returns and its "normal" or average allocation relative to the "typical" fund's "normal" or average allocation. Their conclusion is that changes in the asset mix are relatively less important than suggested by the Brinson study, and that security selection is significantly more important.

APPENDIX K

Calculating Allowable Foreign Content Contributions to RRSPs

Contribution limits are based on the book value of the investment. Book value means the price at which the investment was acquired, as opposed to its market value.

Assumptions
Canadian content fund grows at 10 percent per year.
Foreign content fund grows at 15 percent per year.

Year One
Initial contribution of $10,000. A minimum of 80 percent, or $8,000, must be invested in Canadian content funds. Up to 20 percent, or $2,000, may be invested in foreign content funds.

Year Two
The Canadian content fund is worth $8,800. The foreign content fund is worth $2,300. The total investment is now worth $11,100, but the book value is only $10,000.

A contribution of $10,000 will increase book value to $20,000. Up to 20 percent, or $4,000, may be invested in foreign content funds. The book value of the contribution to foreign content in Year One is $2,000, so a further $2,000 contribution is permitted in Year Two.

Year Three
The Canadian content fund is now worth $18,480. The foreign content fund is worth $4,945. The total investment is now worth $23,425, but the book value is only $20,000.

A contribution of $12,000 will increase book value to $32,000. Up to 20 percent, or $6,400, may be invested in foreign content funds. The book value of contributions to foreign content in Year One and Year Two is $4,000, so a further $2,400 contribution is permitted in Year Three.

Year Four

The Canadian content fund is now worth $30,888. The foreign content fund is worth $8,447. The total investment is now worth $39,335, but the book value is only $32,000.

A contribution of $10,000 will increase book value to $42,000. Up to 20 percent, or $8,400, may be invested in foreign content funds. The book value of contributions to foreign content in Years One, Two, and Three is $6,400, so a further $2,000 contribution is permitted in Year Four.

If a foreign contribution was missed at some point or previous contributions did not maximize the foreign content, an annual contribution could be greater than 20 percent of book value, provided the book value of the total foreign content does not exceed the 20 percent limit.

APPENDIX L

Investment Comfort Level Questionnaire

The purpose of this questionnaire is to help in determining your comfort level. The results are not intended to provide an indication of the maximum, or even the average, volatility that your personal portfolio exhibits. Instead, they are intended to be a guide to the extent to which investments other than equities may alleviate anxiety. This questionnaire differs from most others because it is directed specifically at the psychological component of investing. In our view, the other factors in conventional evaluations of "risk tolerance" are dealt with elsewhere.

1. Your long-term financial priority is–
   a) preserving capital
   b) maintaining current income
   c) staying ahead of inflation
   d) increasing capital growth

2. Which choice would be easiest for you?
   a) a 99 percent chance of winning $100 or a 1 percent chance of losing $10,000
   b) a 75 percent chance of winning $500 or a 25 percent chance of losing $1,500
   c) a 50 percent chance of winning $1,000 or a 50 percent chance of losing $1,000
   d) a 25 percent chance of winning $6,000 or a 75 percent chance of losing $2,000

3. You want to avoid loss of capital above all other considerations.
   a) strongly agree
   b) generally agree
   c) generally disagree
   d) strongly disagree

4. You think the best place to keep your cash is–
   a) savings accounts
   b) GICs
   c) Canada Savings Bonds
   d) T-bills

5. You want the best possible return without risk to capital.
   a) strongly agree
   b) generally agree
   c) generally disagree
   d) strongly disagree

6. A friend who's been successful in the stock market persuades you to buy $5,000 of XYZ Corp., but three months later the value of the investment has dropped $1,000 for no apparent reason. You decide to–
   a) sell the stock and cut your losses
   b) hedge your bets by selling half the shares
   c) hang on and hope the situation changes
   d) buy more shares on the advice of your friend

7. You're prepared to accept some risk to capital if it means staying ahead of inflation.
   a) strongly disagree
   b) generally disagree
   c) generally agree
   d) strongly agree

8. "A bird in the hand is worth two in the bush."
   a) strongly agree
   b) generally agree
   c) generally disagree
   d) strongly disagree

9. You would invest the proceeds of a $100,000 lump-sum pension payout in–
   a) an annuity paying 5 percent for life
   b) trust company GICs

c) a portfolio of government bonds
d) a diversified portfolio of bank, industrial, and utility stocks

10. Higher risk is OK because it provides maximum opportunity for higher returns.
    a) strongly disagree
    b) generally disagree
    c) generally agree
    d) strongly disagree

Scoring your responses:

For each answer	(a) score 1
	(b) score 4
	(c) score 7
	(d) score 10

If your total is–

10–30 –your comfort level requires investments with low volatility

31–50 –your comfort level requires investments with low-to-moderate volatility

51–76 –your comfort level requires investments with moderate volatility

76–100 –your comfort level is consistent with substantial volatility

If you couldn't answer three or more of the questions, it doesn't mean that you will be comfortable with substantial volatility. It means that you haven't given enough thought to what your comfort level really is.

APPENDIX M

Choosing an Investment Adviser

The following checklist identifies the important factors to consider in evaluating an adviser.

1. Resources

- **How large is the organization in which the adviser works?**
  The advantage of large organizations is the availability of support staff to assist the adviser in serving clients effectively. The disadvantage may be the rather impersonal or bureaucratic functioning of such an organization.

- **Is the organization reputable?**
  The reputation of financial services firms varies enormously. The organization must have a reputation for competence and for integrity and customer service.

- **Does the organization have a good research department?**

2. Background

- **How long has the adviser been in the business of advising clients?**
  Many financial advisers have been "in the business" for ten or more years, but have spent the bulk of that time in positions involving no client contact, such as in the accounting department. Choose an adviser with some experience in financial consulting unless there is a compelling reason to do otherwise.

- **Has the adviser had a prior career? If so, what did it involve?**
  Increasingly, the larger organizations are seeking out advisers with experience in sales. While this approach is good for generating business, sales experience is no guarantee of investment acumen.

3. Formal Qualifications

- **Does the adviser have a professional degree or a special designation?** Find out what the qualification means and how it is relevant to your needs Lawyers and accountants, for example, are not necessarily qualified to give investment advice. Find out whether the broker's expertise is compatible with your needs and interests. A single woman in her sixties with a fixed income, for example, does not need a broker whose specialty is trading options.

4. Investment Style

- Is there a fundamental consistency to the adviser's approach

- Is the advice motivated principally by the desire to make a sale or to curry favour with you?
  Avoid advisers who make specific "predictions"—the adviser's self-interest often underlies such predictions.

5. Approach to Clients

- Does the adviser take the time to listen to your concerns and explain issues?

- Does the adviser have a good reputation for customer service with people whose opinion you respect?

- Does the adviser provide regular statements and deal with problems as they arise?

6. Fee Options

- Is the adviser compensated by hourly or block fees?

- Does the adviser charge commissions on the value of transactions or assets under administration?

- What services are included in the compensation "package"?

How the adviser is compensated is much less important than other factors. Traditionally, fee-based advisers have argued that commissions can create conflicts of interest between the adviser and the investor. In fact, many financial planners are also designated as mutual fund brokers or life insurance brokers, and will receive a fee from the purchase of particular securities despite the fact that their planning services are fee based. The fact that an adviser is paid on the basis of commissions does not mean that the advice is biased or unreliable.

Increasingly, the traditional lines between fee- and commission-based compensation are being blurred. A number of brokerages are offering comprehensive asset management programs, charging a "fee" as a percentage of total assets rather than a transaction-based commission.

7. Personal "Fit"

- **What is your "gut feeling" about your interaction with the adviser?** Remember that the adviser has to work *with* you to ensure that your investment objectives are met. If you're not comfortable, the relationship isn't going to work.

APPENDIX N-FUND TABLES

Domestic Balanced Funds

Domestic Balanced Funds include:

- dividend funds (Divid)
  The principal investment objective of dividend funds is to provide a high level of current income through investments in preferred shares, convertible preferreds, and high-yielding common shares. There is some potential for capital appreciation through convertible and common shares.

- balanced funds (Balnc)
  Balanced funds attempt to provide both income and capital appreciation through a portfolio of fixed income and stock market investments

Fund Name	Fund Type	Rate of Return 5 Year	Rate of Return 10 Year
20/20 Cdn Tacticl Asset Allocn	Balnc	9.7	
20/20 Dividend Fund	Divid	14	11.1
ABC Fully-Managed Fund	Balnc	20.8	
AGF Cdn Asset Alloc Service A	Balnc	10.2	
AGF Growth & Income Fund 'A'	Balnc	12.9	9.7
AMI Private Capital Optimix	Balnc	10.8	
APEX Balanced Allocation Fund	Balnc	9.4	8.9
Altamira Balanced Fund	Balnc	11.5	5.8
Altamira Growth & Income Fund	Balnc	10.1	10.6
Atlas Canadian Balanced Fund	Balnc	9.9	
BG Private Balanced Fund	Balnc	13.4	
BPI Canadian Balanced Fund	Balnc	8.4	
BPI Dividend Income Fund	Divid	11	8.6
Batirente - Sec Diversifiee	Balnc	10.4	
Beutel Goodman Balanced Fund	Balnc	10.7	
Bissett Dividend Income Fund	Divid	13.9	
Bissett Retirement Fund	Balnc	13.3	
CCPE Diversified Fund	Balnc	10.1	9.2
CDA Balanced Fund (KBSH)	Balnc	10.3	9.6
CIBC Balanced Fund	Balnc	8.4	
CIBC Dividend Fund	Divid	9.4	
Caldwell Securities Associate	Balnc	13.1	
Cambridge Balanced Fund	Balnc	8.6	8.4
Canada Life Managed Fund S-35	Balnc	10.9	9.5
Canada Trust Balanced Fund	Balnc	10.1	
Capstone Investment Trust	Balnc	10.7	7.9
Cassels Blaikie Canadian Fund	Balnc	10.9	9.8

Fund Name	Fund Type	Rate of Return 5 Year	Rate of Return 10 Year
Cornerstone Balanced Fund	Balnc	9.9	6.7
Desjardins Diversified Fund	Balnc	11.5	
Dynamic Dividend Fund	Divid	10.7	9.3
Dynamic Dividend Growth Fund	Divid	13.5	8.4
Dynamic Partners Fund	Balnc	15.4	
Dynamic Team Fund	Balnc	14.1	10
Elliott & Page Balanced Fund	Balnc	14	
Empire Balanced Fund	Balnc	10.7	
Ethical Balanced Fund	Balnc	10.2	
Ferique Balanced Fund	Balnc	11	10.6
First Canadian Asset Allocatn	Balnc	8.6	
Fonds Desjardins Equilibre	Balnc	10.5	8.5
Fonds Ficadre Equilibree	Balnc	10.2	7.4
Fonds de Professionnels Balanc	Balnc	9.1	9.2
GWL Diversified RS Fund A	Balnc	8.7	
GWL Equity/Bond Fund A	Balnc	10.4	
General Trust of Can Balanced	Balnc	9.5	7.7
Green Line Balanced Growth Fnd	Balnc	9.7	
Green Line Balanced Income Fnd	Balnc	8.8	
Green Line Dividend Fund	Divid	10.1	
Guardian Canadian Balanced A	Balnc	10.2	10.2
Guardian Monthly Dividend Fd A	Divid	9.2	7.7
HRL Balanced Fund	Balnc	7.6	8
Hongkong Bank Balanced Fund	Balnc	12.4	
ICM Balanced Fund	Balnc	12.5	
Imperial Growth Diversified Fd	Balnc	9.8	
Industrial Alliance Diversif'd	Balnc	11.6	
Industrial Balanced Fund	Balnc	11	
Industrial Dividend Growth Fnd	Divid	17.4	9.6
Industrial Income Fund	Balnc	10.2	10.3
Industrial Pension Fund	Balnc	16	8.3
InvesNat Retirement Balanced	Balnc	9.8	
Investors Dividend Fund	Divid	9.4	9.3
Investors Income Plus Prtfolio	Balnc	7.9	
Investors Mutual of Canada	Balnc	11.7	9.7
Investors Retirmnt Plus Prtfol	Balnc	9.6	
Jones Heward Canadian Balanced	Balnc	9.8	8.1
LaSalle Balanced Fund	Balnc	8.6	
Laurentian Canadian Balanced	Balnc	8.3	
Laurentian Dividend Fund Ltd	Divid	9.2	9
Leith Wheeler Balanced Fund	Balnc	11.6	
London Life Diversified	Balnc	11	
Lotus (MKW) Balanced Fund	Balnc	11.1	8.4

Fund Name	Fund Type	Rate of Return 5 Year	Rate of Return 10 Year
Manulife Vista Diversified 1	Balnc	9.5	8.5
Manulife Vista Diversified 2	Balnc	8.7	7.7
Maritime Life Balanced Fund A	Balnc	9.9	8.6
Mawer Cdn Bal Retirement Sav	Balnc	10.8	
Mawer Cdn Diverisfd Invstmnt	Balnc	10.2	
Maxxum Canadian Balanced Fund	Balnc	12.8	
Maxxum Dividend Fund	Divid	19.9	11
McLean Budden Balanced Fund	Balnc	11.7	
McLean Budden Pooled Balanced	Balnc	13.3	11.6
Metlife MVP Balanced Fund	Balnc	8.2	
Mutual Diversifund 40	Balnc	10.2	8.3
NAL-Investor Diversified Fund	Balnc	11.6	
NN Asset Allocation Fund	Balnc	11.6	
National Trust Balanced Fund	Balnc	10.1	
Ontario Teachers Group Balancd	Balnc	11.1	9.8
Optimum Equilibre	Balnc	10.5	9
PH & N Balanced Fund	Balnc	12.4	
PH & N Balanced Pension Trust	Balnc	12.8	
PH & N Dividend Income	Divid	14.3	11.8
Royal Balanced Fund	Balnc	11.4	
Royal Life Balanced Fund	Balnc	9.5	
Royal Trust Advantage Balanced	Balnc	9.9	9
Royal Trust Advantage Growth	Balnc	10	8.3
Royal Trust Advantage Income	Balnc	9.4	8.9
Royal Trust Growth and Income	Divid	11.8	8.1
SSQ - Equilibre	Balnc	10.9	
Saxon Balanced Fund	Balnc	16.8	7.1
Sceptre Balanced Growth Fund	Balnc	13.5	11.1
Scotia Excelsior Balanced Fund	Balnc	10.8	
Scotia Excelsior Dividend Fund	Divid	10.8	8.8
Scotia Excelsior Total Return	Balnc	12.8	
Spectrum United Cdn Prtfl Fnds	Balnc	12.6	
Spectrum United Diversified Fd	Balnc	9.2	
Spectrum United Dividend Fund	Divid	8.9	
Standard Life Ideal Balanced	Balnc	10.7	9.1
Talvest Cdn Asset Allocation	Balnc	9	9.1
Templeton Balanced Fund	Balnc	11	
Trans-Canada Dividend Fund	Divid	8.8	6.8
Transamerica B.I.G.	Balnc	10.7	9.5
Trimark Income Growth Fund	Balnc	14.2	
Trimark Select Balanced Fund	Balnc	13.6	
Trust Pret & Revenu Ret & Baln	Balnc	11.8	9.9
Westbury Balanced Fund	Balnc	10.1	

DOMESTIC BOND FUNDS

Domestic Bond Funds include:

- medium to long-term bond funds (Bond)
  The principal objectives of these funds is income and safety of principal through investments in Canadian bonds and debentures with an average maturity of greater than five years. Capital appreciation through the management of the portfolio's average yield to maturity and bond switching is a secondary objective.

Fund Name	Fund Type	Rate of Return 5 Year	Rate of Return 10 Year
20/20 Income Fund	Bond	7.7	8.1
AGF Canadian Bond Fund 'A'	Bond	10	9.8
AMI Private Capital Income Fnd	Bond	9.4	
APEX Fixed Income Fund	Bond	9.6	10.3
Altamira Bond Fund	Bond	11.6	
Altamira Income Fund	Bond	11	11.8
Atlas Canadian Bond Fund	Bond	9.1	9
BNP (Canada) Bond Fund	Bond	9	
BPI Canadian Bond Fund	Bond	5.9	
Batirente - Sec Obligations	Bond	11.3	
Beutel Goodman Income Fund	Bond	10.3	
Bissett Bond Fund	Bond	9.9	10.1
CCPE Fixed Income Fund	Bond	9.7	9.3
CDA Bond & Mortgage (Canagex)	Bond	9.6	10.1
CIBC Canadian Bond Fund	Bond	8.6	
Canada Life Fixed Income S-19	Bond	8.5	8.8
Canada Trust Bond Fund	Bond	8.6	10.3
Cornerstone Bond Fund	Bond	8.8	9.4
Desjardins Bond Fund	Bond	10.4	11.2
Dynamic Income Fund	Bond	10	10.1
Elliott & Page Bond Fund	Bond	7.1	
Empire Bond Fund	Bond	8.1	8.6
Empire Group Bond Fund	Bond	11.1	11.3
Equitable Life Segregatd Accum	Bond	10.2	10.8
Ethical Income Fund	Bond	9.1	8.9
Ferique Bond Fund	Bond	9.9	10
Fidelity Canadian Bond Fund	Bond	8.5	
First Canadian Bond Fund	Bond	9.3	
Fonds Desjardins Obligations	Bond	9.1	8.9
Fonds Ficadre Obligations	Bond	8.4	
Fonds de Professionnels Bond	Bond	8.6	9.4

Fund Name	Fund Type	Rate of Return 5 Year	Rate of Return 10 Year
GBC Canadian Bond Fund	Bond	10.1	10.3
GWL Canadian Bond Fund (G) A	Bond	8.2	8.7
General Trust of Canada Bond	Bond	9.1	9.2
Green Line Canadian Bond Fund	Bond	10.3	
Green Line Cdn Govt Bond Fund	Bond	9.3	
HRL Bond Fund	Bond	8.9	8.6
Hyperion High Yield Bond Fund	Bond	9.3	
ICM Bond Fund	Bond	9.8	
Industrial Alliance Bond Fund	Bond	8.7	9.5
Industrial Bond Fund	Bond	9.6	
Investors Government Bond Fund	Bond	9.1	9.5
Investors Income Portfolio Fnd	Bond	8.2	
Jones Heward Bond Fund	Bond	8.2	
Laurentian Income Fund	Bond	8.2	8.8
London Life Bond	Bond	9	8.1
MD Bond Fund	Bond	10.5	
Manulife Vista Bond 1	Bond	8.6	9.3
Manulife Vista Bond 2	Bond	7.8	8.5
Maritime Life Bond Fund A	Bond	8.5	
Maritime Life Bond Fund F	Bond	8.6	9.5
Maritime Life Bond Fund G	Bond	9.1	10.1
Mawer Canadian Bond Fund	Bond	9.3	
Maxxum Income Fund	Bond	9.2	9.9
McLean Budden Fixed Income Fnd	Bond	9.8	
McLean Budden Pooled Fixed Inc	Bond	11.2	11.2
Metlife MVP Bond Fund	Bond	7	
Mutual Bond Fund	Bond	8.1	
NAL-Investor Bond Fund	Bond	9.2	
NN Bond Fund	Bond	9.7	8.9
National Life Fixed Income Fnd	Bond	9.3	9.5
National Trust Canadian Bond	Bond	9.6	9.6
OHA Bond Fund	Bond	9.7	
Optimum Obligations	Bond	11.3	10.6
PH & N Bond Fund	Bond	10.7	11.2
Pursuit Canadian Bond Fund	Bond	7	5.4
RoyFund Bond Fund	Bond	9.2	9.6
Royal Life Income Fund	Bond	9.2	
Royal Trust Bond Fund	Bond	9.4	9.6
SSQ - Obligations Canadiennes	Bond	11	11.5
Sceptre Bond Fund	Bond	9.4	10
Scotia Excelsior Income Fund	Bond	9.1	
Spectrum United Long-Term Bond	Bond	9.6	
Spectrum United Mid-Term Bond	Bond	8.7	

Fund Name	Fund Type	Rate of Return 5 Year	Rate of Return 10 Year
Standard Life Ideal Bond Fund	Bond	9.1	9.4
Talvest Bond Fund	Bond	9	9.7
Templeton Canadian Bond Fund	Bond	7	
Top Fifty T-Bill/Bond Fund	Bond	3.6	
Tradex Bond Fund	Bond	7.9	
Trans-Canada Bond Fund	Bond	6	
Trust Pret & Revenu Bond Fund	Bond	9	
Westbury Bond Fund	Bond	8.8	
Westbury Canadian Life 'B'	Bond	9.6	8.9

DOMESTIC GROWTH FUNDS

Domestic Growth Funds include:

- Canadian equity funds (CanEq)
  These funds invest mainly in the shares of companies listed on Canadian stock exchanges. Long-term growth is the principal investment objective.

- small to mid-cap Canadian equity funds (SmCap)
  These funds invest in growth-oriented companies with a market capitalization of less than $500 million. Maximizing capital growth is the principal investment objective.

Fund Name	Fund Type	Rate of Return 5 Year	Rate of Return 10 Year
20/20 Cdn Tacticl Asset Allocn	Balnc	9.7	
20/20 Dividend Fund	Divid	14	11.1
ABC Fully-Managed Fund	Balnc	20.8	
AGF Cdn Asset Alloc Service A	Balnc	10.2	
AGF Growth & Income Fund 'A'	Balnc	12.9	9.7
AMI Private Capital Optimix	Balnc	10.8	
APEX Balanced Allocation Fund	Balnc	9.4	8.9
Altamira Balanced Fund	Balnc	11.5	5.8
Altamira Growth & Income Fund	Balnc	10.1	10.6
Atlas Canadian Balanced Fund	Balnc	9.9	
BG Private Balanced Fund	Balnc	13.4	
BPI Canadian Balanced Fund	Balnc	8.4	
BPI Dividend Income Fund	Divid	11	8.6

Fund Name	Fund Type	Rate of Return 5 Year	Rate of Return 10 Year
Batirente - Sec Diversifiee	Balnc	10.4	
Beutel Goodman Balanced Fund	Balnc	10.7	
Bissett Dividend Income Fund	Divid	13.9	
Bissett Retirement Fund	Balnc	13.3	
CCPE Diversified Fund	Balnc	10.1	9.2
CDA Balanced Fund (KBSH)	Balnc	10.3	9.6
CIBC Balanced Fund	Balnc	8.4	
CIBC Dividend Fund	Divid	9.4	
Caldwell Securities Associate	Balnc	13.1	
Cambridge Balanced Fund	Balnc	8.6	8.4
Canada Life Managed Fund S-35	Balnc	10.9	9.5
Canada Trust Balanced Fund	Balnc	10.1	
Capstone Investment Trust	Balnc	10.7	7.9
Cassels Blaikie Canadian Fund	Balnc	10.9	9.8
Cornerstone Balanced Fund	Balnc	9.9	6.7
Desjardins Diversified Fund	Balnc	11.5	
Dynamic Dividend Fund	Divid	10.7	9.3
Dynamic Dividend Growth Fund	Divid	13.5	8.4
Dynamic Partners Fund	Balnc	15.4	
Dynamic Team Fund	Balnc	14.1	10
Elliott & Page Balanced Fund	Balnc	14	
Empire Balanced Fund	Balnc	10.7	
Ethical Balanced Fund	Balnc	10.2	
Ferique Balanced Fund	Balnc	11	10.6
First Canadian Asset Allocatn	Balnc	8.6	
Fonds Desjardins Equilibre	Balnc	10.5	8.5
Fonds Ficadre Equilibree	Balnc	10.2	7.4
Fonds de Professionnels Balanc	Balnc	9.1	9.2
GWL Diversified RS Fund A	Balnc	8.7	
GWL Equity/Bond Fund A	Balnc	10.4	
General Trust of Can Balanced	Balnc	9.5	7.7
Green Line Balanced Growth Fnd	Balnc	9.7	
Green Line Balanced Income Fnd	Balnc	8.8	
Green Line Dividend Fund	Divid	10.1	
Guardian Canadian Balanced A	Balnc	10.2	10.2
Guardian Monthly Dividend Fd A	Divid	9.2	7.7
HRL Balanced Fund	Balnc	7.6	8
Hongkong Bank Balanced Fund	Balnc	12.4	
ICM Balanced Fund	Balnc	12.5	
Imperial Growth Diversified Fd	Balnc	9.8	
Industrial Alliance Diversif'd	Balnc	11.6	
Industrial Balanced Fund	Balnc	11	

Fund Name	Fund Type	Rate of Return 5 Year	Rate of Return 10 Year
Industrial Dividend Growth Fnd	Divid	17.4	9.6
Industrial Income Fund	Balnc	10.2	10.3
Industrial Pension Fund	Balnc	16	8.3
InvesNat Retirement Balanced	Balnc	9.8	
Investors Dividend Fund	Divid	9.4	9.3
Investors Income Plus Prtfolio	Balnc	7.9	
Investors Mutual of Canada	Balnc	11.7	9.7
Investors Retirmnt Plus Prtfol	Balnc	9.6	
Jones Heward Canadian Balanced	Balnc	9.8	8.1
LaSalle Balanced Fund	Balnc	8.6	
Laurentian Canadian Balanced	Balnc	8.3	
Laurentian Dividend Fund Ltd	Divid	9.2	9
Leith Wheeler Balanced Fund	Balnc	11.6	
London Life Diversified	Balnc	11	
Lotus (MKW) Balanced Fund	Balnc	11.1	8.4
Manulife Vista Diversified 1	Balnc	9.5	8.5
Manulife Vista Diversified 2	Balnc	8.7	7.7
Maritime Life Balanced Fund A	Balnc	9.9	8.6
Mawer Cdn Bal Retirement Sav	Balnc	10.8	
Mawer Cdn Diverisfd Invstmnt	Balnc	10.2	
Maxxum Canadian Balanced Fund	Balnc	12.8	
Maxxum Dividend Fund	Divid	19.9	11
McLean Budden Balanced Fund	Balnc	11.7	
McLean Budden Pooled Balanced	Balnc	13.3	11.6
Metlife MVP Balanced Fund	Balnc	8.2	
Mutual Diversifund 40	Balnc	10.2	8.3
NAL-Investor Diversified Fund	Balnc	11.6	
NN Asset Allocation Fund	Balnc	11.6	
National Trust Balanced Fund	Balnc	10.1	
Ontario Teachers Group Balancd	Balnc	11.1	9.8
Optimum Equilibre	Balnc	10.5	9
PH & N Balanced Fund	Balnc	12.4	
PH & N Balanced Pension Trust	Balnc	12.8	
PH & N Dividend Income	Divid	14.3	11.8
Royal Balanced Fund	Balnc	11.4	
Royal Life Balanced Fund	Balnc	9.5	
Royal Trust Advantage Balanced	Balnc	9.9	9
Royal Trust Advantage Growth	Balnc	10	8.3
Royal Trust Advantage Income	Balnc	9.4	8.9
Royal Trust Growth and Income	Divid	11.8	8.1
SSQ - Equilibre	Balnc	10.9	
Saxon Balanced Fund	Balnc	16.8	7.1

Fund Name	Fund Type	Rate of Return 5 Year	Rate of Return 10 Year
Sceptre Balanced Growth Fund	Balnc	13.5	11.1
Scotia Excelsior Balanced Fund	Balnc	10.8	
Scotia Excelsior Dividend Fund	Divid	10.8	8.8
Scotia Excelsior Total Return	Balnc	12.8	
Spectrum United Cdn Prtfl Fnds	Balnc	12.6	
Spectrum United Diversified Fd	Balnc	9.2	
Spectrum United Dividend Fund	Divid	8.9	
Standard Life Ideal Balanced	Balnc	10.7	9.1
Talvest Cdn Asset Allocation	Balnc	9	9.1
Templeton Balanced Fund	Balnc	11	
Trans-Canada Dividend Fund	Divid	8.8	6.8
Transamerica B.I.G.	Balnc	10.7	9.5
Trimark Income Growth Fund	Balnc	14.2	
Trimark Select Balanced Fund	Balnc	13.6	
Trust Pret & Revenu Ret & Baln	Balnc	11.8	9.9
Westbury Balanced Fund	Balnc	10.1	

DOMESTIC INCOME FUNDS

Domestic Income Funds include:

- short-term bond and mortgage funds (Mortg)
  This category includes funds which invest principally in short-term bonds (term-to-maturity of five years or less), and/or industrial, commercial, or residential mortgages (which also typically have a term-to-maturity of five years or less). These funds offer a combination of high current income plus safety of principal.

Fund Name	Fund Type	Rate of Return 5 Year	Rate of Return 10 Year
AGF High Income Fund 'A'	Mortg	9	
CIBC Mortgage Fund	Mortg	8.3	9.7
Canada Trust Mortgage Fund	Mortg	7.8	9.3
Concorde Hypotheques	Mortg	7.3	
Desjardins Mortgage Fund	Mortg	8	9.7
Dolphin Income Fund	Mortg	11.3	11.5
First Canadian Mortgage Fund	Mortg	8.4	9.9
Fonds Desjardins Hypotheques	Mortg	7.3	8.9

Fund Name	Fund Type	Rate of Return 5 Year	Rate of Return 10 Year
GWL Mortgage Fund A	Mortg	7.8	8.8
General Trust of Can Mortgage	Mortg	7.3	8.7
Green Line Mortgage Fund	Mortg	7.8	9.6
Green Line Mortgage-Backed Fnd	Mortg	7.1	
Green Line Short Term Income	Mortg	6.5	
Industrial Alliance Mortgages	Mortg	7.1	9.1
Industrial Mortgage Securities	Mortg	9.4	10.1
InvesNat Mortgage Fund	Mortg	8.2	
InvesNat Short Term Govt Bond	Mortg	7.7	
Investors Mortgage Fund	Mortg	7.1	8.6
Laurentian Government Bond Fnd	Mortg	7	
London Life Mortgage	Mortg	8	9.2
Ontario Teachers Grp Mortgage	Mortg	9.1	9.4
Royal Trust Mortgage Fund	Mortg	6.7	8.6
SSQ - Hypotheques	Mortg	8.9	
Scotia Excelsior Defensive Inc	Mortg	7.8	
Spectrum United Shrt-Term Bond	Mortg	6.9	7.9
Talvest Income Fund	Mortg	8.3	9
Trust Pret & Revenu H Fund	Mortg	7.4	8.9

FOREIGN BALANCED FUNDS

Foreign Balanced Funds include:

- international balanced funds (InBal)
  These funds invest globally in both bonds and equities with a view to creating both income and capital gains.

Fund Name	Fund Type	Rate of Return 5 Year	Rate of Return 10 Year
20/20 Am. Tactical Asset Alloc	InBal	13	
20/20 World Fund	InBal	10.8	
BPI Global Balanced RSP Fund	InBal	11.3	
Investors Growth Plus Prtfolio	InBal	11.3	
Laurentian Global Balanced Fnd	InBal	8.2	
Protected American Fund	InBal	6.3	
Spectrum United Globl Diversfd	InBal	10.1	
Talvest Global Asset Allocatn	InBal	8.8	

FOREIGN BOND FUNDS

Foreign Bond Funds include:

- international bond funds (IntBd)
  International bond funds invest primarily in the debt instruments of foreign issuers denominated in a foreign currency with an average maturity greater than five years. The objective is to generate income and capital gains. The capital gains can arise from declining interest rates or currency movements. Some funds do not speculate on currency and hedge their investment portfolios against changes in the value of foreign currencies against the Canadian dollar.

Fund Name	Fund Type	Rate of Return 5 Year	Rate of Return 10 Year
AGF Global Government Bond 'A'	IntBd	8.2	8.6
Diversified Bond Fund	IntBd	7.4	
Dynamic Global Bond Fund	IntBd	10.3	
Global Strategy World Bond Fnd	IntBd	7.6	
Guardian Internatnl Income A	IntBd	9.9	6.5
Royal Trust International Bond	IntBd	10.5	
Scotia CanAm Income Fund ($US)	IntBd	5.2	
Templeton Global Bond Fund	IntBd	8.6	

FOREIGN GROWTH FUNDS

Foreign Growth Funds include:

- global equity funds (GloEq)
  Funds which invest in international equities with the mandate to invest in any country where opportunities exist are included in this category.
- U.S. and North American equity funds (UsEq)
  This category includes funds whose investment arena includes the U.S., Canada and Mexico.
- European equity funds (Europ)
  These funds invest primarily in equities of companies listed on European exchanges.
- far east equity funds (FarEa)
  Equity funds which invest primarily in the Asian and Pacific Rim countries are included in this category.

- emerging markets & Latin America funds (EmLat)
  These funds invest in equities of companies located in Latin America or any of the emerging markets around the world such as India, Turkey, South Africa etc.

Fund Name	**Fund Type**	**Rate of Return 5 Year**	**Rate of Return 10 Year**
20/20 International Value Fund	GloEq	14.8	
AGF American Growth Class 'A'	USEq	16.8	11.9
AGF Asian Growth Class 'A'	FarEa	21.3	
AGF Japan Fund Class 'A'	FarEa	1.2	2.4
AGF Special US Class 'A'	USEq	10	10.8
AIC Value Fund	USEq	20.6	
Admax American Growth Fund	USEq	6.5	
Admax International Fund	GloEq	12.8	
Admax Tiger Fund	FarEa	8.5	
Altamira Global Diversified Fd	GloEq	9.7	3.2
Altamira Select American Fund	USEq	18.6	
Atlas American Large Cap Grwth	USEq	13.1	9.4
Atlas Global Value Fund	GloEq	12.3	
BG Private Foreign Equity Fund	USEq	17.1	
BPI American Equity Value Fund	USEq	14.5	
BPI American Small Companies	USEq	22.9	
BPI Global Equity Fund	GloEq	12.8	
Beutel Goodman American Equity	USEq	16.6	
Bissett American Equity Fund	USEq	12.9	9.7
C.I. Emerging Markets Fund	EmLat	8.1	
C.I. Global Fund	GloEq	12	9.1
C.I. Global Sector Shares	GloEq	11.5	
C.I. Pacific Fund	FarEa	16.1	10.9
C.I. Pacific Sector Shares	FarEa	15.6	
CIBC Global Equity Fund	GloEq	9.9	
CIBC US Equity Fund	USEq	13.2	
Caldwell Securities Internatnl	USEq	9.8	
Cambridge Americas Fund	GloEq	10.2	
Cambridge Global Fund	GloEq	2.7	3.5
Cambridge Pacific Fund	FarEa	3.8	-4.5
Canada Life US &Intl Eqty S-34	GloEq	16.2	13.8
Canada Trust International Eqt	GloEq	9	
Canada Trust North American	USEq	10.4	7.4
Canada Trust US Equity Fund	USEq	12.2	
Capstone Intl Investment Trust	GloEq	12.5	
Cassels Blaikie American ($US)	USEq	9.5	12.2
Century DJ Fund	USEq	3.8	3.5
Chou Associates Fund	USEq	16.9	13.1

Fund Name	Fund Type	Rate of Return 5 Year	Rate of Return 10 Year
Cornerstone Global Fund	GloEq	13.1	11.3
Cornerstone US Fund Ltd	USEq	13.7	8.4
Cundill Value Fund	GloEq	16.2	11.6
Dynamic Americas Fund	USEq	13	10.8
Dynamic Europe Fund	Europ	13.9	
Dynamic International Fund	GloEq	13.1	4.3
Elliott & Page American Growth	USEq	12.8	8.9
Empire International Fund	GloEq	13.9	
Ethical North American Equity	USEq	15.1	8.8
Fidelity Far East Fund	FarEa	23.9	
Fidelity Growth America Fund	USEq	18.8	
Fidelity Int'l Portfolio Fund	GloEq	14.4	
First American Fund	USEq	4.5	
Fonds Desjardins International	GloEq	11.3	9.9
GBC International Growth Fd	GloEq	4.3	
GBC North American Growth Fd	USEq	16.7	11.8
General Trust International Fd	GloEq	8.4	
General Trust of Canada US Eqt	USEq	11.3	11.3
Green Line US Index Fund ($US)	USEq	13.7	13.2
Guardian American Equity Fd A	USEq	16.5	12.4
Guardian Global Equity 'A'	GloEq	12.7	5.2
Hansberger European Fund	Europ	7.4	
Hyperion Asian Fund	FarEa	17.8	
Hyperion European Fund	Europ	12.7	
Hyperion Value Line US Equity	USEq	16.5	
Imperial Growth N American Eqt	USEq	13	8.7
Industrial American Fund	USEq	14	10
Investors European Growth Fund	Europ	12.5	
Investors Global Fund	GloEq	11.3	8.4
Investors Growth Portfolio Fnd	GloEq	14.2	
Investors Japanese Growth Fund	FarEa	4	2.9
Investors North American Grwth	USEq	13.1	12.6
Investors Pacific Internationl	FarEa	18	
Investors Special Fund	USEq	12.7	12.7
Investors US Growth Fund	USEq	16.8	13.6
Jones Heward American Fund	USEq	8.6	8.9
Laurentian American Equity Fnd	USEq	11.4	8.8
Laurentian Commonwealth Fund	GloEq	9.3	8.6
Laurentian International Fund	GloEq	9.6	8
London Life US Equity	USEq	12.2	
MD Growth Fund	GloEq	17.4	11.9
Mackenzie Sentinel Global Fund	GloEq	10.4	

Fund Name	Fund Type	Rate of Return 5 Year	Rate of Return 10 Year
Margin of Safety Fund	USEq	12.1	
Mawer World Investment Fund	GloEq	13.1	
McLean Budden American Growth	USEq	13.1	
McLean Budden Pooled American	USEq	15.4	14
McLean Budden Pooled Offshore	GloEq	10.9	
Mutual Amerifund	USEq	14.2	9.8
NAL-Investor Global Equity Fnd	GloEq	11.4	
National Life Global Equities	GloEq	14.3	
Ontario Teachers Group Global	GloEq	10.5	
Orbit World Fund	GloEq	5.9	
PH & N US Equity	USEq	18.4	14.8
PH & N US Pooled Pension	USEq	20	16
RoyFund US Equity Fund	USEq	18	
Royal European Growth Fund	Europ	13.7	
Royal Japanese Stock Fund	FarEa	1.5	-0.6
Royal Trust American Stock Fnd	USEq	14.5	12.2
SSQ - Actions Americaines	USEq	13.8	
Saxon World Growth	GloEq	19.5	12.6
Sceptre International Fund	GloEq	17.5	14.6
Scotia Excelsior International	GloEq	10.9	7.9
Scotia Excelsr American Growth	USEq	12.5	
Spectrum United American Eqty	USEq	14	11.3
Spectrum United Americn Growth	USEq	20	13.3
Spectrum United Global Equity	GloEq	9.7	
Spectrum United Global Growth	GloEq	8.6	2.9
Templeton Emerging Markets Fnd	EmLat	14.2	
Templeton Globl Smallr Compnes	GloEq	15.9	
Templeton Growth Fund, Ltd.	GloEq	17.1	12.3
Templeton International Stock	GloEq	19	
Top Fifty US Equity Fund	USEq	9.3	
Trimark Fund	GloEq	21.2	15.4
Trimark Select Growth Fund	GloEq	19.2	
Trust Pret & Revenu American	USEq	12.8	9.9
Universal Americas Fund	GloEq	12.8	9.7
Universal World Equity Fund	GloEq	11.4	7.4
University Avenue US Growth Fd	USEq	4.3	3.6
Vision Europe Fund	Europ	14	

FOREIGN INCOME FUNDS

Foreign Income Funds include:

- funds which primarily in the debt instruments of foreign issuers denominated in a foreign currency with an average maturity less than five years. There are no such funds with a minimum five year track record currently available from Canadian fund companies

GLOSSARY

active investing investing that attempts to produce returns superior to those of the broader market by choosing investments selectively on the basis of various strategies and techniques. Contrast with: **passive investing.** See also: **bottom-up investing; top-down investing.**

adjusted cost base the cost of an asset plus (or minus) any "adjustments" permitted by tax legislation. The adjusted cost base is important in calculating capital gains (or losses).

ADR see: **American Depository Receipt**

all weather fund a **mutual fund** which does equally well in **bull markets** and **bear markets.** Contrast with: **fair weather fund; foul weather fund.**

alpha a measure of the *actual* performance of an investment relative to the performance that would be *anticipated* on the basis of its **beta.** See also: **risk-adjusted returns.**

American Depository Receipt a **security** representing the shares of a foreign corporation which are held on behalf of investors by a U.S. bank or trust company. Investors may purchase ADRs instead of purchasing the shares directly. There are ADRs for hundreds of companies from many foreign countries. They allow investors to avoid the inconvenience of dealing with foreign markets and currency **exchanges.**

amortization the gradual repayment of a debt over a period of time.

amortized cost pricing a method for pricing a mutual fund (especially money market funds) in which the unit cost is held constant and changes in net asset value are reflected in the amount of the periodic interest payment. Contrast with: **mark-to-market pricing.**

analyst an individual who studies a number of companies and makes recommendations on their **securities.**

annualized the **rate of return** expressed as if the investment were for one year.

annual information form a document required by securities regulators that supplements the information in a **simplified prospectus.**

annual report a summary of a company's activities including its financial results issued to shareholders following the end of the **fiscal year.**

appraisal determination of the value of an asset or investment by estimation.

arbitrage the purchase and sale of investments at different prices in different markets.

asset anything owned by a person or company. Assets may be tangible (real estate, jewellery, cash, and so on) or intangible (patents, computer programmes, and so on).

asset allocation the distribution of investment **assets** into various categories, such as **stocks, bonds**, and real estate. Also, the *active* distribution of assets in response to expectations regarding future economic and market conditions. See also: **tactical ~; strategic ~.**

asset allocation fund a mutual fund that attempts to adjust the mix of investments in the **portfolio** between stocks, bonds, and other assets in order to achieve the highest possible **return.** See also: **balanced fund.**

attribution analysis the breakdown of return into various components in order to determine its basis.

auditor the accredited professional who reviews the financial statements of a business to ensure that they accurately reflect the financial status of the business.

average the quantity intermediate to a set of numbers. Also, an indicator of the performance of the **market** as a whole: eg. the *Dow Jones industrial average.*

average term to maturity a measure of the time to **maturity** of a **portfolio** of fixed-income investments. Used as a measure of **volatility.**

back-end load a sales charge levied at the time mutual funds are sold or redeemed by the investor. The amount of the charge typically declines with the number of years the fund is held. See also: **deferred sales charge; rear load; redemption charge.**

back testing a process for establishing the validity of an investment technique by applying the technique to past data in order to determine what performance would have been if the technique had been used.

balance sheet a financial statement showing the **assets** and **liabilities** of a company or individual on a specific date. See also: **income statement; net worth.**

balanced fund a **mutual fund** that invests in both **stocks** and **bonds** in order to provide the investor with both **capital gains** and steady **income.** See also: **asset allocation fund.**

bankers' acceptance a promissory note drawn for payment by a corporation on a certain date that has been guaranteed by a chartered bank. The terms range from 30 to 90 days and they are backed by the credit standing of both the issuer and the guaranteeing bank.

bear market a market that is generally declining, as measured by an **average** or **index.** Contrast with: **bull market.**

benchmark a standard against which investment performance is measured.

beta a measure of the degree to which the price of a **stock** fluctuates relative to a **market average**, or **index**. A stock with a beta of 1.0 fluctuates in price as much as the market. A stock with a beta less than 1.0 fluctuates less dramatically than the broader market, while a stock with a beta greater than 1.0 has greater price fluctuations than the market as a whole. See also: **volatility; standard deviation.**

blue chip stock the **shares** of big, well-established companies with good records of earnings, and a history of regular **dividend** payments.

bond a **security** issued by governments and corporations that constitutes a promise to pay a debt. See also: **debenture; mortgage.**

bond fund a mutual fund that invests primarily in **bonds.**

book value the stated value of a company (**assets** minus **liabilities** and the value of **preferred shares**).

~ per share the book value divided by the number of **common shares**. This is often used by **value investors** as an indicator for selecting shares priced below their true value.

bottom-up investing an investment style that focuses on the merits of individual companies rather than the industry **sector** or economy as a whole. It assumes that particular companies can do well even though their competitors, or the economy generally, may be doing poorly. Contrast with: **top-down investing.**

break-up value the value of a company that would be realized if the assets of the company were sold off individually. See also: **liquidation value.**

broker a representative who provides investors with advice and acts as agent in the purchase and sale of securities. See also: **investment adviser.**

bull market a market that is generally rising, as measured by an **average** or **index**. Contrast with: **bear market.**

business cycle the alternating periods of strength (expansion) and weakness (recession) in the economy. Contrast with: **market cycle.**

call an **option** that gives the holder the right, but not the obligation, to buy a security at a specified price for a period of time. Contrast with: **put.** See also: **derivative.**

callable the feature of a **bond** that gives the **issuer** the right to **redeem** prior to **maturity**. Compare with: retractable. Contrast with: extentible.

call risk the possibility that a **bond** will be called by the issuer.

Canada Deposit Insurance Corporation the agency of the federal government that insures **deposits** against the insolvency of member institutions. The maximum coverage is $60,000 per person per institution.

Canada Mortgage and Housing Corporation an agency of the Canadian federal government that plays various roles in the housing market including the provision of guarantees on some residential mortgages offered by financial institutions.

capital cost allowance a deduction from income allowed on **assets** to reflect the fact that they typically decrease in value with use.

capital appreciation the increase in the value of an investment.

capital distribution see distribution.

capital gain the profit resulting from the sale of an **asset.**

capital markets **markets** that deal in long-term (greater than one year) **securities,** both **debt (bonds)** and **equity (stocks).**

cash flow the net income of a business together with expenses not actually paid (such as depreciation, **amortization** and deferred taxes). It reflects the capacity of a business to fund its operation, and is frequently used as a measure of its efficiency.

CDIC see **Canada Deposit Insurance Corporation.**

charting the process of plotting the trading volumes and price movements of share prices in order to discern any trends. Charts are the basic tool of **technical analysis.**

closed-end fund a fund with a fixed number of **shares** or units, which are traded on an **exchange.**

CMHC see **Canada Mortgage and Housing Corporation**

collateral **assets** pledged as security for the repayment of a **debt.**

collateralized mortgage obligation a **derivative** based on **mortgages.**

commercial paper a short-term promissory note issued on the strength of a corporation's general credit standing.

commission the fee paid to a **broker** or other agent for buying or selling **securities** on behalf of an investor. Typically a percentage of the amount of the transaction. See also: **sales charge.**

commodity a tangible asset (such as grain, oil, etc.).

commodity future a **derivative** based on a **commodity**. See also: **future.**

common share a class of **stock** that represents the basic unit of ownership or **equity** in a company. See also: **common stock.**

common stock

1. the basic unit of ownership or **equity** in a company.
2. stock that has no special privileges. Contrast with: **preferred shares.**

compound annual rate of return the **rate of return** of an investment including reinvestment of profit, expressed as if the return were constant. See also: **rate of return; simple rate of return.**

compound interest **interest** paid on interest.

consumer price index a statistical yardstick showing the rate at which prices have risen. Often used as an indicator of the rate of inflation.

continuous disclosure disclosure on an on-going basis of all material facts related to an investment.

contrarian an investor who takes a position opposite or contrary to the consensus.

convertible a feature of **securities** (such as a **bond** or **preferred shares**) that can be exchanged for common shares of the same company.

core investing an investment approach for **bonds** in which the duration and credit quality are varied only within relatively narrow limits around a **benchmark.**

corporate bond fund a **mutual fund** that invests primarily in bonds issued by corporations.

correlation the degree to which price changes in one investment are matched by price movements in another investment.

counterparty the opposite side or party in a **derivative** transaction.

coupon the **interest rate** on a bond. Also, individual documents forming part of the **bond** certificate, which are detached and presented for payment of **interest** as they come due.

CPI see **consumer price index.**

credit rating an evaluation of the quality of a debt investment made by an independent agency.

credit risk the risk that a debt investment such as a **bond** will not pay interest as required. See also: **default risk.**

currency risk the risk that an investment denominated in a foreign currency will decline in value as a result of devaluation of that foreign currency.

current yield the interest income of a **bond** divided by the **market price.**

custodian the agency that holds the assets of a mutual fund for safekeeping.

cyclical stock stock of a company within an industry sector that is particularly sensitive to economic or business cycles.

debenture a **bond** without security other than the general credit-worthiness of the **issuer.** Government bonds are really debentures, although they are conventionally called bonds.

debt an obligation to pay money, goods, or services.

deemed disposition the sale of property imputed by tax legislation in the absence of an actual transaction. See also: **disposition.**

default risk the possibility that a borrower of money will not repay the debt. See also: **credit risk.**

deferred sales charge see: **back-end load.**

deflation a general decline in the prices of goods and services. Contrast with: **inflation.**

derivative an investment based on or *derived from* another, underlying, investment or **security.**

disclosure documents documents that are intended to provide investors with "full, true and plain" disclosure of all material facts about an investment. They include: the prospectus (or **simplified prospectus**) and **financial statements.**

discount the amount by which an asset sells below its **nominal** value. Contrast with: **premium.**

disposition the sale of an investment. See also: **deemed disposition.**

distribution the payment to investors of the **income** or realized **capital gains** of a **mutual fund.**

distribution fees fees levied by a few mutual fund companies on **shares** or **units** of funds purchased with a **deferred sales charge.**

distributor the person, business, or agency responsible for making a mutual fund available to investors.

diversification investment in a variety of different **securities** in order to spread, and thereby reduce, the **risk** of investing.

dividend a share in the profits of a company paid to holders of **common** or **preferred shares** in an amount determined by the company's Board of Directors.

dividend fund a **mutual fund** that invests primarily in securities that pay **dividends.**

dividend tax credit a **tax credit** allowed on **dividend income** to reflect the fact that the corporation has previously been taxed on the amount it pays in dividends.

dollar cost averaging an investment technique involving the purchase of **securities** at regular intervals in a fixed amount. More **shares** are purchased when prices are lower, and fewer are purchased with prices are higher.

Dow Jones Industrial Average **market indexes** based on 30 stocks listed on the New York Stock Exchange. The Dow Jones Industrial Average is the most widely quoted, but there are several others: the Transportation Average; the Utilities Average; and the Composite Average. See also: **index.**

duration a measure of **risk** for fixed income investments that reflects the size, frequency and timing of **interest** payments.

earned income generally income from employment, including self-employment.

earnings per share a company's **net income** (less **dividends** on **preferred shares**) divided by the number of **common shares** outstanding.

efficient market theory the belief that the price of an investment reflects all information known about it, and that it is therefore impossible to outperform the market by identifying undervalued investments.

effective interest rate the actual **interest rate** on a debt once the frequency of compounding is taken into account. See also **compound interest.** Contrast with: **nominal interest rate; real interest rate.**

effective return the **nominal rate of return** adjusted for the effects of taxes.

effective yield the yield on a **money market fund** expressed as if the **indicated yield** would continue into the future. Contrast with: **indicated yield.**

equities **securities** representing ownership in a company. See also: **common stock; preferred shares.**

equity the value of the ownership in an **asset** after deducting the value of any claims against it.

equity fund a mutual fund that invests primarily in **equities.** See also: **growth funds; stock funds.**

exchange an organized **market** on which **securities** are traded by the members of the exchange.

exchange rate the relationship between two currencies.

~risk: The possibility that the relationship between two currencies will change, affecting investment **return.**

face value the value of a bond or debenture that appears on its face as the amount due on **maturity.** The bond or debenture may **trade** in the **market** at face value or at a **premium** or a **discount.**

fair weather fund a **mutual fund** that has better than average returns in **bull markets** and poorer than average returns in **bear markets.** Contrast with: **foul weather fund; all weather fund.**

family of funds a group of **mutual funds** with a common **manager.**

financial adviser an individual who provides investment advice. Compare with: **broker; investment adviser; financial planner.**

financial institution a business that collects money from investors for the purpose of placing it in financial **assets.** Depository institutions (such as banks) pay **interest** on deposits. Non-depository institutions (such as insurance companies) provide services for the money they receive.

financial planner an individual who provides clients with advice regarding investment and retirement plans. Some are compensated on the basis of hourly or project fees; others receive **commissions** from the sale of investment products.

financial planning a systematic approach to developing and meeting financial goals.

financial statements written records of the financial status of an individual or company. See also **balance sheet; income statement.**

fiscal year the 12-month period that is the basis of accounting. The fiscal year of some businesses does not correspond to the calendar year.

fixed-income investments **securities** such as **bonds, debentures,** and **mortgages,** which provide stable, regular payments.

fixed-income fund a mutual fund that invests primarily in **fixed income securities.**

formula investing investing according to mechanical techniques. See: **life-cycle investing; dollar cost averaging.**

forward contract a **derivative** investment that gives the holder the right to purchase an asset at some future time at a previously agreed price. See also: **future.**

foul weather fund a **mutual fund** that performs better than average in **bear markets** and poorer than average in **bull markets.** Contrast with: **fair weather fund; all weather fund.**

front-end load a sales charge levied by many mutual funds at the time fund units are purchased. Typically, the commission rate decreases as the size of the purchase increases. See also: **acquisition fee.** Contrast with: **back-end load.**

fundamental analysis an approach to determining the value of **securities** based on examining the basic circumstances of the issuer—sales, **earnings, dividend** payments, etc. Contrast with: **technical analysis.**

fundamental investment objectives the most important objectives identified in the **prospectus** of a **mutual fund.** They cannot be changed without the approval of the **unitholders.**

future a contract that provides the buyer the right, and the obligation, to purchase or sell securities or commodities at a specified price and time. Futures are typically **traded** on **exchanges.** Compare with: **options.** See also: **derivatives; forward contract.**

GIC see: **guaranteed investment certificate**

growth fund a **mutual fund** with the principal objective of **capital appreciation** which invests primarily in **common stocks.**

growth investing an investment strategy based on seeking out **growth stocks.**

growth stock common shares of a company with earnings that are expected to grow at an above-average rate in the future.

guaranteed investment certificate (GIC) an **interest** bearing deposit contract usually issued by a trust company or other **financial institution** in which the investor commits funds for a specified term and receives a fixed rate of interest for that term. Early **redemption** typically entails penalties.

hedge a technique used to reduce investment **risk** by pairing securities with opposing price movements. See also: **derivatives.**

high yield bonds bonds that are rated below "investment grade" (BBB). They typically offer a higher yield than investment grade bonds to compensate for their higher default risks. Also known as **junk bonds.**

illiquidity see: **liquidity**

income periodic receipts from employment or investments. Contrast with: **capital gains.**

income distribution see: **distribution**

income fund a **mutual fund** with the principal objective of providing a stable income which invests primarily in **securities** that pay a regular **income** such as **bonds, mortgages,** and **preferred shares.**

income statement a written record outlining the revenues, expenses and profit (or loss) of a business or individual over a period of time. See also: **financial statement; balance sheet.**

index a statistical "yardstick" against which performance is measured.

market~ is a **portfolio** of **securities** chosen to represent a broader **market.** See also: **average.**

market timing the attempt to buy stocks prior to price increases, and sell stocks prior to price declines in order to increase returns. Compare with: **asset allocation.**

index fund a **mutual fund** that holds a portfolio which mirrors an **index.**

indexing an investment strategy that involves a portfolio chosen to match an **index.**

closet~ is a strategy of indexing that is undisclosed.

indicated yield the **annualized** rate of return on a money market fund over the preceding seven days.

inflation the erosion of the purchasing power of money. Contrast with: **deflation.**

inflation risk the possibility that inflation will reduce the purchasing power of an investment's return.

institutional investor a large corporate investor, often with special expertise in areas such as pension plans financial institutions or **mutual funds**. These investors dominate trading on most **exchanges**. See also: **sophisticated investor**.

interest the payments (sometimes comparable to rent) that a borrower of money is required to make to a lender for the use of money.

interest rate the cost of borrowing money expressed as a percentage of the borrowed amount. The interest rate is typically expressed on an annualized basis. Compare with: **real interest rate**.

interest rate anticipation an investment strategy for **bonds** based on modifying the **term to maturity** of a **portfolio** on the basis of expectations about the future direction of **interest rates**.

interest rate sensitivity the degree to which the value of an investment is affected by changes in interest rates.

intermediate term the time frame between long term and short term. In the analysis of **stocks**, it typically means 6 to 18 months. In the analysis of **bonds** it typically means 3 to 10 years. See also **medium term**.

international fund a mutual fund that invests in securities from both the domestic and foreign **markets**.

inverted yield curve describes a situation in which the normal **yield curve** is disrupted so that long-term **interest** rates are lower than short-term **interest** rates. See: **yield curve**.

investment adviser
1. the person or entity with responsibility for investing the assets or providing investment advice to a mutual fund or other large investor. In the case of mutual funds it may be the fund **sponsor**, or a person or organization hired by the **sponsor**. See also: **sponsor**.
2. an employee of an investment firm licensed to give investment advice to the public. See also: **broker**; **financial adviser**. Compare with: **financial planner**.

investment company a company that earns income by investing in the **securities** of other companies. See also: **closed-end fund**; **mutual fund**; **unit trust**.

investment grade securities (usually bonds) that are rated BBB or better and that are suitable for trusteed investments.

investment horizon the period of time over which an investor expects to make an investment.

investment income income earned from investments. Contrast with: **earned income**; **capital gains**.

investment manager the person or entity who make decisions about the **securities** included in the **portfolio** of a **mutual fund** or pension fund.

investment mandate the **fundamental investment objectives** and **investment policies** of a **mutual fund.**

investment policy
1. the kinds of investments and assets a **mutual fund** will include in its **portfolio,** and the degree of **risk** the **portfolio manager** is prepared to accept.
2. the framework of goals and constraints that influence the specific investment decisions of an investor.

issue a specific offering of **stock** or **bonds.**

junk bonds see: **high yield bond**

LSIF see: **labour sponsored investment fund**

LSVCC see: **labour sponsored venture capital corporation**

labour sponsored investment fund a mutual fund that is not subject to many of the usual investment restrictions, and which is eligible for special tax treatment. See also: **labour sponsored venture capital corporation.** Compare with: **segregated fund.**

labour sponsored venture capital corporation an investment corporation which invests in small- and medium-sized businesses, and which is eligible for special tax treatment. It is similar to a mutual fund in some respects, but it is not subject to many of the investment restrictions of mutual funds.

laddering an investment strategy based on combining **bonds** and other debt investments with different **maturity dates.**

large-capitalization fund a mutual fund that invests primarily in large-cap stocks.

large-capitalization stocks stocks in companies with a market capitalization greater than $1 billion. Contrast with: **small-cap stocks; mid-cap stocks.**

leverage the artificial enlargement of an investment to increase **returns.** The most common form of leverage is the investment of borrowed money.

liability an amount owed. Contrast with: **asset.** See also: **balance sheet.**

LIF see: **Life Income Fund**

life cycle investing an **investment policy** based on the belief that different stages in life require different approaches to investing.

Life Income Fund a plan, similar to a RRIF, which is created from the assets of a terminated **Life Income Retirement Account.**

Life Income Retirement Account a plan registered in accordance with the Income Tax Act (Canada) which is funded from an investor's irrevocable entitlement under a pension plan

liquidation value see: **break-up value**

liquidity the ease or readiness with which an **asset** may be sold for cash. Highly liquid assets can be converted to cash without significantly affecting price: **illiquid** investments may be sold only by **discounting** their price.

LIRA see: **Life Income Retirement Account**

listed stock **common shares** or **preferred shares** of a company that have been accepted for **trading** on an **exchange**.

load a **sales charge** charged on the purchase of mutual funds. See also: **acquisition fee; front-end load; back-end load; rear load; deferred sales charge.**

load fund a mutual fund on which purchasers pay a **sales charge**.

long term when applied to **stocks**, a time frame greater than 18 months. When applied to **bonds** or debentures, a time frame greater than ten years. Contrast with: **short term; medium term.**

MBS **mortgage-backed security**.

management expense ratio the total of all expenses associated with the operation of a mutual fund, expressed as a percentage of total **assets**.

management fee the fee paid to the **manager** of a mutual fund for administering the operation of the fund and providing advice respecting the fund's investment **portfolio**.

management risk the possibility that the actions of a business manager will negatively affect the value of the shares of the business.

manager the persons responsible for overseeing the operation of a **mutual fund**. Compare with: **investment manager; portfolio manager.**

marginal tax rate the rate of tax imposed on any additional dollar of income received by the taxpayer.

market the network of institutions and people in which products and services are bought and sold. Also applied to describe securities **exchanges**.

market capitalization the value of a company measured by the number of shares multiplied by the share price. Often used as an indicator of a company's size and risk profile. See also: **large capitalization; small capitalization.**

market cycle the alternating periods of strength and weakness in the financial markets. Contrast with: **business cycle**.

market exposure rule a general principle regulating the content of investment portfolios, which limits a mutual fund to holding 10 percent of any class or series of securities, or investing more than 10 percent of the portfolio's assets in any class or series of securities.

market price the last reported price at which a **security** was sold on an **exchange** or by other public transaction.

market risk the possibility that the markets as a whole will decline. See also: **bear market.**

mark-to-market pricing a method for pricing a mutual fund in which the value of the units fluctuates with the net value of the fund's portfolio of assets. Contrast with: **amortized cost pricing.** See also: **net asset value.**

maturity the 'life expectancy' of a bond or other fixed interest investment. See also: **term to ~ ; average ~.**

maturity date the date on which the principal amount of a debt becomes due.

modern portfolio theory an investment approach based on the belief that it is rational and possible to structure a portfolio which offers the greatest return for a given level of volatility (or the lowest volatility for a given level of return) by modifying the mix or **allocation** of assets. Compare with: **asset allocation.**

momentum investing an investment approach based primarily on the use of trading statistics to identify securities with rising price trends.

money market the **market** in **debt securities** maturing in one year or less.

money market fund a mutual fund with the principal objective of safety of capital, and which invests in **money market securities.**

money market securities **debt** investments with a term to **maturity** of one year or less.

mortgage a contract in which the borrower of money pledges real estate as collateral for the loan.

mortgage backed security a **security** based on a 'pool' or 'bundle' of **mortgages** packaged and resold or re-issued by **financial institutions.**

mutual fund a professionally managed **portfolio** of investments which offers **shares** or **units** to the public on a continuous basis. See also: **open-end investment company; unit trust.** Contrast with: **closed-end fund.**

mutualization the process of converting a **closed-end fund** to an **open-end mutual fund.**

net asset value the price of shares or units of a **mutual fund,** established by dividing the total value of the **securities** in the fund's **portfolio** (less any **liabilities**) by the number of outstanding units.

net worth the value of an individual's (or company's) **assets** less any **liabilities.** See also: **balance sheet.**

no-load fund a **mutual fund** that imposes no **sales charge** for the purchase of its **shares** or units.

nominal the **face value** or **stated value.**

~ interest rate: The face value or stated interest rate paid on a **debt security** without taking into account the effects of **compounding** or **inflation.**

non-prepayable a **mortgage-backed security** based on **mortgages** which do not permit mortgagors the privilege of early re-payment.

non-systematic risk **risk** which is specific to an individual investment. Non-systematic risk can be reduced through **diversification.** Contrast with: **systematic risk.**

non-registered investment an investment which does not qualify as Canadian content for inclusion in tax-advantaged plans such as **RRSPs.** Contrast with: **registered investment.**

offering memorandum a document that describes the characteristics of an investment which is available only to large or sophisticated investors in **private placements.** Compare with: **prospectus.**

open-end fund a fund with no limit on the number of investors, or the amount of money that may be invested in it. Open end funds typically trade at **net asset values.** See also: **mutual fund.** Contrast with: **closed-end fund.**

open-end investment company a mutual fund organized as a **corporation.** Compare with: **unit trust.**

opportunity cost the difference between the **rate of return** actually realized and the rate of **return** available from an alternative course of action.

option a **derivative** giving the holder the right, but not the obligation to trade in a specified **security** or commodity at a pre-determined price for a fixed period of time. Compare with: **future.**

overvalued a security whose current price is not justified by **fundamental analysis.** Contrast with: **undervalued.**

par value face value

passive investing investing which attempts merely to replicate the returns of the broader market. See also: **indexing.** Contrast with: **active investing.**

permanent information record the collection of documents which describe the way in which a mutual fund is organized and operated; its **portfolio;** and its reported performance. See also: **prospectus; financial statements; annual information form.**

permitted derivatives derivatives for which a reasonably clearly identifiable market exists. They include clearing corporation options, futures contracts, options on futures, over-the-counter options, forward contracts, debt-like securities and listed warrants.

P/E ratio price-earnings ratio

portfolio a collection of various different **securities** held by an investor.

portfolio adviser an individual or company which makes investment *recommendations* to the **manager**, but is *not* responsible for actually executing investment transactions. See also: **investment adviser.** Contrast with: **portfolio manager.**

portfolio manager the person or persons with direct responsibility for investment decisions relating to assets of an investment fund. Contrast with: **portfolio adviser.**

portfolio turnover the degree to which the investments in a mutual fund **portfolio** are traded, expressed as a percentage of the total value of fund assets.

preferred share **stock** in a company which entitled the owner to certain specified rights (notably the right to receive **dividends**) "in preference" to the rights of holders of **common stock**. Often, they have a **par value** at which they may be **redeemed** by the issuer.

premium the amount by which a bond, debenture or preferred share sells above its **par value**. Also, the amount by which the **market price** of an asset exceeds its **book value**. Contrast with: discount.

pre-payable a **mortgage-backed security** based on **mortgages** which permit mortgagors the privilege of early repayment.

pre-payment privilege the opportunity for a mortgagee to repay some or all of the principal; debt prior to the end of the mortgage term.

pre-payment risk the possibility that a mortgage will be prepaid, depriving an investor of some portion of the interest income.

present value the current value of a sum of money to be received at some future time. It is **discounted** to reflect the fact that its value can **compound** between the present and the future time.

price-earnings ratio the **market price** of a **share** divided by the company's annual **earnings** per share. The ratio is a basic tool in **fundamental analysis.**

principal the amount of money borrowed or lent.

private placement a sale of securities made by way of offering memorandum to a group of no more than 50 purchasers who are by virtue of their net worth and investment experience able to evaluate the investment.

prospectus the legal document which describes the nature and characteristics of a **security**. See also: **simplified prospectus; annual information form; offering memorandum.**

purchasing power a measure of the goods and services a dollar can buy.

put an **option** which gives the holder the right but not the obligation to sell a security at a predetermined price for a specified period of time. See also: **option**. Contrast with: **call.**

qualified investments investments which may be included in registered tax plans such as **RRSPs.**

quality an expression of the likelihood that the issuer of a **bond** will **default.**

quantitative analysis a method for evaluating the value of assets based on the assessment of measurable factors such as sales, **earnings, book values,** volumes of share transactions, etc. Practitioners are often called "quants".

quartile one-quarter of the data points in a sample. "Top quartile" means the top 25% of the sample. Contrast with: **quintile.**

quintile one-fifth of the data points in a sample. "Top quintile" means the top 20% of the sample. Contrast with: **quartile.**

random walk theory the idea that it is impossible to consistently earn a return which is greater than that of the broader market by identifying superior investments because there is no pattern to price movements which can be relied upon as a basis of selection.

rate of return the profit realized from an investment, calculated as a percentage of the cost of the investment. It is most often expressed on an annual basis. Compare with: **actual ~; real ~; nominal ~; compound ~; simple ~; effective.**

real estate investment trust a security which issues **units** to investors representing an interest in a portfolio of **real estate.** A REIT is similar to a mutual fund trust because the tax advantages which the investments in the trust enjoy are passed through to investors. A REIT is also similar to a **closed-end fund** because the units of the trust are **traded** on **exchanges** rather than being bought and sold from the trust itself.

real interest rate the interest rate adjusted for **inflation.**

real rate of return the **nominal rate of return** adjusted for the rate of **inflation.**

rear-load fund a commission charged on the purchase of mutual funds, levied at the time the fund is sold or **redeemed.** See also: **back-end load; deferred sales charge.** Contrast with: **front-end load; acquisition fee.**

recession a downturn in economic activity, generally defined as at least two consecutive quarters of decline in a nation's gross national product.

redemption charge
1. a charge levied by a few mutual funds to redeem units.
2. a sales charge levied when a mutual fund is sold.

redeem sell securities back to the issuer. Also: redemption.

registered education savings plan an investment program registered in accordance with the Income Tax Act (Canada) used to save for a child's future post-secondary education expenses. Assets contributed to the plan up to specified limits **compound** tax free. See also: **tax shelter.**

registered investment an investment which qualifies as Canadian content in tax-advantaged plans such as **RRSPs.**

registered retirement income fund an investment program registered in accordance with the Income Tax Act (Canada) which operates to minimize the tax consequences of terminating an RRSP.

registered retirement savings plan an investment program registered in accordance with the Income Tax Act (Canada) used to save for retirement. Assets contributed to the plan up to specified limits are deductible from **taxable income,** and returns **compound** tax free. See also: **tax shelter.**

re-investment risk the danger that the the proceeds of an investment cannot be invested again at same rate as before.

REIT see: **real estate investment trust**

RESP see: **registered educational saving plan**

return see: **rate of return**

risk the possibility that an investment will not achieve its anticipated return.

risk-adjusted returns the measurement of return which reflects the degree of **risk** required to achieve the return.

risk free rate (of return) In **modern portfolio theory,** the return which can be obtained with no volatility. Usually, the 3 month T-Bill rate.

risk tolerance the capacity of an investor to handle the consequences of an investment which does not achieve its anticipated return.

royalty trust an investment that consists of an interest in a royalty-paying asset such as a mine, oil or gas field.

RRIF see: **registered retirement income fund**

RRSP see: **registered retirement saving plan**

S&P 500 Standard & Poor's 500. A **market index** based on 500 of the largest stocks on the New York Stock Exchange. Compare with: **Dow Jones Average.** See also: **index.**

secondary market the transactions between buyers and sellers in **securities** following their initial sale by their **issuer.**

sector fund a **mutual fund** which invests in a particular segment or sector of the market: eg: precious metals.

sector rotation an investment approach which invests the assets of the **portfolio** on the basis of projections about which economic sectors will provide the greatest returns in the future. See also: **top-down investing.**

securities acts provincial legislation regulating the **issuing** and **trading** of **securities**.

security risk the danger that an investment in a single investment will not provide the anticipated return. See also: **single issue risk**.

security a document or note which signifies ownership or indebtedness, or a right to ownership to indebtedness.

segregated fund an investment offered by insurance companies which is similar to a **mutual fund**. In reality, segregated funds are variable value insurance policies.

self-directed ~RRSP. A plan in which the investor makes investment decisions. Contrast with Group RRSP. Self-directed plans are offered by a wide variety of **financial institutions**.

settlement date the date on which a transaction for the purchase or sale of securities is completed (by payment).

share the basic unit of ownership in a company or **mutual fund** organized as an **investment company**. See also: **unit**.

short-selling the sale of an investment or **security** before it is purchased.

simple rate of return the change in the value of an investment expressed as a percentage. Compare with: **compound return**.

simplified prospectus a short form of prospectus permitted by securities regulators for many **mutual funds**. Contrast with: **prospectus**.

single issue risk the danger that an investment in a single investment or **issue** will not provide the anticipated return. See also: **security risk**.

small cap. fund a **mutual fund** that invests primarily in **small-capitalization stocks**.

small capitalization stocks **stocks** in companies with a **market capitalization** of less than $500 million.

small stock effect the fact that **small-capitalization stocks** outperform **large-capitalization stocks** over the long-term.

sophisticated investor an investor with special expertise, or an investor who makes a very large investment in a single security. See also: **institutional investor**; **offering memorandum**.

specialty fund a **mutual fund** which invests in securities with a specific theme. See also: **sector funds**.

speculation high risk investing based on concentrated positions in anticipation of dramatic or sudden changes in price.

sponsor the company which establishes a **mutual fund**, and is responsible for its ongoing operations, including the filing of the **prospectus** and **financial statements**, and the overall administration of the investment portfolio.

spread trading an investment approach for **bond portfolios** which attempts to increase returns by capitalizing on disruptions in the historical relationships in the relative yields of different **issues.**

Standard & Poors 500 Index See: **S-P 500**

standard deviation an indicator of the volatility of an investment which measures fluctuations in the price of the investment around its average price. Contrast with: **beta.**

standard performance data performance data which is calculated in accordance with securities regulation.

statement of earnings a **financial statement** which indicates the profitability of a business.

statement of portfolio transactions a **financial statement** required of **mutual funds** showing the purchases and sales of investments in the portfolio over the preceding six months.

statement of investment portfolio a **financial statement** required of **mutual funds** showing the investments in the fund portfolio on the reporting date.

stock the equity of a company contributed by investors. See: **share.**

strategic asset allocation the process of allocating investments among asset classes in order to meet an investor's needs.

strip bond a bond from which the interest coupons have been detached or 'stripped'. The remaining component pays the face value at **maturity.** See also: **strip coupon; zero-coupon bond.**

superfluous diversification **diversification** which does not contribute to the reduction of risk.

swap a **derivative** in which the income streams of two (or more securities) are exchanged without exchanging the underlying securities.

Switching the privilege of moving assets from one **mutual fund** to another with the same group of funds.

systematic risk **risks** which are common to all investments, and which cannot be reduced by diversification. Contrast with: **non-systematic risk.**

TSE Toronto Stock Exchange

TSE 300 a **market index** of 300 companies traded on the TSE. See also: **index; benchmark.** Compare with: **Dow Jones Average; S&P 500.**

tactical asset allocation the allocation of investments among asset classes on the basis of expectations about market developments. Contrast with: **strategic asset allocation.**

taxable income the amount of **income** subject to tax after subtracting allowable deductions.

tax advantaged plan an investment program such an **RRSP, RRIF**, etc. which permits the deferral of tax. See also: **tax shelter.**

tax bracket the range of income to which a particular tax rate applies. See also: **marginal rate.**

tax credit an amount which is deducted from tax otherwise payable. Contrast with: **tax deduction.**

tax deduction an amount which is deducted from the income on which tax is payable. Contrast with: **tax credit.**

tax deferral the legitimate postponement of tax until at later date.

tax shelter an investment offering variously **tax deferral, tax credits,** or **tax deductions.**

taxable income the portion of total income subject to tax.

technical analysis an approach to determining the value of **securities** based on examining patterns in the price and volume of shares traded. Contrast with: **fundamental analysis.**

term to maturity the time remaining on a **bond.** Often used as a rough indicator of a bond investment's volatility. See also: duration.

Term Deposit an interest paying investment with a specified term and fixed rate of **interest.** See also: **GIC.**

theme fund a mutual fund which invests according to a specific theme or set of themes.

theme investing an investment approach that identifies securities on the basis of "themes" which are expected to stimulate economic activity.

top-down investing an investment approach based on anticipating the **sectors** of the economy which will display the strongest growth in the future, and identifying the most profitable investments within those sectors. Contrast with: **bottom-up investing.**

Toronto Stock Exchange Composite Index 300 see TSE 300. See also: **benchmark.**

trading the process of buying and selling **securities.**

trailer fees continuing commissions paid to brokers by some mutual funds.

treasury bill a short-term government debt investment, also referred to as a "T-Bill". Treasury bills are sold at a **discount** and **mature** at **par,** and are available with **terms** from one month to one year.

trust a formal legal relationship in which property in held by a **trustee** on behalf of others, called beneficiaries.

trustee the administrator of a **trust.**

unit the basic element of ownership of a mutual fund. See also: **share.**

unit trust a mutual fund which is organized as a **trust.** Contrast with: **investment company.**

value investing an approach to choosing investments which looks for situations in which the **book value** of the company exceeds its **market price.** Contrast with: **growth investing.** See also: **bottom-up investing.**

value stocks stocks with low **p/e ratios,** low debt ratios and/or high cash per share.

venture capital funds pools of capital which invest in new or unproven technologies, processes or enterprises. Typically higher risk because the likelihood of success for any individual investment is limited.

volatility the tendency of the price (and **return**) of an investment to fluctuate.

wasting assets assets (such) as mines or oil wells that gradually decline in value.

wrap account a comprehensive asset management programme offered to investors with higher net worth by financial institutions. The charge for such a service is usually as percentage of assets.

yield the **rate of return** of an investment in relation to its price. See also: **yield to maturity; coupon; current yield.**

yield curve the relationship between short-term and long-term **interest** rates. Usually, long-term rates are higher. Compare with: **inverted yield curve.**

yield to maturity the **rate of return** on an interest-bearing investment such as a **bond** taking into account, the purchase price, **coupon rate** and **term.**

zero coupon bond a bond which makes no periodic interest payments. The rate of return is reflected in the **discount** of the purchase price below the bond's **par** or **face value.** See also: **strip bond.**

INDEX

D

E

J

K

L

M

U

V

W

Y

Z